A Million Green Flags

by Sia Stevens

Table Of Contents

A Story of Two Birds

Chapter 1: Connection

When I first began to think seriously about relationships, it was not out of curiosity or academic interest. It was out of longing. I was heartbroken, missing the man I loved, replaying the heartfelt moments we had shared and the silence that followed after he was gone. I remember wondering if what I missed most was him, or the way I felt in his presence.

On one of those mornings, I sat in my garden, staring at the world as if it might reveal something I had overlooked. Beyond the roses and stone wall, at the edge of the property, stood an old fig tree, its branches sprawling wide. That day, two birds had taken their places among its leaves.

One bird began to sing. Her song was light and melodic, flowing through the air as though it belonged to the morning itself. The other bird sat nearby, not singing, not moving, simply watching her. The singing continued for a while. The listener did nothing but remain, attentive and still. Together they seemed lost in a trance, each held by the presence of the other.

I found myself wondering whether the bird sang for her own joy or for the pleasure of her companion. Would she still sing if the other flew away? Or was her song sustained only because she had an audience, a witness to her music? I couldn't tell. Yet one thing was clear: the beauty of the moment lay not only in the song itself, but in the way it was received. One sang, the other listened, and in that *shared engagement* the song became more than sound. It became a *connection*.

Watching them, I felt the echo of my own ache. What I missed most about my lover's absence wasn't his smile or his touch. It was the feeling of being seen, mirrored and understood in his presence. Without someone to witness my life, I felt as though I had lost my own reflection. Who was I singing for now? Was anyone listening? Did anything I did matter if no one was there to receive it?

And so, beneath the branches of the fig tree, I realized that the question at the heart of every relationship is not *"Do you love me?"* but *"Do you see me?"* It is *engagement* that makes us come alive, the recognition of our song by another soul. Without it, we are left to wonder:

If no one is watching, if no one is listening, would we still sing?

Chapter 2: Attention

What makes us truly enjoy someone's company? Is it the satisfaction of being seen, or of seeing someone else?

Perhaps it is a little bit of both. You see, companionship cannot be one-sided. If one refuses to be attentive to the other, the joy quickly drains away. A good companion, at the very least, is someone who notices us, just as we notice them. This simple exchange of *attention* is what allows a connection to spark between two people.

Attention, therefore, can be thought of as the *currency* needed to form a connection. Just as you cannot trade without money, without some token that holds *value*, you cannot form a relationship without attention.

To connect with another person, you must see them, listen to them, engage with them, and respond to them. Your attention is the signal that they matter, that their presence registers in your world. When this attention is reciprocated, even in the smallest way, a connection is made.

A connection and a relationship are essentially two expressions of the same thing. The word "relationship" is generally used to describe a deeper, more established, multilayered connection, but at its root *every relationship begins with that first exchange of attention.*

Think about sitting across from a stranger in an airport or a coffee shop. You look up, your eyes meet, and you offer a smile. In that moment you have given them a token of your attention.

If they return it with a smile of their own, you instantly feel a connection with the stranger. It may be brief, it may never be woven into something larger, yet even in its simplicity it matters. For in that instant your presence has been acknowledged. You feel *seen*.

Do not underestimate the power of such small exchanges. What begins as a fleeting smile has the potential to ripple outward in ways you cannot predict. A tiny connection may evolve into a friendship, a partnership, even a love that reshapes a lifetime. Or at the very least, it can add color and richness to the fabric of your day.

Think about how extraordinary that really is. There are billions of people on this planet, each carrying their own burdens and dreams, each preoccupied with the endless details of daily life. Yet every so often, two people pause. They choose to step outside their own concerns and take notice of one another. They choose to think of someone besides themselves. To celebrate another's joy. To bear witness to another's life. And in those small but powerful choices, we make someone else feel alive.

You can see this truth reflected everywhere. Children crave their parents' attention because it reassures them that they are seen and loved. When parents fail to notice them, even in the smallest ways, the child begins to feel invisible, and that invisibility quietly shapes their sense of worth. Couples drift apart when they stop truly seeing each other. They may share a home, routines, even laughter, but if their eyes no longer meet, the relationship begins to starve. The same is true in friendship: what sustains the bond is not simply time spent together, but the feeling of being deeply understood. Relationships may grow layered and complex, yet their foundation never changes: *the simple, essential act of noticing one another.*

The two birds in my garden seemed to understand this far better than we do. The 'watching' bird could have been doing anything else—plucking figs from the tree, hunting for prey, gathering twigs for a nest, or simply resting in the shade. Yet instead, he chose to sit and listen. He chose to be there. To bear witness to the 'singing' bird, to listen to her song, to ensure her moment did not pass unseen. And in that simple choice, a connection was born.

This is why giving attention is more than a casual act. It is the essential currency of connection. Without it, nothing lasting can be built. Yet somehow, the very word *attention* has become tainted in modern times. It carries a shadow, as if to seek attention is to be weak, needy, or self-centered. Isn't that strange?

Why is it that we hesitate to ask our friends, our families, or our partners for more presence, more engagement, more acknowledgment, when those are the very things that make a relationship feel alive?

People today fear being labeled an *attention-seeker* or someone desperate for validation. So they learn to swallow their longing. They pretend not to crave a gaze, a listening ear, or the simple recognition of their existence. And in doing so, their relationships fade, one small neglect at a time. They stop asking, convinced that the desire to be seen is a flaw. Yet what could be more natural?

The question, then, is not whether it is bad to ask for attention, but have we learned to ask for it in the right way? How do we earn the attention of others in a natural and convincing way without forcing it? I feel like that itself would solve a lot of our relationship problems, isn't it?

Chapter 3: Value

The sweet song of the bird continued in my garden drifting through the morning air, pouring its joy into everything it touched. It was the kind of joy that didn't bind you with gratitude, but simply offered itself, without asking for anything in return. The *other* bird, perched nearby, remained still, listening to the song, spellbound by its melody.

The simplicity of their exchange carried a strange weight. I found myself wondering how long it could last. How long could *the other* stay attentive before it grew restless and flew away? How long could *the one* keep singing before her voice tired or her song no longer drew interest? Because the truth, in the end, is that attention is fragile. It must be sustained, yet it cannot be forced.

That thought pierced me because it echoed my own story. My own relationship had followed the exact same arc— beginning with undivided attention, ending when that attention quietly slipped away.

I remember the night we drove to the coast, three months into us. He had surprised me—picking me up after work without warning, a duffel bag already packed in the trunk. "We're going somewhere," he'd said, that slow grin spreading across his face, the one that made my stomach flip.

We drove for hours, windows down, his hand resting on my thigh, the radio playing songs we'd already forgotten. By the time we reached the beach, the sun was setting—streaks of orange and pink bleeding into the Pacific. He spread a blanket on the sand, and we sat there, shoulders touching, watching the light die.

"Tell me something you've never told anyone," he said.

I told him about my fear of being ordinary. Of living a small, forgettable life. He didn't laugh or offer empty reassurance. He just listened, his eyes steady on mine, like I was the only person in the world worth hearing.

Then he kissed me—slow, deliberate, tasting of salt and coffee. And in that kiss, I felt it: I mattered. Not because of what I did or how I looked, but because I existed, and he saw me.

That was the night I fell.

In the beginning, attention was abundant. We were absorbed in each other, eager for every word, every glance. It felt effortless. He'd text me good morning before I woke up. He'd listen to my stories about work like they were the most fascinating thing he'd ever heard. When I walked into a room, his eyes would find me first, always.

But slowly, the attention began to fade.

He stopped asking questions. Stopped listening like my answers mattered. His eyes would drift to his phone mid-sentence. Our dinners grew quieter. When I reached for his hand, it was there, but limp—present but absent.

I told myself it was normal. That passion fades. That I was being needy.

But then came the night I knew.

We were sitting on his couch, a movie playing neither of us watched. I turned to him, needing to feel close, and said, "So what's next for us?"

He looked at me, confused. "What do you mean?"

"Like... where this is going. What we want."

He shrugged. "I don't know. I guess I haven't really thought about it."

That shrug—casual, dismissive—cracked something in me. I realized: I had been building us in my mind, brick by brick, while he'd been... coasting. Comfortable. Present but not invested.

Two weeks later, it ended. Not with a fight, not with betrayal. Just a slow fade, like a song turned down until you can't hear it anymore.

He said he "needed space." I said I understood.

But I didn't. I didn't understand how someone could make you feel like the center of the universe, and then drift away like you were nothing. I didn't understand how love could feel so real and then just... evaporate.

A gust of wind moved through the fig tree, and the bird's song broke through—bright, untouched, as if my heaviness meant nothing to the morning. She was still singing. He was still watching. Their world hadn't paused for mine.

I wiped my eyes and looked at them again, differently this time. Because now I could see my own story playing out on that branch. The singing, the listening, the slow unraveling—it was all there. And sitting in the ache of that recognition, I began to understand something I couldn't see while I was living it.

It wasn't that we wanted to hurt one another or end things. It was simply that the desire to notice and engage with one another was no longer there. And without that desire, love becomes an empty shell. What follows is a series of disappointments.

When attention slips, we grow restless. Insecurity seeps in. It's only human. We try to reclaim what's fading, often by force. *But attention should never be seized by force.* That's where things begin to go wrong.

In the weeks after we ended, I changed my hair. I started posting more on social media—curated shots of dinners I barely tasted, sunsets I watched alone, laughter that didn't reach my eyes. I went to parties I didn't want to attend, wore clothes that didn't feel like me, laughed louder than I needed to. All of it a silent scream aimed at one person: notice me. See that I exist without you. See that I'm fine.

I wasn't fine. And none of it worked.

We do this more than we'd like to admit—try too hard to stand out, act different, look different. We stir up drama, pick fights, adopt different personalities, even alter who we are—all in the hope of being noticed, of feeling seen. And we may get attention that way, yes, but not the kind that nourishes. Not the kind that lasts. We mistake noise for notice, never realizing how quickly it all fades once the spectacle ends.

There's no shame in admitting it. We all crave to be seen, especially when we feel invisible. The difference lies not in the desire itself, but in how we choose to fulfill it.

As I watched the bird sing, I began to understand the most natural way to draw attention and how simple it had always been. You don't need to be loud, demanding, or extravagant. You only need to offer something of *value*—something useful, beautiful, or soothing, like the bird's own song. When what you hold has genuine value, attention comes to you effortlessly, as naturally as morning light finds the dew.

The fault isn't in seeking, but in how it's sought. When attention is demanded through force or intimidation, it grows heavy, suffocating, and inevitably drives people away. But when it's earned naturally, it becomes a bridge, drawing people closer. Think of a flower: it never demands attention. It earns it. Through its beauty, its color, its gentle fragrance. That is the most natural way to draw people toward yourself.

I watched the bees in my garden drift from flower to flower, never hesitating, never forced. The flower didn't call them. It simply held what they needed, and they came.

This isn't just philosophy, it's science too. Our brains are wired to focus on two things above all else: *reward and fear*. These are the twin forces that command our attention. When you see a bright red apple hanging from a tree, your eyes are drawn to it. It promises sweetness, nourishment, something of *value*. On the other hand, if you see a snake coiled at your feet, that too will seize your attention, but it would do it differently.

Both reward and fear capture attention, but only one of them draws us closer. *Reward makes us want to engage with it because it offers value. Fear, by contrast, makes us cautious, hesitant, ready to pull away.* In relationships, this distinction matters more than we often realize.

I couldn't help but think of how often we try to hold on to each other in all the wrong ways. People say things like, "*If you don't call me back, I'm done*" or "*This is your last chance*" believing that fear will make someone stay. But fear only tightens the grip for a moment; it never sustains love. Others reach for guilt: "*I guess I just don't matter to you*" or "*After everything I've done for you*". Yet real, lasting attention can't be coerced. It's drawn naturally, the way the singing bird drew it, not through demand but through value, through something genuine that makes you want to stay and listen.

That is the secret. In relationships, attention endures when *both partners continue to offer value to one another*. When value is no longer *given* or no longer *appreciated*, the attention fades, and with it the relationship does too.

Looking back on my own breakup, I sometimes wonder: did we simply stop offering value to each other? Or did the value we gave stop being recognized? Perhaps what I offered was being offered elsewhere too. Perhaps what he gave was no longer meant for me?

I do not hold grudges; I only carry questions.

What matters to me now is not the blame—who did it, or whose fault it was—but rather what I can learn from it: how to move forward without letting the heaviness of the loss weigh me down? How do I resist sinking into the emptiness that lingers after love ends? Dating again does not interest me, not yet. What I want is clarity. The clarity of how not to repeat the same mistakes again and again, not to fall into patterns and loops.

And for that, I need to fully understand human relationships. What do we truly desire from our partners? Is it connection? Is it Love? Is it Attention? And what do we fear most? Is it feeling invisible? Feeling disconnected? Feeling alone?

And most importantly, the question that has crossed my mind time and again:

How do we build lasting relationships in today's world?

****

Conversations With My Professor

Chapter 4: Superpowers

My fascination with the human mind began, unsurprisingly, after my own breakup, but what kept it alive was something bigger. It wasn't just heartbreak. It was heartbreak multiplied by observation. Everywhere I looked, people seemed unhappy. Friends spoke about anxiety and loneliness as casually as they once spoke about movies or dinner plans. People were signing up for therapy in droves, not as a last resort, but more of a lifestyle, something you signed up for like a gym membership. Social media was flooded with self-help slogans, quick fixes for mental health, and confessions of despair disguised as memes.

It made me wonder: how did we get here? How did a species that built airplanes, pyramids, and the internet end up feeling so lost inside our own heads? Why is depression spreading so quietly yet so rapidly, especially among the young, who supposedly have "everything"?

Everyone had a theory. Some blamed technology, some the economy, others the collapse of culture. But I wanted answers from someone who'd spent his life decoding the human mind itself. Which is how I ended up, one afternoon, at a café in

Capitol Hill, across from my old college professor—Dr. Alan Meyer.

He was the sort of man who could make even existential dread sound like a fun seminar. Decades of psychology had etched fine lines of curiosity around his eyes, the kind that come not from age, but from paying attention. I trusted him to untangle the questions I couldn't shake.

Dr. Meyer sat across from me, hands wrapped loosely around his cup. He had a way of being entirely present. Never hurried, never restless, as if time itself slowed down when he entered a room. Outside, Seattle exhaled a slow drizzle, the kind that never quite becomes rain.

I watched him for a moment, then finally asked my question: "Why is it, Professor, that people feel more lonely and depressed these days, even as the world seems more developed and prosperous than ever?"

He held my gaze for a moment, as if deciding whether to answer or to make me find the answer myself. Then smiled faintly and tilted his head, the slight mischief that comes just before a teacher drops a truth he knows will rearrange your thinking.

"What is it that birds enjoy the most, Sia?"

I blinked. "Flying?"

"And fish?"

"Swimming."

"And bees?"

"Making honey?"

"And cheetahs?"

"Running."

He smiled. "Exactly. Every species has its way. Goats climb, dolphins dive, wolves howl, squirrels dig. Each one evolved with a particular gift—its own built-in *superpower*. Now, what do you think would happen if you took that away from them?"

"They'd lose themselves. They'd go mad."

"Exactly," he said, leaning closer. "Now tell me, what is *our* special gift, our superpower?"

"Our brain?"

"Sure, but what about it, specifically? Plenty of animals have large brains. What's that one thing that truly makes us different?"

I hesitated. "I don't know. Innovation?"

He clasped his hands together and smiled like a magician about to pull a rabbit out of a philosophy book:

"It is *Connection*," he said softly. "Our superpower is *connection*. Our ability to bond, to form deep, lasting relationships. That's what built everything.

"'Really?' I said, surprised. I thought he would say human intelligence or problem solving, or something along those lines. But relationships? That wasn't even remotely on my bingo card. But still it felt unexpectedly... true.

He leaned back, the teacher in him waking up. "Humans are capable of forming the most complex, long-lasting relationships on the planet. Deeper than any other species. You know why...? It is because of how our brains evolved. We were never the fastest or strongest, nowhere near it. If it came down to muscle, lions would've had us for lunch. But what brought us this far is our ability to form relationships. We hunted together, raised children together, built fires together. Social bonding was our evolutionary edge. That was our superpower. This is how we came to become the most dominating species of the planet."

I let his words settle in, trying to picture the evolutionary trajectory of human beings in my head. "So basically what you're saying is, we're the friendliest apex predators!"

He laughed. A deep, unfiltered laugh. "Exactly! People like to say intelligence got us here. But intelligence *is* social. Intelligence and relationships are two sides of the same coin. The two evolved together."

I raised an eyebrow. "Not sure about that. What about the classic nerd stereotype? You know, the math genius who can barely talk to another human, the trope we see in every movie?

"Eh, Hollywood nonsense," he said, waving a hand as if to swat the idea away. "Intelligence isn't about calculus or a perfect IQ score. From an evolutionary lens, intelligence means thriving in the jungle of life. It's the ability to protect yourself *and* your tribe. To lift others with you. True intelligence isn't isolation. It's expansion"

"Look at any successful person around you. Or pick any prominent figure from history. Leaders. People who could move others. Do you think any of them would ace a modern IQ test? Probably not. But they had social intelligence in spades, the ability to rally people, to inspire, to create trust. That's the highest form of intelligence."

Something clicked in me, as if a dissonance I'd long absorbed from pop culture was finally starting to align. "You know, I always hated how pop culture divides 'nerds' and 'popular kids,' as if you can be smart *or* social, but never both," I said, shaking my head.

He sighed. "That's a tragic side effect of our education system. Back in the day, intelligent people weren't tucked away in labs. They were philosophers, warriors, poets, statesmen. They were thinkers *and* connectors. Now we churn out obedient employees, not well-rounded humans. Schools train for jobs, not for life."

I nodded, reflecting on his words, and slowly realizing the truth in it. Real cognitive growth happens through interactions. Our ability to connect, listen and inspire is how we learn. Every conversation, every argument, every shared story expands collective intelligence. Without that exchange, our brilliance would wither.

But unfortunately our generation has been taught to see these things very differently. We've come to think of relationships as something belonging solely to the realm of emotions, distant and separate from intellect or logic. They're often painted as instinctive, chaotic, even irrational.

This, however, was the first time someone had uttered the words: relationships and intelligence, in the same sentence, as if they were not only related, but inseparable. And now that the door was open, I wasn't ready to close it. I wanted to step through.

"How did we come to develop this extraordinary superpower? I mean, why only humans, out of millions of species, are capable of forming such intimate, one-on-one relationships, while the rest of life feels so untouched by the same longing for connection?"

"Seriously, we even try to form bonds with plants and animals. And not just that... think of *Cast Away*—how he draws a face on a volleyball and starts talking to it when there is no one else to bond with. What the heck is that? Where does this strong need to connect come from?"

Dr. Meyer caught my look. "Now you're getting somewhere," he said with a knowing smile. "Good. That's a sign of curiosity." He paused, as if weighing how best to guide me into the next layer of his argument.

"Our ability to connect didn't come first. It was built on something deeper. Long before we learned how to connect, our brain developed *four* unique capabilities, *the four superpowers of our brain*, that made everything else possible.

I leaned in. "Four superpowers of our brain?"

He nodded, eyes glinting. "Do you want to know what they are?"

"Yes, of course. If you have the time," I said, unable to hide the excitement in my voice.

He finished his coffee with a theatrical flourish. "Then settle in. Once you understand them, you'll understand why humans are the way we are, and why we're so miserable in our modern lifestyle."

Just then, the barista appeared with two chocolate croissants we'd ordered earlier, setting it on the table like an offering. "You two look like you'll need fuel for this," she said with a grin.

Dr. Meyer smiled. "Perfect. Superpowers and croissants. Let's begin."

Chapter 5: Memory

The rain droplets had gathered on the window beside us, merging and sliding down in slow, deliberate trails. I tore a piece of croissant, the steam curling faintly in the chill. Morning moved at its unhurried pace, while our conversation deepened, like the city itself was listening.

"First superpower," Dr. Meyer began, waving his fork like a magician about to reveal a trick. "*Long-term memory*. Without it, human relationships would evaporate like morning mist."

"Really?"

"Yes. Think about it. Most animals disperse the moment they're self-sufficient. A bird flies the nest and never looks back. A cub leaves its mother once it can hunt. But humans? We remember. We remember our parents' care, our friends' laughter, even our enemies' betrayals. That memory is what allows us to sustain bonds for years, even decades."

"But animals remember things too, right?", I asked, raising an eyebrow.

"Some do, yes. Elephants can recognize family members; some even mourn their dead. Dolphins can remember the unique whistles of their pod mates. Chimps are good at remembering past alliances and betrayals. And perhaps that is why these animals also show signs of social bonding. But our memory? It outstrips that of any other species by a wide margin. It's not even comparable."

I nodded slowly, struck by the image of an elephant caressing bones in the dust.

"This is why our relationships outlast those of any other species: because we remember. Every kindness remembered, every sight retained, every running joke stored in memory. Together they weave continuity and trust. Memory is the glue that holds societies together. It's why civilizations exist. It's how knowledge travels across generations. We don't simply forget our past. We remember it. Our families, our childhoods, past relationships. Because, *forget your people, and you forget yourself.*"

"But here's the problem," he said, raising a finger. People squander this gift in the modern world. 'Live in the moment' is the new mantra, fine for sunsets, but terrible for civilizations. Because when you only think short term, you don't allow anything to build over time. People switch jobs, places and partners like clothes; Old friends are traded for new ones, family ties weaken over time. We rarely hold anyone in our memory for long. Our memory has become a hard drive for trivia instead of a tool to nurture relationships."

"And why is that Professor?", I asked, wanting to get to the root of the issue. "Why are people no longer investing in long term relationships? Why is everyone looking for cheap thrills, laughing over cocktails, forgetting faces by the morning. " My question reflected the pain of my own forgettable encounters over the years.

"Have you ever heard of Dunbar's Number?", he asked.

I shook my head, curious where this was leading.

"It's a theory by an anthropologist named Robin Dunbar. He suggested that humans can maintain about 150 meaningful relationships at once. That's our cognitive limit. Beyond that, things break down. But what do people do now? Collect thousands of online 'friends' while barely nurturing ten real ones. It's like loading up a buffet plate with every dish and still going home hungry. Our brains evolved for depth, not endless variety."

"So social media is relationship spam?"

He slapped the table, nearly spilling his coffee. "Yes! Memory spam. We are overloaded with the possibility of connections, but hardly any turn into strong ones. And weak connections, Sia, don't stick in our memories. You may vividly remember a small interaction you had on a flight with a stranger for a lifetime, while some might even forget thirty years of marriage if the connection isn't there."

His words settled heavily in me, stirring a thought I couldn't keep in. "It's so unfortunate, Professor, isn't it? We are built for lifelong bonds, maybe even enduring love, yet we date as if memory is a burden we can't wait to drop. Casual everything. Names forgotten by morning. Connect, consume, discard. A rabbit probably doesn't remember who it paired up with an hour ago. He simply can't. His little brain is not built for that. But ours is. And yet what's the point if we still choose to forget? What's the use of memory if no relationship is deep enough to even leave a mark?"

He grew quiet, studying me. I could tell he heard more than my words. He heard the ache beneath them. He didn't press, didn't prod, just smiled warmly, as if to say he understood.

"You're beginning to see it," he said softly. "You don't just listen; you wrestle with it. And that wrestling, that honesty, teaches me too."

Then his voice turned poetic, almost reverent. "Imagine you have the power to grow a magnificent garden, filled with a variety of plants and trees, flowers that return season after season, fruits that grow year after year. But what do you do? You plant a new flower every day and dazzled by its novelty, you neglect the ones from before. You forget to water them or take care of them. At first, your garden looks lively, a variety of flowers smiling at you. It's all so exciting. But without persistent care, nothing roots. No fragrance deepens, no fruit grows, no shade forms. Eventually, the garden dries out, empty despite all its potential. We are doing the same with our relationships today. We forget to nurture what we already have. Instead, we rush to chase new ones. A new friend request, a fresh face, a viral post, an exciting DM. We are drowned in options and in that noise, nothing settles long enough to become memory. That is the tragedy of modern life."

Dr. Meyer was right in his assessment. Humans are built to create lifelong memories and store them like a treasure chest. That is our superpower. Without those fond memories, life feels empty. But are we really doing that?

My own memories of the past few years have become a blur of faces, with no one standing out and no particular moment to look back on fondly.

Strange how memory works. I could still feel the warmth of my mother's hand on my forehead when I was sick, still hear my college roommate's laugh echoing down the hallway at 2 a.m., still remember the weight of my lover leaning into me on a quiet Sunday morning, his breath warm against my neck. But the random parties, my days working at my office, those hours scrolling on my phone, those had dissolved into nothing.

I didn't remember what I saw. I remembered what I felt. And in the moments I didn't feel anything, the memory simply disappeared.

Perhaps others experience this too. This could be why so many people feel empty. As if they have missed life, as if it slipped through their fingers. Most likely, because they stopped feeling.

Most of our fondest memories are shared experiences because that's when we feel most intensely. They are created with people, not things. And so, the answer to creating those treasured memories again surely lies in strengthening our connections with people. That is how we can truly utilize our first superpower.

Chapter 6: Language

Dr. Meyer set his cup down with a decisive *clink*. "The second superpower, *Language*."

"Language?" I said, frowning. "That feels more like a skill than a superpower."

At first, I wasn't convinced. Animals communicate too. Birds sing, dolphins whistle, wolves howl. Humans just happen to have more vocabulary, right? But the more he talked about it, the clearer his point became. Human language isn't just *more words*. It's another dimension entirely.

"Imagine a world without words," he said, lowering his voice. "No *'I love you'*. No *'I forgive you'*. No *'I miss you'*. Only grunts and gestures. You'd never truly know the person sitting across from you. Their inner world would stay locked away. You might live beside them for years and still remain strangers."

His emphasis on language made me think of all the times words had been the only lifeline: late-night conversations with friends, a whispered comfort from my mother, even the silly texts shared with my siblings. Without language, all of that would have been silence. How would relationships flourish in silence? How would love blossom without words?

"Picture early humans. A hunter comes back from the plains. Without language, he can only grunt, mime, point. But with words, he can *tell* the story: the size of the animal, the terrain, the fear in his comrade's eyes. Suddenly, survival knowledge becomes collective. It can be passed on. Shared stories are what turned tribes into civilizations."

"Words aren't just empty vessels, Sia. They carry emotional fingerprints. They carry our inner world outward. Without them, every face would be a mystery. With it, every face becomes familiar. Every silly joke, every whispered fear, every midnight confession, it all builds intimacy."

"So going by that logic," I said, "can we say pillow talk is an evolutionary strategy?"

He threw his head back laughing, nearly toppling his chair. "Exactly! Pillow talk is survival. It's bonding. It's the open door to the soul."

I paused, thinking of all the doors that had stayed closed in my own relationships. "But what if the other person doesn't open up? We have language precise enough to name the subtlest thought and the most tangled feeling, so why do some people still fail to communicate, Professor? Why is it so hard to say things as they are? Why are there misunderstandings everywhere? Why this communication gap?"

"Well Sia, communication is a two way street. It has to be mutual. If one talks and the other doesn't respond back it is like hitting your head on the wall."

"No, but seriously, why are some people so bad at communicating? Why don't they reply to texts or pick up the phone? Did God forget to give them the superpower of language?" My voice had turned sarcastic.

Dr. Meyer didn't flinch. "Have you considered that maybe they're just not interested in talking to you?"

I froze, expecting a smirk, waiting for him to laugh it off. But his expression didn't budge. He meant it.

"So you're saying... if they wanted to talk, they would?"

"Absolutely," he said, without hesitation.

His certainty hit harder than I expected. I felt the sting before I could stop it. Maybe the silence I'd been interpreting as confusion in my past relationships, was just... apathy. Maybe it wasn't that he *couldn't* communicate, it's that he *didn't care to*. Love can make you delusional at times. You start making excuses for them: he's busy, he's shy, he's bad at texting. When really, the translation might just read: he doesn't want to.

I thought of all the messages I'd sent into silence. The ones I crafted carefully, the ones I sent impulsively at midnight, the ones that ended with a question mark and never got an answer. I used to think he didn't know what to say or that he needed time. But he didn't need time. He just didn't need me.

My thoughts spiraled inward, pulling me into a pause. I hadn't come here to dissect my personal life. I simply wanted clarity about human nature. But clarity has a way of arriving uninvited, slipping in quietly when you least expect it, the way light finds its way beneath a closed door.

Dr. Meyer noticed my quiet retreat inward. He watched me for a moment, debating whether to let it pass. Then, with that uncanny professor timing, he reached into his coat pocket, pulled out his phone, and tapped a few times.

He turned the screen toward me: a photo of a cave wall, covered in ochre drawings. Bison, hunters, human silhouettes mid-motion.

"These are thirty thousand years old," he said. "We call them cave paintings, but that's not quite right. They weren't decoration. They were language. The language of the ancients. The first attempt to turn thought into permanence."

I traced the lines with my eyes, imagining the flicker of torchlight across stone as if I was exploring the ancient caves.

"Think about it. The thunder of hooves, the rush of the hunt. All trapped inside one person's head until he painted it. *That* was the first *I was here*. The first *remember me*."

"Expression isn't optional, Sia. When something matters, it demands to be spoken. It bursts out of you, you can't help it. Caveman or a CEO, the impulse is the same"

"Those cave people were desperate to be understood. They scratched their thoughts into stone. And now we, armed with phones, Wi-Fi, education, entire dictionaries, say *we can't communicate*? Oh please! If people could speak across millennia with smoke and pigment, they can surely send a damn text."

He sat back, shaking his head. "This whole 'communication gap' thing everyone talks about? It's bullshit. *It's not a gap in skill... it's the lack of will.*"

"When someone really feels something, they'll say it. They'll find the words, paint them if they have to. When people stay silent, it's not because they can't, it's because they don't care enough to."

I kept listening to every word he had to say. His words felt heavy, almost ancient, but they also made sense. His reasonings were beginning to unlock a fresh perspective in my brain. A perspective that finally made sense, words that I could easily understand.

It was not really a communication problem that our generation faces. It's a connection problem. When the fire's there, words flow like oxygen. When you're in love, poetry writes itself. When you're heartbroken, your tears become sentences. But without feeling, language withers. And that's the real tragedy: *we've lost that depth of connection.*

That's why people no longer tell their parents how much they love them. That's why partners 'internalize' all of their feelings instead of proclaiming them to their lover, shouting from mountaintops, carving them into stone. That's why friends keep their stories to themselves. It isn't because they are shy. It isn't because they are afraid. It's because the passion has drained away, and with it, the urge to express.

This loss of passion helps explain the avoidance tactics we see everywhere today. No wonder ghosting has become so common. Not because people are scared to say it to your face, but because they simply have nothing substantial to say. The connection was never strong enough to deserve a reply, let alone the closure you hoped for.

I sighed at the thought. "I miss the late-night phone calls,the long conversations that stretched until dawn. Now everything feels... superficial, like a formality. Honestly, those cavemen might've used language better than we do." I said with a smirk. "At least they made paintings. We just send emojis and memes."

That broke the heaviness. "Hey, don't you dare say anything bad about memes," Dr. Meyer said with mock indignation wagging his finger. "I like memes. The only good invention of your generation!"

Dr. Meyer lifted his cup in a small, wry toast. "To language: the bridge between souls."

He held my gaze for a beat longer. "Now," he said, "are you ready for the third superpower?"

Chapter 7: Empathy

The café had grown quieter. The playlist had slipped into soft jazz, and the hiss of the espresso machine pulsed like a heartbeat beneath our conversation. Outside, the drizzle had finally stopped, leaving the streets glazed in silver. Through the window, Capitol Hill shimmered: a patchwork of murals, vintage shop signs, and rain-speckled glass.

A man in a beanie walked his dog past a record store; two students hurried by with coffee cups and tote bags covered in protest pins. Capitol Hill was always like that, half bohemian, half restless intellect. Artists, baristas, tech workers, and musicians all packed into the same square mile, their lives overlapping like verses of the same unfinished song.

It was the kind of place where people cared deeply about things—music, causes, ideas—and, beneath all their differences, carried an unspoken kindness toward one another. Strangers offered directions, shared smiles, left notes on bulletin boards for lost cats and open mics. Everyone seemed part of something larger than themselves, even if no one ever said it aloud.

Inside the café, I was eager to keep the conversation going. I leaned in. "So," I asked, "what's the third superpower?"

Dr. Meyer smiled. "Third superpower, *Empathy*," he said. "And let me tell you, this one changes everything."

For once, he didn't start with a riddle. His voice turned measured, almost reverent. "Every living thing competes. Trees fight for sunlight, lions fight for prey, even bacteria fight for space. But competition alone doesn't create superior species. The real leap in evolution happens when creatures learn to *collaborate*. And collaboration only exists because of this extraordinary gift: *empathy*."

I agreed. "Because without empathy why would anyone ever put the group above themselves?"

"Exactly. Plenty of species show flickers of it. Dolphins protect wounded podmates. Wolves in a pack hunt together. Ants and bees of a hive coordinate like they share a single brain. But humans can push empathy far beyond the boundaries of bloodlines. We can feel for people beyond our own tribe. We can care for strangers. We can grieve for animals, tend to plants, feel for the planet, even worry about future generations yet to be born."

"Think of your body. Billions of cells, dozens of organs, all working as one. When you stub your toe, your whole body winces. When your stomach aches, your mind slows down in sympathy. Why? Because your nerves connect everything to one brain. Empathy is that *nerve* for humanity. It lets us feel each other's joy and pain.

I liked that image. A giant human body, stitched together by invisible nerves of care. "Like a rowing team?" I said. "Each person pulling an oar, but the rhythm belongs to the group."

He nodded. "Yes. Empathy is the thing that keeps the oars from clashing. It is not just about feeling what others feel, it's *synchronizing*. It's *simulation*. Or if you want me to be more precise... empathy is *imagination* turned inward, our ability to imagine someone else's emotions inside our own."

"That's why books make us cry? And why movies stick with us for days?"

He nodded approvingly. "Studies show that women, on average, score higher on measures of empathy than men. Which might explain why women tend to enjoy books and films more, and why they're often better at relationships, while men are better at writing philosophy books trying to figure women out," he added with a smirk.

I laughed. "I'll quote you on that"

When the laughter faded, I found myself piecing together Dr. Meyer's words. "Empathy is what makes us human, isn't it? And maybe, when it fades, that's what makes us unhappy. Maybe that's what's happening to us now."

"Yes, because when empathy dies, collaboration dies. And without collaboration, we fall back into competition. Every man for himself. And that," he added with a sigh, "is the state of modern life."

He wasn't wrong. Loneliness has become its own epidemic, a public health crisis, according to recent research. Everyone was "connected," yet everyone felt so distant at the same time. It was exactly why I'd come to him, to trace this ache to its source.

"Why is empathy fading, Professor?" I asked finally.

He leaned back slightly. "Is it fading, or just misplaced?"

"I think it's fading," I said, frowning. "Look around. People can't even sustain friendships, let alone their love lives. Everyone's self-focused, impatient and so guarded."

"Empathy is just a tool, Sia, like memory, like language. You use it when you *can*. When life gives you that space, the opportunity to use it. But modern life offers none of that. It rewards speed, isolation and efficiency. Robot traits, not human ones. People aren't becoming heartless. They're just living in systems that leave no room for their hearts."

"So we blame the lifestyle?"

"Partly. But who built that lifestyle? We did. Society is just a mirror of our collective choices. When two people share an experience, empathy flows naturally. That's why classmates bond, why teammates click, why people at concerts feel like family. *Shared experience* synchronizes emotion. But now..." He shrugged. "Now everyone's tuned to a different channel. Everyone's doing their own thing. Different shows, different timelines, different worlds. Families used to sit around one TV. Friends used to debate the same headlines in cafeterias. We used to *experience life together*. Now we stream alone, scroll alone, cope alone. How can empathy survive when we barely inhabit the same reality?"

I didn't say it out loud, but I felt complicit. My own screen time was a confession. I'd convinced myself that constant connection was the same as closeness, but it wasn't.

Dr. Meyer must've read my expression. "Your generation," he said, pointing a playful finger at me, "needs to come out from behind those little glowing bricks. TikTok, Reels, whatever you call them. Throw them away! Go outside. Touch grass. Touch *people*. Look into someone's eyes. Laugh, cry, argue, flirt! Whatever you do, just do it *together*. You'll see how empathy blooms instantly."

I smiled. "Touch grass? That's your official prescription?"

"Absolutely," he said, mock solemn. "Doctor's orders."

Just then, the barista placed two biscotti on our table. "On the house," she said with a grin. "You two look like you're rewriting the Constitution of Humanity over here."

Dr. Meyer raised an eyebrow. "Article One," he declared, "Empathy for all."

By the time we finally paused, the sun had climbed higher, slanting warmer beams through the café windows. The vibe in the café had softened as people proceeded on with their day. Our conversation had run far longer than either of us planned. Unexpectedly long, but every bit fascinating.

Dr. Meyer glanced at his watch. Duty flickered in his eyes. "I have a class to teach," he said, pushing his chair back reluctantly. "But I don't want this conversation left unfinished. Come to my house for lunch on Sunday. We'll conclude properly." With that, he slipped on his coat, waved to the server, and disappeared into the thinning afternoon crowd.

The invitation caught me off guard. In all the years I'd known him, he'd never once invited me to his home. I wasn't sure if it was the caffeine or the honor, but my heart lifted a little.

As I walked out into the crisp Seattle air, I couldn't help thinking about how far back our connection stretched. It started years ago at the University of Washington. I'd wandered into his office hours after a lecture on social psychology, and what was supposed to be a ten-minute chat became an hour-long conversation about mirror neurons and the architecture of love. And then it kept happening. Week after week, year after year.

Even after I graduated, we stayed in touch. We'd send each other research papers, debate over email, sometimes just trade curiosities we'd found online. He once told me that what he appreciated most about me was that I never took an answer at face value. "You dig into the cracks," he said. "That's what keeps you interesting."

But he'd never let me into his personal world, not until now.

The thought of sitting at his table, seeing him not as the academic sage but as a husband, maybe a father, felt strangely intimate. Like he was inviting me beyond the classroom, into the living experiment of his own life.

And as I drove home through the rain-streaked streets, I found myself smiling. The third superpower had been empathy, and somehow, by the end of that day, I realized he'd been practicing it with me all along.

Chapter 8: Creativity

The following Sunday I drove out to the professor's house on the edge of the city, where traffic noise thinned into birdsong and the streets relaxed into green. A hedged boundary kept the world at a respectful distance. Inside the gate, a garden unfurled like a well-kept secret. Tulips and daffodils bright at the borders, cherry blossoms nodding along the path, an old oak presiding with the kind of authority you don't question. It wasn't just a big house; it was a thoughtful one. The details were the grandeur.

His wife answered the door with a warm smile and a calm, quick energy. "You must be Sia," she said. "We've heard a lot about you." I stepped in, and any remaining stereotype of the aloof academic evaporated. The professor was lighter here, playful even. Home loosened his tie you couldn't see.

He bantered easily with his wife in the kitchen, teasing her about burning toast ("the only scientific experiment she ever fails"), and she rolled her eyes, laughing as she swatted him with a dish towel.

Their teenage children, two boys and a girl, were sprawled across the living room, one working on homework, another strumming a guitar, and the youngest building something out of Legos. The professor floated between them, dropping bits of knowledge like candy: a quick fact about how guitar strings vibrate, a math trick for solving a problem faster, a story about dolphins that had his youngest giggling. He wasn't lecturing; he was engaging. Playful and present.

It struck me how right he had been when he said intelligence wasn't about test scores or math problems alone. Real intelligence was about lifting everyone around you, making life richer for those closest to you. He wasn't just saying stuff in the cafe that day. He really meant every word he said. He lived by his words.

After a hearty Sunday lunch, we settled in the gazebo area in the garden, with warm afternoon sun and dessert plates in front of us. His wife insisted I take the last slice of pie, while he protested dramatically until she finally relented, serving it to me with a wink.

"Tell me, Sia," the professor said, working his way through the pie, "have you ever watched little kids play? Really watched them?". The professor gave a quick glance toward his youngest son who was still building something out of Legos.

I smiled. "Of course. My nephews once spent three straight hours playing house. At one point the dog became the 'policeman' and the sofa was apparently the local jail. And don't even get me started on hide-and-seek. They never hide properly, but the thrill is all in the pretending."

He nodded enthusiastically. "*Pretend play*. That's the common thread in all their games. Kids don't need much, just *imagination*. A stick becomes a sword, a cardboard box becomes a spaceship, and suddenly they're bonding through a world they've built together. *Children connect through imagination and creativity.*"

"But as adults, we stop doing that. We stop being playful. No more castles out of pillows, no more dragons to slay. Do you know why?" he asked.

"Maybe because we get smarter?" I wasn't sure what answer he was expecting.

He laughed loudly. "You probably don't have much experience with little kids, do you? You think they don't know the difference between pretend and real? Oh they do. They know the difference really well. But they play with their imaginations simply for fun. Because, and it's not any kind of a mystery, but kids simply like to have fun. They love being creative."

I smiled looking at his son. "Are you saying as adults we forget to be creative? Wait, is that the fourth superpower? *Creativity?*"

"Bingo! You are absolutely correct. Our most celebrated and revered superpower. *Creativity*," he said, almost reverently. "The crown jewels of the brain. It lives right here," he tapped his forehead, "in the prefrontal cortex. Many cultures mark this area of their forehead with bright colors reminding themselves never to forget the power of it."

His words gave me goosebumps. Fascinating to see how it's always the most powerful of things that we take for granted. Never before had I seen someone talk about creativity with so much reverence.

"Do you think AI can copy our superpowers?"

He chuckled. "No way it can. AI can simulate patterns, but it can't *feel wonder*. It can't imagine itself in *love*. It can't *create for joy*. That's uniquely human."

Dr. Meyer was never a big fan of AI anyway but his words weren't just pessimistic rants, they indeed were true. *Creating for joy* is uniquely human. I mean, creation itself is amazing in the first place. Who else can create something original other than humans? And even if we assume AI can create things out of its own imagination, would it ever create for joy? Perhaps this is what Dr. Meyer meant about a child's play.

I glanced at his youngest through the window, still hunched over his Lego tower, completely absorbed. No one was paying him. No one had assigned it. He was building because building felt good—because the act of creating something from nothing was its own reward. No algorithm would ever do that. Not because it couldn't stack the bricks, but because it would never feel the joy of stacking them.

When we grow up, we get so engrossed in *creating for pay,* that we forget how to create for joy. Humans are the most creative species on this planet, perhaps even the universe for all we know. And yet what do we do with this creativity? Our creativity gets funneled into PowerPoint decks and Excel sheets.

"Most people think creativity means art, music, literature, or scientific invention," he said. "Sure, those are important. But the deeper purpose of creativity is *creating connections.* Think of humor. Think of a pickup line that makes someone laugh. Think of surprising your partner in a way they didn't expect. That's creativity at work. That's how bonds form."

I realized how true that was. But somehow, we've been conditioned to believe that the best audience for our creativity isn't our spouse, our children, our family or our friends, but rather we are told our creativity should be best presented to our teacher or our boss. Think about that. The people closest to us, the ones who know our soul, are rarely the ones we create for. Instead, we perform for authority figures. Seeking approval, chasing validation, presenting our best ideas to those who grade or promote us, not those who love us.

"Humans are instinctively designed to be creative for bonding purposes and when this need is not met creativity feels hollow, life feels hollow."

He talked about all kinds of ways we are creative for connection. Sports, team rituals, theatre, performance. All of them are forms of imaginative play. Games, after all, are filled with pretend rivals, pretend quests, pretend challenges. And the real joy is never in the win, it's in the bond that forms along the way.

This concept of *creativity for connection* applies at work as well. It made me realize that the jobs I loved most were the ones where my creativity brought me closer to people. And the ones that drained me were those where I worked all day without any human interaction. Just tasks and outputs. I was beginning to understand his point.

This is why even high-paying jobs can feel meaningless without acknowledgment, appreciation, or connection. We're not bees or ants, able to work mindlessly for the hive. We're humans. We need interaction. We need spark. Without it, our creativity dries up before we even get home. And then we show up to our families empty. No jokes, no surprises, nothing playful left.

The more he spoke, the more the pieces aligned. Creativity, similar to empathy, was clearly a powerful tool for bonding, but it took bonding even further.

Empathy simply enables you to feel what the other is feeling at any given moment. But creativity? It doesn't just stop there. It goes a step further. It gives you the ability to anticipate how the other might feel next, how they will react, what they'll need in the future, even before they ask. It allows you to *design* joy for someone else, solve problems on their behalf, surprise them, delight them, just as instinctively as you would for yourself.

This is the hidden magic of creativity: it personalizes connection. It's how you plan the perfect birthday, write the right words in a tough moment, pull someone out of their sadness with a joke, only you knew would land just right. It's how you turn a mundane Tuesday into a memory.

"To feel truly connected to someone," Dr. Meyer said, "you must be able to simulate their thoughts inside yours, predict their next move, foresee their actions, anticipate their hidden desires. It's like two consciousnesses merging into one."

I shivered a little at the thought. That's what I craved most in love. That sense of oneness. The sense of being not just alongside someone, but intertwined with them.

Without creativity, relationships would be functional, transactional at best. You give, I take. You help, I repay. A loop of needs and duties. But with creativity, relationships become more than survival. They become *playful, exciting and full of color.*

In that sense, creativity is the heartbeat of every lasting relationship. It's what keeps love fresh, friendships alive, families close. We often blame breakups and divorces on cheating, lying, or losing interest. But what usually slips away first is the *fun of it.* When a relationship stops being enjoyable, every small challenge starts to feel heavier. If the joy is gone, so is the motivation to fight for it. Without playfulness, laughter, and shared ease, there's little reason to stay. The will to stay together fades. The desire disappears. And everything else falls apart from there.

He saw the realization land. "Think about it," he said, "when's the last time you did something interesting for your mother or your sibling beyond the usual routine? When's the last time you made your friends laugh so hard they couldn't breathe? Humor is disappearing from our relationships, Sia. And why? Because we've spent every ounce of our creative energy at work, doing tasks that mean nothing when we get home."

I thought of my own evenings. Coming home after a long day, too exhausted to do anything but scroll. "That's true. Sometimes it feels like the people closest to me get the dull leftovers of my day."

The professor smiled knowingly. "Our advanced cerebral capacity wasn't meant only for building skyscrapers and robots, or for sending rockets to Mars", he said softly. "It was also for sketching a silly drawing for your partner, coming up with an inside joke, or creating moments that makes the other person feel understood. That's what imagination and creativity are truly for. For the simple, timeless act of making each other feel alive. Connection is in the heart of every creation."

Dr. Meyer was not exaggerating with his concept of creativity for connection. After all, if you look at all the modern gadgets we rely on, all the major inventions, all the breakthrough scientific advances, at the heart of it the purpose is to stay connected with the world around us. Phones, internet, satellites, radio, GPS, social media, dating apps, transport systems: planes, trains, ships, automobiles. What is the purpose of them? Basically to connect with more and more people in the world. People are what matter, not technology.

"What good is your phone if you have no one to call?" I said aloud. "Or a social networking app if you have no friends? Or a mansion if you have no one to invite in?"

I paused, letting the thought settle. "This is Maslow's hierarchy, isn't it?" I went on. "You can pile all the success, money, and achievements you want. But at the end of the pyramid, what people crave is connection. To love and be loved. That's the only thing that makes the rest of it worth anything."

"Absolutely. All our devices, all our knowledge, all our possessions, none of it means anything without someone to share it with. A phone finds its purpose in the voice of someone you love. A million-dollar home, in the laughter of its guests. A fancy car, in the joy of riding alongside another. Fine clothes and accessories, in the sparkle of someone's eyes when they notice. And even a joke," he added with a smile, "finds its meaning only in the laughter of others."

Dr. Meyer leaned back, satisfied. "That's why creative people often succeed in relationships. Humor, playfulness, surprise, these are tools of bonding."

I found myself nodding. Maybe that's why I've always found funny men so attractive. Humor makes connection effortless. It's a form of intelligence, an instant bridge between two minds. When someone can make you laugh, they pull you out of your defenses and into the present.

How many close friends we have often depends on how interesting, creative, or funny we are. How well we can entertain, engage, and draw others into our little world. *People don't just want to be understood; they want to be delighted.*

It all began to make sense now. How relationships, intelligence, and creativity were deeply interconnected. Relationships, I realized, had less to do with heart and emotions than with mind and skills. The subtle art of understanding, responding, and entertaining together.

He pointed his spoon at me like a judge passing a verdict. "Our primal drive is to compete, but our *superpowers* taught us to collaborate. Animals work against one another, they fight for resources, but we Sia, we humans, we have these superpowers that makes us ask: what if we did this together? What if we connect? What if we share? That's how humans survived. That's why we thrive."

And maybe that's what modern life is missing. Not more technology. Not more tools. But *more connection, more empathy, more play*. More jokes. More sparks of creativity, where they matter most.

I sat quietly, taking it all in, watching his family move around the kitchen, teasing, laughing, sharing pie. *Memory, language, empathy, creativity*. Not just brain functions. Not just evolutionary quirks. But the superpowers that had carried humanity this far, and the very ones we seemed to be forgetting. And not just forgetting, in fact, we've created systems that numb it. Endless scrolling, carefully curated feeds, those make us spectators of each other's lives, not participants. We watch, but we don't feel. We comment, but we don't connect.

And the tragedy is that modern culture actually promotes this kind of an isolated lifestyle. There is no work life balance. Most people live and work like robots with little to no human interaction. While animals can thrive perfectly well in instinct-driven survival, humans cannot.

The deer grazes, the wolf hunts, the bird builds its nest. None of them wonder if life could be more. They are bound to instinct, and instinct is enough. But we are built for something else. Humans are equipped with superpowers that allow us to build not only strategies but whole civilizations and when we ignore it, the soul begins to wither.

The hidden source of modern despair is nothing but the gap between what we are capable of and how we actually live. Deep down, people sense that they are not using their gifts, not living to their full potential. That knowledge gnaws at them, even when they cannot name it.

The Harvard Grant Study, a decades-long examination of human happiness, confirms this. The study revealed that the greatest predictor of well-being was not wealth, fame, or achievement, but close, meaningful relationships. Another study on empathy and mirror neurons, shows how our brains light up when we see the emotions of others, urging us toward compassion. It is as though our biology itself is crying out for connection, but our culture dulls that cry with constant distraction.

As my conversation with Dr. Meyer wound down, I grew quiet. For the first time, depression did not seem like a mysterious shadow but like a mirror reflecting our own neglect.

The professor's children soon invaded the gazebo like a wave of energy. One tugged on his sleeve with a Lego tower that refused to stand. Another waved a math problem at him with a look of pure desperation. The third strummed a guitar chord that was clearly out of tune and wanted him to fix it.

What struck me wasn't their chaos but his response. He gave each of them his full attention, as if the Lego tower were a nuclear equation, as if the math homework were a matter of state, as if the guitar string were the hinge of civilization itself. His face, his focus, his patience, all of it was absolute.

I couldn't help but laugh softly, amused in the most tender way. To me, it was poetry in motion. Perhaps this was as important as making rockets or going to Mars. After all, who decides what matters and what doesn't? *We do.* And his choice, at that moment, was his children.

I let my eyes wander around the house. Sunlight spilled across family photos on the wall, a bookshelf with worn spines, fresh flowers in a vase. The professor was still surrounded by his kids, leaning into their questions, their noise, their laughter. He had it all. Not just the financial security earned through decades of hard work, but the kind of wealth you can't measure.

A loving wife, children who adored him, respect from his students, a home that felt alive.

This was a life that looked whole, wholesome, complete. I could already see his future: retired, with grandkids playing on this very lawn, a peaceful energy surrounding his day. He would leave his mark on both his family and the wider world.

Anyone can give us advice, intellectuals, online experts, authors, therapists, family, pretty much anyone. But whose advice do we actually take to heart? We listen to the people not with degrees or citations, but those whose lives we admire. Because by following their path, we hope to shape a little of that fullness for ourselves. And Dr. Meyer was surely one of them.

"Was I able to answer your question, Sia?" The professor's voice cut through my reflection. He had popped his head out from the swarm of children, still half-occupied with fixing a Lego roof.

I smiled, my heart unexpectedly full. "You did, professor. You really did!"

I noticed the Lego piece in his hand was turned the wrong way. "But now," I said, taking it gently from his hand, "let me help you with this problem." I flipped the piece, and it clicked perfectly into place, making his son beam with excitement. I looked back at my professor, silently thanking him with my eyes, for his time, his wisdom, and the incredible warmth he had shared with me while patiently answering my questions.

As I stepped outside and walked toward my car, my world felt lighter, as if a cloud had been lifted. For the first time, my own heartache didn't seem like a struggle, but a challenge instead, something that I didn't have to fight with weapons, but with knowledge instead.

****

The Library

Chapter 9: Education

After that conversation with my professor, something settled in me with crystal clarity: loneliness isn't cured by money, hobbies, or even Netflix marathons. To not feel empty and to experience life at its fullest, you need relationships. You need people. You need connection. I was convinced this was the superpower we all had to use if we wanted our lives to mean something.

But then came the harder question: *What makes a good relationship?* How do you know if someone is right for you, before you hand over your heart like a fragile package on overnight delivery? What are the signs of a healthy relationship? That's when my brain made the strangest leap—straight to tomato shopping.

Think about it. You don't walk into a store and close your eyes and hope for the best. You thump a watermelon, press a tomato, sniff an orange. There's a whole secret science in how shoppers pick fruits. A PhD in produce selection. Yet when it comes to choosing people, arguably more important than a good tomato, we're all like amateurs buying mystery boxes off the internet.

Dating today feels like online shopping: you scroll, you order, it looks perfect in the pictures, then it arrives and...

nope. Return. Refund. Repeat. Somewhere out there, Tom Hanks' line from *Forrest Gump* is laughing at us: life isn't a box of chocolates anymore, it's an Amazon Prime nightmare, you never know what you're gonna get, but hey, 30-day returns!

I didn't want that to be my life. I didn't want to spend years "ordering and returning" until maybe, one day, the right one stuck. Why should I have to learn through heartbreak after heartbreak? Why should scars be the tuition fee for wisdom?

That's not how we do it with anything else. Is that how they teach you driving? "Here, take the car, crash it a couple times, you'll figure it out." Of course not. We don't unleash teenagers on highways with the optimistic shrug of "good luck, kid." We give them manuals, training wheels, instructors who yell at them when they forget the turn signal. Only when they've studied and practiced do they earn the keys.

So why do we treat relationships, the thing that defines the quality of our entire lives, as the one skill you're supposed to master by wreckage? Where's the manual? Where's the training course? Who's teaching us how to love without self-destructing? High school? College? Our parents? Hollywood? Taylor Swift?

The truth is, we used to learn by watching. Families lived close, communities were tight, and you could see partnerships up close: the good, the bad, the endurance of it. But now? Families are scattered, divorce rates are high, even the "happily married" couples you know are often bickering under the surface. And so we grow up with no clear models, no real apprenticeship in how to love.

Instead, our "teachers" are celebrities and influencers. We scroll through their polished pictures, their perfect captions, their red-carpet divorces. And we're supposed to figure out what love looks like? It's like studying nutrition by looking at a cake on Instagram.

No wonder heartbreak wrecks us so deeply. It's not just the pain of loss, it's the confusion, the unanswered questions. Why did it end? Was it me? Was it them? Could it have been prevented? It's the not knowing that drives people mad. If a project fails at work, there's a post-mortem. If a relationship fails, you're told: *shut up, move on, stop overthinking.* And you drag your unanswered questions into the next relationship, like carrying broken glass in your pockets.

After my breakup, I decided I wanted better than that. People want to master coding, painting, cooking, even knitting sweaters for their cats. Me? *I wanted to master relationships.*

What Dr. Meyer had given me were tools—memory, language, empathy, creativity. But tools alone don't build anything. A hammer doesn't construct a house by itself. You need to know *how* to use it, *when* to swing it, *what* you're building.

The professor had given me the instruments. Now I needed to figure out the blueprint, a manual of sorts for building a lasting relationship. And I figured: if there's knowledge, there must be somewhere it's stored. If there's a manual, there must be somewhere it's hiding. And for that, I knew exactly where to go: *The Library.*

At least that's what I told myself when I drove back to my old campus at the University of Washington. If there's a secret textbook out there with chapters titled *"How to design your happily ever after"* or *"Page 42: How to find a perfect match"*, surely it would be tucked away in some dusty aisle between Psychology and Anthropology.

The UW library, by the way, is not just any library. Step inside and you feel like you've walked straight into *Harry Potter*. Soaring gothic arches, tall stained-glass windows, rows upon rows of books stretching like cathedrals of wisdom. If only they also came with moving staircases and an old wizard whispering, "Ah, yes... aisle three for the spell of eternal commitment."

Instead, what I found was a former classmate, now a full-time lab rat doing a PhD on something that sounded important but, the more he explained, the more it sounded like corporate Sudoku. He was studying a tiny molecule that, if manipulated correctly, could make shampoo foam better or make laundry detergent last longer. I kid you not, he was devoting six years of his life to making bubbles slightly bubblier, so that one day a corporation could charge you an extra $2.99 for "new improved lather."

When I teased him about this, he bristled.

"Hey, it's useful! These advancements trickle down into products people use every day."

"Sure," I said, "but nobody's depression has ever been cured because their shampoo foamed a little better."

He didn't laugh. That's when I noticed: the sparkle he used to have in college, the witty one-liners, the ridiculous puns, had been slowly drained away by the lab. Back in the day, he was the guy who could turn any boring lecture into stand-up comedy. Now, his jokes had been replaced with phrases like "enzyme pathway" and "funding proposal."

In a way, he was a victim of his own success. Too smart for his own good. *Because* he could get into the elite programs, he did, and in doing so, he bound himself to whatever projects the university could get corporate funding for. You don't say no when Bill Gates funds your program. You nod politely, put on your lab coat, and devote your twenties to molecules that will one day make someone else's shareholders richer.

The irony hit me hard. Here was one of the most brilliant people I knew, unraveling molecular mysteries with a microscope, but when I asked him about his own life, his voice faltered. I pressed him gently:

"Come on, tell me. What's your biggest problem in life right now?"
He scratched his head, avoided my eyes, and muttered something about stress, exhaustion, not having time to meet anyone. Translation: *brilliant in lab, lost in love.*

It's strange how universities train you to conquer molecules, but not loneliness. They'll hand you a PhD in how to fold proteins but nothing on how to hold a hand without fumbling.

I told him I was on my own quest. Not for molecules, but for manuals. "You basically live in this library," I teased. "You know every nook and cranny. Help me find the section on love and relationships. Not the mushy novels, I want the real stuff. If you can study detergent bubbles, then I can study why couples burst."

He rolled his eyes, but he smiled. For the first time in our conversation, I saw the old him peek through.

Chapter 10: Therapy

He finally gave in. With a sigh that carried all the weight of his unfinished dissertation, he got up and motioned for me to follow. "Fine. You want books on love? Let's see what the great library of human knowledge has to say."

First stop? Romance novels. He pointed proudly at an entire wall of them. Glossy covers, couples kissing in the rain, titles like *Love at Sunset*, *Forever and Always*, and *The Billionaire's Reluctant Bride*.

I stared at him. "Seriously?"

"You said relationships. This counts."

"Yeah, and if I want to learn about surgery, should I start with *Grey's Anatomy* fan fiction?"

He laughed, but I was dead serious. "I don't want fairy tales. I want formulas. Equations. The Newton's laws of dating. Something I can actually use."

So he tried again. This time, he led me to the self-help aisle, and oh boy. Breakup survival guides. Coping with loneliness. Divorce recovery. Titles screaming *'It's Not You, It's Him'* and *'How to Get Over Anyone in 30 Days'*. It felt less like education and more like a trauma ward.

"This is depressing," I muttered, running my fingers across the spines. "Where's the section on how to actually build a good relationship before it falls apart? Prevention, not damage control."

"See, this is the problem," I told him. "Therapy is like a bandage. Useful, sure, but it doesn't fix the potholes in the road. You fall, you scrape your knees, you go get patched up. But then you walk the same road again and trip over the same damn pothole. Why don't we get enough people together to actually fix the road? Wouldn't that save us all from the repeated falls?"

He nodded slowly. "So you're saying all this is... reactive. Nothing proactive."

"Exactly! It's like having classes on how to use painkillers but no one teaching us nutrition so we don't get sick in the first place. Look at these shelves. It's heartbreak, heartbreak, heartbreak. Coping, surviving, moving on. Where's the education on how not to break in the first place?"

I picked up a title: *Moving On Gracefully*. The irony wasn't lost on me. In corporate life, when a project fails, they hold postmortems. They dissect every detail to figure out what went wrong, so the same mistakes aren't repeated. But in relationships? You're told to stop thinking about it, move on, don't look back. No analysis, no clarity, no closure. Just drag your broken heart into the next round and hope this one works out better.

I shook my head. "It's insane. Why do we treat our jobs with more seriousness than our hearts? If your marketing campaign fails, you get a whiteboard and a team meeting. If your marriage fails? You get a therapist who tells you to journal and wait for time to heal."

He gave a bitter little laugh. "At least campaigns don't file for alimony."

I grinned, but inside I was frustrated. The truth is, this aisle was proof of how backward we've gotten. Whole shelves dedicated to patching wounds, but none to preventing them.

And then he admitted it: he'd been seeing a therapist himself. This was the same friend who, back in college, was so full of life, cracking jokes even at 3 a.m. in the library when everyone else was sleep-deprived and delirious. To hear him say that he now needed therapy just to stay afloat... it stunned me.

"What happened to you?" I asked, not unkindly. "You're one of the brightest people I know. How did it come to this?"

He gave a bitter little shrug. "Grad school happened. Research happened. Life."

I looked at him then, really looked. The long hours in labs, the endless funding proposals, the weight of corporate-driven research, it had stripped him. The sparkle, the mischief, the old humor... all dimmed. He wasn't just studying molecules anymore. He was trapped by them.

And that's when the thought struck me hardest: universities hand out manuals for enzymes, atoms, and galaxies. But for life itself? For love, connection, relationships...? We get nothing. No syllabus, no textbook, no manual. Just trial and heartbreak.

I turned back to the sad row of breakup books and felt an almost comic frustration. *This is the best humanity has to offer? Shelf after shelf of coping mechanisms?*

I whispered it out loud before I could stop myself: "Even after all our progress, our knowledge of relationships, still feels as primitive as in the times of Adam and Eve. We've mapped glaciers, split the atoms, decoded genomes, walked on the moon, even stretched till Mars. But the thing that determines whether we're lonely or loved? Still a total mystery."

My friend glanced at me. "And yet, that's the one thing everyone actually cares about."

"Exactly."

Chapter 11: Overload

We left the heartbreak aisle behind and wandered deeper into the stacks. I couldn't help laughing at the absurdity of it all. "So this is what human civilization has achieved? Thousands of years of evolution, the printing press, the internet, and our greatest contribution to understanding love is... *'How to Get Over Him in Ten Days'*?"

My friend smirked. "Well, when people don't find answers in books, they find them in podcasts."

That opened the floodgates. "Oh my god, yes. Podcasts. We live in an age where every barista with Wi-Fi thinks they're a philosopher. Half the world is trying to tell you how to live, how to date, how to breathe correctly. It's like a never-ending infomercial for life hacks nobody asked for."

He chuckled. "At least radios had music."

"Exactly! Podcasts are just radios, except now it's your ex's roommate explaining attachment theory."

We walked past shelves labeled *Psychology* and *Sociology,* and I kept going. "The crazy part is, the advice is always contradictory. One guru says women should never text first. Another will say women should absolutely text first. Some say wait three days to reply. Others will say to reply instantly or you'll look disinterested. It's like dating has turned into assembling Ikea furniture without the manual, and everyone online has their own opinion on which Allen wrench works best."

He burst out laughing. "True, true."

"And don't get me started on personality tests," I added. "If Myers-Briggs types really determined compatibility, psychiatrists would be the new Cupids. ENTJ + INFJ equals happily ever after? No it's not! It's more like OMFG + STFU."

He laughed so hard people turned to stare. It felt good to see his old self flicker through again.

"And love languages," I pressed on. "Supposedly the holy grail of relationships. Words of affirmation, quality time, gifts... blah blah. Let's be real: who doesn't want all of those? But now people use them as excuses. Don't want to spend time with your partner? Just say, 'Quality time isn't my love language.' Bad with words? 'Sorry babe, affirmations aren't my love language.' Like... really? When did love languages become a 'get out of effort free' card?"

"Okay, that one hits close to home," he admitted, still grinning.

For a moment, it was fun to tear it all apart. The endless flood of contradictory, click-bait wisdom. But as our laughter settled, the silence afterward was heavier.

"Still," I said softly, "the scary thing is people actually depend on this noise. They're lost. Schools don't teach this stuff. Families don't talk about it anymore. So where do people go? Podcasts. YouTube. Twitter threads. They drink from the firehose of advice. And the more they drink, the thirstier they get."

He tilted his head. "Information overload."

"Exactly. Everyone shouting, nobody agreeing. Imagine if science had evolved this way. If there were no laws of physics, just TikTokers with theories on why apples fall from trees. That's literally what relationships are right now. A giant free-for-all of opinions."

I thought of how it used to be. Once upon a time, wisdom passed down through communities, families and mentors. Grandmothers would tell you what to look for in a husband, uncles would warn you about red flags. But today? Our social structures have fractured. Divorce rates are high, families are scattered, and young people grow up never having seen a healthy partnership even in their own homes. Instead of learning from the community, we learn from algorithms.

And the algorithms don't care if advice is useful. They care if it's viral. A toxic hot-take travels faster than a thoughtful truth. Some teenager on TikTok screams that all men are trash; another says women are irrational chaos demons. Both hit a million views. And millions of confused, heartbroken people gulp it down, wondering if maybe their misery is their fault.

"You know," he said finally, "for all my papers, I've never once seen a serious study on what makes relationships succeed. Not in psychology, not in sociology, not in science conferences. Nothing."

I looked at him. "And yet... isn't that the thing that decides whether people live fulfilled lives? Whether they wake up happy or miserable?"

He didn't answer, but he didn't need to. His silence was its own confession.

Chapter 12: Structure

By the time we circled back to the library's entrance, I couldn't shake the thought that this place, this cathedral of knowledge, had everything except the one thing people need most. Physics? Check. Chemistry? Check. Even books on how ants organize their colonies. But an actual *academic study* on relationships... the glue of our existence? Still treated like gossip in a women's magazine.

I turned to my friend. "You know what blows my mind? Humanity can predict weather patterns down to the minute. We can use AI to forecast stock markets. But no one can tell you if the person sitting across from you at dinner is going to break your heart in six months."

"True. But people say feelings are subjective, you can't quantify them."

"Please. That's just lazy. We once thought weather was subjective too. Gods were angry, Zeus threw lightning bolts. Then someone bothered to study it, and surprise! Turns out storms have patterns. Same with relationships. We just haven't invested in them, because they don't make corporations richer. A cure for loneliness doesn't sell shampoo."

He leaned against the oak table, thoughtful.

I pressed on. "Do you know the U.S. Surgeon General literally called loneliness an epidemic last year? More dangerous than smoking fifteen cigarettes a day. We're living longer, richer, smarter... and lonelier. It's not just sad; it's killing us. And yet... look around. Still no manual, no solution, nothing that the scientific community can collectively endorse."

His shoulders dropped. "And still no funding."

"Exactly. Billions go to consumer products, inventing apps that deliver tacos faster, or teaching algorithms how to sell you things you don't need. But where's the billion-dollar project for teaching humans how to stay married, how to raise healthy families, how to be good partners? Isn't that what determines the actual quality of our lives?"

He didn't answer. He didn't need to. I could see it in his face. He craved that knowledge as much as I did.

So I looked straight at him and, by extension, at anyone who would one day read these words. "We need a new field. Not psychology as an abstract, not therapy as a bandage. A science of relationships. Universal principles, like Newton's laws. Not the vague advice of influencers, but foundations that hold. Imagine a future where libraries had entire shelves on this: *The Principles of Love. The Theory of Relationships. The Architecture of Commitment. The Mechanics of Connection.* Where we don't wait for heartbreak to learn, but we prevent it by understanding how things actually work."

He smiled faintly. "If that existed, I'd enroll tomorrow."

In his words, I realized he wasn't speaking only for himself but voicing the hunger of a generation. The generation that had dismantled the old systems. We tore up all the rulebooks, the ones that said: marry at a certain age, date a specific type. The ones that said *no sex before commitment, no kids before marriage.* We shattered the stereotype of men working and women raising children. We broke gender roles, marriage norms, and the rules of intimacy. We challenged timelines for commitment and the expectations of families.

Bravo. Pat on the back. We did a hell of a job.

But then what? Did we replace those rules with anything better?

Not really.

Did we create new standards to live by? New expectations, new boundaries, new values to anchor us?

Nope. We said, *no rules, no timelines, no norms, no expectations.* And now we're left wondering why we feel so lost?... why we're so confused, why we no longer know how to do life, love or commitment.

We ask ourselves: what are the benchmarks now? What standards remain by which we can hold ourselves, or anyone else, accountable? How do we even make sense of people's actions anymore?

But we get no answers. Because the truth is, we've built nothing of our own. No rules, no norms, no expectations.

Breaking an old structure is always welcome, especially if it no longer holds relevance in the present context. But every broken structure must be replaced by a new one. Because without structure, without order or rules, a society where *anything goes* eventually collapses, like a building without beams or a foundation.

We said biology doesn't determine gender, then it's fair to ask, what does?

We said commitment doesn't require marriage, then it's fair to ask, what binds a promise when there's no consequence for breaking it?

We said both men and women should work, then it's fair to ask, who will raise the children?

We said both partners should earn, then it's fair to ask, who pays for the date?

Somewhere between the questions and the silence that follows, we realize how far we have gotten lost. And perhaps that's why what our generation needs most today is *direction*— a structure, guidance to look up to.

Yes, it's true, the old rules cannot keep pace with the changing times, the rapid evolution of culture and technology. In this new renaissance, the old patriarchal order had to be rejected. But to reject order entirely is misplaced logic. Because removing order invites chaos, and chaos invites stress, and trust me, nobody wants that.

That's why we want a *manual*—a real training guide for love, for life, for relationships. A framework that offers both structure and compassion. Structure to set hard boundaries, and compassion to keep them humane. With the right balance of both, harmony can return.

Everyone is craving for this manual. Because learning through endless heartbreaks is an expensive way to master a lesson, especially when the currency is your soul.

I sat in silence for some time, the great hall around us echoing with the faint rustle of pages. For once, the library felt less like a place of answers and more like a reminder of everything still missing.

My friend watched me, then said something I didn't expect.

"You know what's funny? You've been here for hours, pulling books off shelves, arguing with me about love languages and podcasts and Newton's laws of dating—and you're more passionate about this than anyone I've met in six years of grad school." He paused. "Maybe the manual doesn't exist because no one's written it yet."

I looked at him.

He shrugged, smiling faintly. "I'm just saying—you're the one asking all the questions. Maybe you're the one who's supposed to find the answers."

I laughed it off. But the words lodged somewhere deeper than I expected. Maybe the manual was not something I would find, but something I would have to write myself.

When I finally stepped out of the gothic arches, the spring air greeted me—soft, fragrant, impossibly gentle after the weight of my thoughts. The cherry blossoms were in full bloom, their pale pink canopies lining the Quad like clouds that had drifted down and decided to stay. Petals floated on the breeze, settling on benches, on backpacks, on the shoulders of students who walked beneath them without looking up.

I stopped beneath the nearest tree and watched the petals fall. A month ago, these branches had been bare. A month from now, the petals would be gone. But the trees wouldn't be dead. They'd be green, gathering energy for the next bloom. And then autumn would strip them. And winter would still them. And spring would wake them once more.

The same cycle. Over and over. Not a straight line—a spiral.

And suddenly I saw it everywhere. Day follows night follows day. Tides rise and fall and rise. Seasons don't march forward and stop—they return. Nothing that endures moves in a straight line. Everything that lasts is cyclical.

A seed germinates, grows, and either reproduces or dies. A fire sparks, burns, and either spreads or extinguishes. Civilizations rise, flourish, and either renew themselves or collapse.

Three phases. Always three. And the things that last? They cycle back. They begin again from within.

Standing beneath the falling blossoms, I felt something click into place. If this pattern held true for seeds, fires, seasons, empires—then surely relationships followed the same law.

There had to be three phases to every relationship. Something that begins it. Something that sustains it. And something that determines whether it renews—or ends.

I didn't know what those three things were yet. But I knew they existed. And I knew the secret wasn't just in understanding the phases—it was in understanding how to keep the cycle turning.

I kept walking, petals drifting in my wake, the arches of my old university shrinking behind me. I had come to this library looking for a manual someone else had written. I was leaving with something better—the first page of my own.

****

The Launch Party

Chapter 13: Drive

It arrived on a Tuesday afternoon, tucked among the usual stack of bills and glossy catalogues. The envelope was heavier than the others, the paper thick, embossed with a silver crest that caught the light. Not the kind of thing you toss on the counter and forget about. I slit it open and pulled out a card so elegant it almost seemed out of place in my modest apartment, the kind of invitation that belonged in a movie scene rather than real life.

A launch party. The name of an old friend printed in bold— Richard Collins—announcing the debut of his new company.

I set the other mail aside and held that card for a moment longer than I should have. There's something about a real invitation, not a Facebook event or a group text, that makes you stop in your tracks. A small artifact of intention. It was as if my day had paused for a second to ask me: *do you still remember what it feels like to show up?*

I hadn't gone to parties or events since my breakup. I simply hadn't wanted to. As Dr. Meyer would say, my superpowers were gathering dust. Memory, language, empathy, creativity, all of it sitting unused. I laughed at the thought, but not without a sting of truth. He is right, *we already have the superpowers we need, so why aren't we using them?*

I was still very grateful for the conversations I had with my professor. Even though I was still looking for answers, he definitely got me one step closer. There is something beautiful about knowing the reason behind your sadness. It's no longer a dark room you're afraid to enter. You can see it, even if you don't yet know how to face it. I knew the demon; I just needed to learn how to tackle it. I knew if I wanted to be happy again, I had to step back into the world, to make connections again, to find that drive I'd somehow lost.

Where? Where did that drive go? Somewhere along the way, we all seem to have lost it. We live in a world where connection has become absurdly easy. I could FaceTime someone in Tokyo while sitting in a café in Seattle. A car, a plane, a train, any of them could take me wherever I wanted to go. Dating apps offer a parade of faces with the swipe of a finger. We're wired, networked, surrounded by endless opportunities to meet, to love, to belong. And yet, we drift. We scroll instead of speak. We watch instead of touch.

The numbers back it up, though I hardly needed them to know it was true. Young people are pairing off less, marrying less, having children less. A U.S. survey reported that nearly one in three men under thirty hadn't had sex in the past year, triple the rate a decade earlier. Marriage rates are at historic lows, fertility at its weakest in a century. We are a generation raised on infinite possibility, and somehow the possibility itself has hollowed us out.

When I pressed Dr. Meyer on it, asking him why the hunger to date had gone missing, why the fire to connect had burned so low, for the first time I saw a blank stare in his eyes: *"I don't have all the answers, Sia."*

That answer stunned me more than I expected. Professors are supposed to have answers, especially *him*. But then I realized: perhaps he couldn't know. His generation had already lived through it: married, raised families, built communities. They had *used* their superpowers. Ours was the one stumbling, fumbling, wasting them. No wonder he couldn't explain it; the problem belonged to us.

The library had confirmed as much. All those shelves, all that knowledge, and still no manual for why my generation can't seem to fall in love, or stay in love, or even want to try. The answers weren't in the books. Not yet.

Still, I couldn't shake the determination. If the drive had disappeared, I had to know where it went. And why.

So when the invitation slid into my inbox, it felt like a flare in the dark. A party. A launch. And not just any party—this one thrown by an old college friend who had just sold his startup and was unveiling his new company. A multimillionaire now. Out of everyone I had known in those years, he had gone the farthest, climbed the highest. I had always known he had the spark—restless, ambitious, brimming with ideas even as a student. But this far? Even I wouldn't have guessed.

And suddenly, I wanted to see him. Not just out of curiosity, not just to celebrate, but because if anyone could tell me about *drive*, it was him. The fire I had lost after my breakup, the apathy that had bled into my work and my life, maybe he had carried his flame all the way through. Maybe he could remind me how.

We hadn't spoken much in years, not really. A birthday message on Facebook. A half-joking comment on a photo. A heart tapped on a story. That was it. But I imagined us in a quieter corner of his party, a drink in hand, him flushed with the satisfaction of victory. That sweet moment of triumph when people feel most like the main character in their own story.

When they let down their guard and pour out the truth. That's when I wanted to catch him.

Not for my book. Not even for the answers. But to rekindle the drive within my own self that once fueled me.

Chapter 14: Value

Seattle has its own kind of charm, a city that manages to be both restless and serene at once. That evening, Lake Washington stretched out like a silver mirror, its surface trembling with the last hints of daylight. His house sat proudly along the waterfront, all glass and cedar, blending into the evergreens as though it had grown there naturally. Modern, yes, but softened by the water's reflection and the glow of the setting sun.

As I walked up the drive, I could see the inside spilling with warm light, laughter leaking through the open doors. No velvet ropes, no corporate stiffness. This wasn't a party for investors or employees. It was friends, only friends, the ones who had known him before he was somebody.

Behind the house, a wide staircase led down toward the water. The railings draped with small golden lights that blinked against the twilight. I stood there with a mutual friend, both of us watching the sun bleed pink across the lake, when I felt a tap on my shoulder.

"Richie Rich," I said, turning with a grin.

He laughed, shaking his head. "That's new. You never called me that before!"

"Well, you weren't rich back then. I had to update the nickname."

"Guess I'll allow it," he smirked. "Though it makes me sound like a cartoon."

"And yet it fits," I teased, raising my glass.

That was the thing about college friends, no matter how much time passed, when you met again it felt like yesterday.

We hugged, and for a moment it was as though nothing had shifted between us. He had always been warm with me. Always. Ours was a delicate friendship, the kind that tiptoes near the line of something more but never crosses it. I had always known he liked me. The compliments that came a little too easily, the way he offered to help with homework, the lunches he paid for, the concerts he'd surprise me with. I hadn't forgotten any of it. But he had never pushed, never risked breaking the friendship we both cherished.

And that made it beautiful. Every woman treasures a friendship like that, part validation, part possibility, part reminder of her own charm. In college, it had been a boost to my confidence. Tonight, for the first time, it felt like a possibility.

He hadn't changed much. Same smile, same demeanor. And yet, for the first time, I felt a spark. A faint tickle I hadn't expected. After my breakup, I thought that part of me had been buried for good. But here it was again, flickering quietly to life.

He pulled me aside, handed me a drink, and we fell into reminiscing. The concerts, the late night study sessions, the jokes only we would still remember. Then, as though picking up on my urgency, he asked, "So, what have you been up to lately?"

This was my chance. He would get busy later, drift back into the crowd. I had to ask him now. Our friendship had always allowed blunt questions, silly or serious, so I leaned into that tone—playful, dramatic, familiar.

"Oh, you know, I've been searching for answers," I said, raising my glass as though reciting lines from a film. "Looking how to solve the equations of life."

He smirked and played along. "And what is it that Miss Sia is searching for these days? Maybe, this seemingly ordinary man can help!"

I rolled my eyes with a small laugh, then with a thoughtful gaze asked him. "I want to know what keeps the drive alive? What keeps the passion burning? Look at you, Richie. You've achieved everything. What fueled you? Race cars? This fancy yacht?" I pointed toward the gleaming beast tied up at his dock. "Or maybe this luxury lakeside house?"

He tilted his head, his grin softening into something almost shy. "You want me to be honest? It was none of that. I just wanted to be noticed. I wanted to be someone. Back in college, I was invisible. Nobody saw me. Nobody cared. I was just... there."

He hesitated, then exhaled like he was letting out a truth he hadn't shared before. "There was this girl I liked, Rachel, you remember? She'd kind of nodded when I asked her to the spring formal. Not a yes, not a no, just enough to keep me hoping. I thought I had a shot. I even bought flowers. Stood outside her dorm like an idiot, rehearsing lines in my head." He gave a short, humorless laugh.

"She came down the steps that night, all dressed up, looking incredible. And then, she walked straight past me, got into another guy's car, one of those golden boys on the basketball team. She didn't even look at me, Sia. Not once. I remember ducking behind the bushes with those stupid flowers so nobody else would see me standing there like a fool. That's when it hit me—I was the backup. The invisible one. The guy you only remember when the first choice isn't available. And I swore to myself, never again. I would make damn sure people noticed me."

I cut in quickly. "That's not true. I noticed you."

"Did you, Sia? Did you really notice me?" His eyes locked on mine, steady and unflinching.

And he was right. I may have noticed him as a friend but not in the way he had wanted me to. My eyes softened, and I gave him the gentlest nod I could.

He went on, quieter now. "That emptiness became my fuel. I didn't dream about yachts or houses. Those came later, sure, but they were never the goal. I just wanted to matter. I wanted to walk into a room and have people know I existed. I wanted to be someone people looked at and thought—he counts."

"So," I asked softly, "people notice you now?"

"Yes," he said with a grin, mischief returning. "Especially women." He winked, and I couldn't help but laugh.

As the evening wore on, I watched him move through the party. He hopped from friend to friend, clasping hands, giving hugs, offering that easy smile. And the more people noticed him, the more his confidence seemed to swell, as if each spark of attention fed the next. He had always carried some of this confidence, even back in college, but nothing like the kind he showed now. It snowballed with every nod, every laugh, every admiring glance.

We usually try to force confidence. We are told to act confident, to "pretend" to be confident. To say affirmations in front of the mirror: *I am great. I am beautiful.* Maybe it works for some, but that sort of trick never worked for me. What works is when you add value to your life—through skill, through hard work, through consistency, through discipline. Once you hold value, people automatically take notice. You don't even have to try. You don't have to be loud. You don't have to be flashy. Value will draw attention organically, the way bees are drawn to honey, the way the bird in my garden was drawn to the song. And that attention will give you all the confidence you need.

Back in college, I remember how I had to push Richie to go talk to girls. *Don't worry, you're looking great. Your outfit is perfect, don't overthink. She likes you, don't stress, just go and talk to her.* But none of that worked. He was still shy, still hesitant, still unsure of himself. And look at him today—talking effortlessly to beautiful women around him, not with bravado but with ease, with charm, without needing any pep talk from me. His confidence was shining through his smile. And why would it not? After all, he had worked so hard to get here. Those late nights in the lab, the endless hours of preparation for job interviews, the steady discipline, the relentless focus on his craft—all of it had paid off. He always had that drive in him, that passion to do something big, that hunger to become someone who people value, and not just look past.

And I thought: *isn't this what drives all of us?* Not the objects themselves but the value they represent. The cars, the houses, the titles, the money—they are all signals, tools to make others turn their heads and say, *I see you.* The hunger inside us isn't for things. It's to be noticed. We strive all our lives to raise our value. The endless working hours, the career, the job interviews, the splashy makeup, the fancy clothes, the diets and the exercise. To raise our value so we can be noticed. Because when people notice you, you feel that you *matter.* Your life has *meaning*. And that, more than money, more than trophies, more than comfort, is what keeps the human drive alive.

Chapter 15: Attraction

It was almost funny to watch. Richie had barely moved a few steps before another woman appeared at his side—laughing at something he said, touching his arm as if the joke were physical. Phones flashed, selfies snapped, a pair of women leaned in close to him as though he were some rare exhibit worth documenting. Their laughter drifted like ribbons in the air, and he collected them easily, one after another.

The contrast struck me. In college, Richie was never the attractive guy. Hardworking? Sure. Consistent? Yes. A good friend? Absolutely. He had plenty of friends, but the women... well, they never hovered around him like this. They would talk if he approached, but rarely the other way around. Back then, he didn't stand out in a crowd of young men with sharper cheekbones, louder voices, and better reputations.

But watching him now, I could tell something had changed. He suddenly seemed more attractive, even to me. Because in all honesty, I had never felt a spark with him in those years. He was the friend, the helper, the steady presence, but never the one to ignite desire. Tonight though, I did feel it. A flicker, small but real. He hadn't changed much in appearance, and yet the women at the party seemed to orbit him as though he were the most attractive man in Seattle.

I chuckled quietly, shaking my head. "You didn't get more handsome, Richie," I thought, "but your value definitely went up."

And maybe that's what attraction really measures—the perceived value. Flowers draw bees with their colors, ripe fruit lures animals with sweetness, rivers pull us with the promise of water. In every case, life is drawn toward what sustains it. Humans are no different. We gravitate to what feels valuable: *beauty, intelligence, strength, kindness.* Because value promises enrichment. And once we sense it, we don't just want to admire it from afar. We want to move closer, to touch it, to weave it into our lives. That is the essence of attraction: *It is the force that awakens our drive.*

Without attraction, there is no drive. No desire. No desire to move closer, to talk, to reach out a hand, to connect. The desire to connect—in romance, in friendships, in business, in art—always begins with attraction.

Attraction has always been the first step of a relationship. The first spark. Without it, no relationship ever begins. You don't sign up for long talks, shared silences, or future plans with someone who doesn't first make your head turn. All the rest—commitment, companionship, trust—comes later.

Have you experienced that invisible charge in the air that makes you lean forward rather than step back? That's *attraction* at work. It lights up your whole system. The thrill of the first glance, the stomach flipping at a laugh, the glimmer of possibility. It is because your brain is instantly hit with millions of dopamine telling you, this is the direction you need to move. Most times, we are not even aware of it, it works in the background pushing us slowly toward the person.

Even my friendship with Richie must have started off that way. Not romantic attraction, but the recognition of some value in him, and a desire to connect with that. Out of hundreds of students at college, I didn't befriend everyone. I befriended those who had something I noticed, something I wanted near me—beauty, intelligence, humor, kindness, status, talent. Attraction doesn't only open the door to intimacy; it opens the door to every relationship we choose.

And here's the truth we rarely say aloud: attraction, in many ways, *is* superficial. Not necessarily physical, but perceptual. We notice what shines—the energy, the presence, the physique, the talent. We notice what is valuable, especially to us. Pretending otherwise is dishonest. When you see value, you want to be close to it.

I looked at Richie again, his circle swelling, his voice rising over theirs in laughter. Attraction in motion. Not just his looks, not just his confidence—but the value they sensed in him now. Money, success, energy, presence, all wrapped together in a way that made them want to stay close.

Chapter 16: Beauty

Richie appeared again. His arm slipped lightly around my shoulder, his voice bright. "Come on, Sia. I want you to meet someone."

I followed him through the clusters of guests, and then he stopped, smiling with a softness I hadn't seen in him before. "This is Lena," he said. "My girlfriend."

She extended her hand, and for a moment I was caught off guard. Lena was... breathtaking. She had the look of someone who stepped right out of an Instagram reel—perfectly symmetrical face, large almond eyes, proportions that almost made you doubt they were real. Her hair fell in glossy waves, her smile disarming and practiced at the same time, her posture elegant without stiffness. She was the sort of beauty that feels inevitable, like of course she would end up with Richie now.

Yet as I exchanged pleasantries with her, I caught whispers weaving around the party like smoke: *She's a gold digger. She's only here for the money. Classic move.*

I felt a pinch inside me. Really? A gold digger? That's such a tired accusation, and it sounded unfair. Because if Lena was looking at Richie's value—his success, status, and security— wasn't Richie doing the same in reverse? Wasn't he also looking at her value—her physique, her youth, her beauty? He chased traits that promised fertility, charm, and softness. She chased traits that promised protection, resources, and power. Put away the judgment and both were doing the same thing: choosing value, just in different currencies.

This was the unspoken truth of attraction. Men and women see value in different things. Always have. Always will. His worth was measured in what he could build and protect; hers in what she embodied and nurtured. Both were valid. Both were survival. To dismiss this human instinct is unfair. Do we shame men for chasing beauty and charm? Then why shame a woman for chasing wealth and power?

And it's not just about men and women either. We all find attraction in different things. This is because we all value things differently. Some value beauty. Others value personality. Some value humor, or kindness, or intelligence. Every magazine, every self-help catalogue has a different "Top 10" attributes of what men or women find irresistible. If attraction had a universal checklist, then the prettiest girls would never be single, and the wealthiest men would never be lonely. But that isn't true.

That is not to say that beauty is all subjective either. "Everyone is beautiful in their own way," we say—and yes, there is truth in diversity. But denying hierarchy altogether drains beauty of its meaning. If sunsets were endless, would we marvel at them? If every day were summer, would we treasure warmth? Contrast gives value. Hierarchy gives direction. Without it, we are left in chaos—like abstract art where anything goes, and most of it a mess.

I do believe that beauty has an objective component to it. Even science agrees. Symmetrical faces, balanced proportions, and the golden ratio are often found to be more attractive. In women, beauty is commonly associated with large eyes, fuller lips, healthy hair, soft voices, and similar traits. In men, it is linked to broad shoulders, a sharp jawline, tall stature, and deep voices, among other things. We are all evolved to be attracted to it. They promise resilient genes and promising offspring, increasing the chances of your survival. So in that sense beauty can be objective. But then what about the thing we say: "beauty lies in the eyes of the beholder"? Is it just a poetic lie we tell ourselves or does it hold some deeper truth? The more I observed Richie that evening, the more I began to think it was the latter.

I remembered college, how Richie always hovered near me. I may not be the most beautiful girl in our class. But at that time, in his circle, I was the one he noticed. Options were scarce, and so my ordinary aura became luminous to him. He gave me his full attention then. And now, here I was watching him casually leave Lena, his stunning girlfriend, standing alone in the corner while he bounced from one friend to another, basking in the glow of the crowd.

It was jarring. But it also made sense. Attraction has an objective component, but it also has a subjective one, built from context and comparison. The desire feels stronger during scarcity, while it can disappear in abundance. This is because *attraction is not just about beauty, but value.* You are attracted to the overall value a person carries. And value, after all, is never just intrinsic. It is always relative. The value of something shifts with time and context, with demand and supply, with abundance and scarcity.

Think about value in the context of a business. A restaurant with average food but no competition in the neighborhood thrives, while a five-star restaurant can struggle during a recession. Ratings and reviews matter, but demand and supply matters more. Success is not only about quality—it's about timing and context. That's economics. Turns out attraction isn't much different either.

To prove this, psychologists once ran an experiment that revealed this fluctuating nature of attraction. Men were asked to rate their wives' attractiveness on a scale of 1 to 10. Then they were shown images of highly attractive women. Supermodels, actresses, covergirls. When asked to re-rate their wives immediately after, their ratings dropped. Nothing about their wives had changed, only the context did. Surrounded by comparison, attractiveness shifted.

Comparison skewed perception, lowering their value in this case. That was exactly what I was watching unfold at this party—Lena's beauty was constant, but Richie's attention was diluted, spread thin by the surplus of admiration flowing his way. I was not there critiquing or judging Richie for his behavior but rather was fascinated by the complexities of human attraction. On surface it looks so simple, but down deep it can be quite nuanced, especially when you start looking at it from a value perspective.

And then a darker thought landed, sharp as glass. If one man in one room could devalue even the most beautiful woman simply by being surrounded with options, what happens in the age of social media... where beauty is endless, scrollable and abundant? What happens in the age of internet and pornography, when attraction is reduced to tab-switching and skin is served instantly, on demand? What happens when a man can see hundreds of faces more attractive, more polished, more glamorous than the women he knows? What's the effect of watching thousands of bodies more sculpted, more enticing, more sensual than all the women he would ever get to meet? Would it not curb his drive? Would it not smother the fire that fuels desire—to come closer, to engage, to connect?

Chapter 17: Power

Lena was not an ordinary woman. Her presence was almost angelic, the kind that reminded me of the legendary beauties of the past. She and Richie had been dating for more than two years—two years, and still not a trace of her on his social media. His Facebook said "single." His feed had no pictures of her, no stories, no mentions. As if she were invisible. Shouldn't he have been elated? Shouldn't he have wanted to show her off? Even in the way he introduced her to me, there was no spark.

I thought of Richie's past, the humiliation of being overlooked by Rachael in college, hiding behind bushes in shame. That sting had become his fuel—the hunger to be noticed, to matter. It pushed him to build companies, buy mansions, dock yachts. And now, the moment he has options, the moment he gets the power, what does he do? He does the same thing. The girlfriend—the kind of woman he would once have killed to be near—stood ignored. The very prize he would have once fought for now felt ordinary. Not because she was any less radiant, but because her beauty no longer felt like treasure.

It made me wonder: does beauty still hold the same power it once did? Or has its value—once rare and magnetic—been flattened by overexposure?

There was a time when beauty could topple empires. Cleopatra's allure wasn't just her throne; it was her presence, her face, her ability to bend men's wills with a glance. Helen of Troy was said to have launched a thousand ships. In ancient Greece, sculptors immortalized symmetry and proportion in marble because they believed beauty itself was divine, a force capable of shaping destiny. Back then, beauty wasn't just decoration. It was currency. It was agency. It was power.

But what happens to power when it stops being rare? It goes away.

And what might be responsible for the decline in the power of beauty?

The curse, I realized, was the camera.

For most of history, if you wanted to see someone's face, you had to stand near them. If you wanted to see them smile, you had to make them smile. To hear their laugh, you had to sit close enough to feel it in your chest. Proximity used to require effort. Attention used to require intention.

But now, at your fingertips, you can see more faces in a minute than your ancestors saw in a lifetime. More smiles, more bodies, more perfectly edited images than perhaps even Cleopatra or Helen. And our brains—ancient, unevolved—still light up the way they once did when a rare beauty appeared at the village well. Dopamine, hit after hit, until it gets tired. Saturated.

Back then, to see beauty up close was a reward you worked for. Men went to war for it, wrote poetry for it, crossed oceans for it. Today, you open a browser. You scroll. You see skin, faces and bodies, like an avalanche of what was once sacred.

Instagram alone delivers more flawless faces in a morning than Rome or Athens saw in a century. We were never built for this kind of oversaturation. What we are experiencing is *cultural lag*, where our brain isn't able to adapt fast enough with technology. The result is mental and emotional fatigue.

Numbness. The loss of drive. It's like when you feed too much and your body is unable to move.

I looked at her again, standing by the railing, bathed in the gold spill of sunset. Her body nearly perfect, her skin radiant even without the filter—and yet ignored. Not just by Richie, but by half the room. What should have been divine blurred into the noise of a thousand curated feeds.

This, I thought, is what happens when *abundance dulls desire*. Gold loses its value if it rains from the sky. Beauty loses its power when it floods the market. The hierarchy still exists—some faces will always outshine others—but the impact is diluted. What once could launch ships now barely holds a man's gaze beyond a few seconds.

It isn't fair to her. It isn't fair to us, us women. Because once, beauty was her power. Like men had muscles, women had beauty. This was our leverage in society, our form of currency, our means of influence.

But today, beauty has been commodified, mass-produced, and sold back to us by corporations, significantly reducing its worth. Meanwhile, the power exercised by men remains unchanged, perhaps even amplified. Money and muscle still determine status and influence, while female beauty is increasingly reduced to decoration. Perhaps that is why so many of us feel replaceable. Why desire feels thinner, more conditional. Why being seen no longer guarantees being valued.

I sipped my drink and wondered, not without sadness, whether our culture had stripped women of one of their oldest powers: the power of beauty.

Chapter 18: Personality

I watched Lena standing alone, her expression dulled with boredom. She swirled her glass half-heartedly, the kind of gesture that says *I'm here, but not really here.* It was Richie's success party, his girlfriend should be on his side, but instead he was out there flirting with other women. I could see her confidence slowly cracking bit by bit. Her legs restlessly moving, her finger fidgeting the ring, eyes darting back and forth at her phone. She was clearly unsettled.

I wanted to talk to her, get to know her thoughts. How she was feeling at the moment. So I walked up beside her, lowering my voice into a mock-conspiratorial tone. "Men, I tell you... always chasing the shiny thing. It doesn't matter if they already have gold in their hands."

She glanced at me, eyes widening for just a second before she laughed softly. "Yeah, I know," she said, almost shyly.

The ice cracked. I nudged further. "So... how did you two meet?" I asked, tilting my glass toward her. "Don't tell me it was some epic love story with a violin soundtrack."

She grinned, finally looking straight at me. "He slid into my DMs."

I let out a laugh. "Ah, of course. That's how all great love stories start these days. Once upon a time... in the DMs."

She chuckled but quickly returned her gaze to her phone, thumb flicking across the screen with mechanical precision. A notification lit her face more than the lake's glow. I tried again—"Did you grow up in Seattle, or did you move here?"—but her responses came clipped, distracted, her attention locked in the black mirror, perhaps trying to post something.

I stood there, watching her curate herself for strangers, while I was right beside her, flesh and blood. It wasn't that she wasn't striking, of course she was luminous, magnetic even. But I couldn't find a personality in her, not in that moment. She was a stark contrast to the women Richie used to like: loud, witty, alive, chatter spilling out faster than the wine. They had personalities that filled a room. She, though... She felt curated, trimmed to fit within a frame.

What do they even talk about? I wondered. Their backgrounds, their humor, their interests—so different, so misaligned. Then again, maybe that was the point. Social media had collapsed the rules of attraction. You didn't have to share a world anymore. You just had to look good in one.

And that's the trap most people don't understand? In the online world, attraction has flattened into appearance alone. Fifteen second reels carefully crafted, a few filtered photos, and suddenly that's the whole story. We obsess over aesthetics: the face, the style, the fashion, the makeup. Every curve and angle is scrutinized. No wonder insecurities are at an all-time high. The standards are raised so far beyond reach that women chase them with lashes, fillers, nails and surgeries, burning half their salaries just to become scroll-stopping versions of themselves. Keeping up with the Kardashians isn't a metaphor anymore; it's become the daily grind!

Attraction today has been reduced to the purely physical. We've been conditioned by the internet, through porn and social media, to value only superficial beauty. That's become our standard. Looks alone give us the rush—the thrill of seeing someone's flawless, tempting, photo-ready body—and we mistake that for attraction.

Real attraction, however, the kind that sustains, needs much more: personality, presence, humor, intelligence, charm. It's the way they carry themselves. It's the aura that emerges only with time. Even a voice can be magnetic, the way someone says your name, the rhythm of their laugh, their mannerisms, their gestures, even their silence. These are the textures that make a person whole. You only get to experience that when you actually date someone in real life, when you see *all* of them, not just a smiling face. And sometimes, that's when the truth hits you: the attraction was never real, the connection was never there. It was all an illusion crafted by the internet.

"Can you take a picture of me?" she asked, handing me her phone as if it were a sacred object.

I laughed and nodded, watching her step back into position by the staircase. She adjusted her hair, then tilted her face toward the lake so the last orange streaks of sunset hit her cheekbones just right.

"Wait, lower the camera a little. No, angle it upward. Yes, perfect. Hold it. One more. Oh, and make sure the glass in my hand shows. Good, now one where I'm looking away like I'm laughing at something."

She knew exactly what she wanted. Pose, angle, lighting. The choreography of digital desire.

I snapped a dozen photos, handed the phone back, and within seconds she was scrolling, editing, and posting. Her fingers moved fast, as though she'd done this routine a thousand times—which of course, she had. Notifications pinged in rapid bursts. Comments poured in.

Curiosity tugged at me, so I pulled out my own phone and found her account. I hit "follow."

Her feed was an endless kaleidoscope of images: laughing on rooftops, sipping coffee in Paris, yoga at sunrise, chic outfits in perfect framing. A digital persona buzzing with life and vibrancy. And for a moment, I thought, *Had I not met her in person, I'd believe she was exactly that. Lively, witty, a character straight out of a rom-com.* Maybe this was what Richie had fallen for. Not the quiet girl half-lost in her phone tonight, but the version of her that glowed on the screen.

As I looked at her photos, I realized the saddest part: it wasn't her fault. The system rewards superficiality, she has simply learnt to adapt to it, certainly better than me. Social media trains us to strip our value down to only aesthetics. That's what gets the likes, shares and follows. So that's what we do. The more revealing the picture, the more likes. The more outrageous the post, the more shares. So that's what we offer. A pleasant personality doesn't trend. A deep laugh doesn't translate in a filtered reel. Authenticity doesn't sell. So we train ourselves, almost unconsciously, to value only what is desired, what is popular and what the algorithm picks up.

Women were always good at adapting to the times. In the ballroom era, they learned grace, elegance and dancing. During the war, when courtship unfolded through letters, they mastered the art of language, charming with poetry and handwritten vulnerability. In agrarian societies, they brought skill: craftsmanship, resourcefulness, homemaking and survival.

And today? Today, courting happens on Instagram. On Tinder. On DMs and OnlyFans. On the internet, where still images and short videos decide your worth in seconds. So they've mastered that too. Angles, filters, editing, styling, makeup, beauty—all of it. Because in the online world, no one waits long enough. They reward what's immediately visible. Personality gets overlooked. Intelligence gets ignored. Skills go unrecognized. All the attention goes to physical attraction. That's what the market demands. So that's what gets delivered.

And yet men have the audacity to call women *superficial*? No, we are not. We are simply catering to the demands of the market. We are simply responding to *your* very needs. *You* stopped rewarding personality, so we stopped offering it. And without personality, connections will always remain on the surface.

Connection, after all, can go either wide or deep, but not both. When you spread yourself thin across thousands of faces and look only at the exterior, how deep can any bond really go? That is the problem with the internet. That is the problem with online dating. People these days connect primarily through physical attraction. Such connections rarely run deep. But outside the world of filters and swipes, when you actually connect through personality, bonds form that can endure. Those are the connections that can last a lifetime.

Chapter 19: Frosting

The firepit was the last light in the garden, burning low against the dark sweep of Lake Washington. The crowd had thinned to the core—Richie's closest college friends, all a little drunk, jackets off, voices softened by wine and memory. Above us the stars blinked like they'd been waiting all night for their turn, and the breeze off the water carried that cool, tired sweetness that only comes when a party is nearly over.

Richie appeared with a tray like a magician with his final trick. "Last course," he announced. "Custom cake. I stood in line for an hour to get this, so no excuses."

Groans rose around the circle. "Too much sugar."

"Do you know how many calories are in that?"

"Sugar is poison."

The debate sparked instantly, like we were back in the dorms. Someone quoted the latest diet book. Someone else waved their fork and declared dessert a human right. Someone tossed in a half-serious quip about how even healthy foods like apples had tons of sugar.

But then the talk shifted, as drunk conversations do, from sugar to companies, to marketing, to how everything was engineered to hook us. Candy in bread, candy in drinks, candy even in everything. *It wasn't just food, though, was it?* I thought as I listened. It was everything. Smiles. Sex. Drugs. The whole economy had learned what we craved and served it back to us in endless doses until we gorged ourselves into numbness.

Modern life presents us with so many options, every option so tempting, so enticing. We've become kids in a candy store, dazzled by choice, grabbing tastes of everything, committing to nothing. Our systems are overstimulated, our attention stretched thin, our bodies high on the rush until the crash comes. And then we crave again. Tempted, but never satisfied.

Richie was still going around the group, making sure everyone had the cake. When he finally reached me, he asked playfully, "Permission to tempt you?"

"Just a bite," I said, leaning in and stealing a forkful straight from his plate instead of taking my own.

He grinned as he sat next to me with his plate between us. "You still do that! Remember in college? You never ordered your own food. You'd just eat off mine."

"No I didn't!" I said, laughing, as I took another bite from his plate. "Ok, maybe sometimes. Portion control, you see. If I ordered for myself, I'd end up eating too much."

He pointed his fork at me. "You still finished all of mine. I'd look away for a second and half my fries would be gone."

"That's because you ate so slow," I shot back. "Anyone would starve waiting for you."

He smiled, that old half-smirk I remembered too well. "Or maybe," he said lightly, "I was too busy staring at you."

And there it was again, that delicate tension between us. Not tension exactly, but the memory of it. It was the kind of line that slips out between people who share too much history to call it flirting, yet too much feeling to call it nothing. His gaze lingered a second too long—curious, searching—and for a heartbeat, it felt as if the air itself had paused to listen. It was harmless, yet it stirred something inside me at the moment—a quiet awareness of all the years that might have gone differently. I wanted to play along, to say something that might let that warmth unfold. Something soft, something playful, maybe even kind.

But I didn't.

Because I knew Richie. I always had. I knew his kind of longing, the kind that chases the next shiny thing. Back in college, it was Rachael. Today, it was Lena. Tomorrow, maybe someone else. I'd seen him move through desires like stepping stones, always crossing, never pausing to sit by the water. And maybe that's why I'd never let anything happen between us. I wasn't afraid of falling, I was afraid of being another glittering stop along the way.

So instead, I did what I always do when a moment threatens to deepen. I shifted the conversation. "So..." I said, nudging his plate back toward him, "what's the best part of the cake?"

He cleared his throat lightly, the moment slipping back behind his easy smile. "The frosting, duh," he replied, grinning, happy to be back on familiar ground.

I looked down at the slice sitting on the plate. The frosting was elaborate, sculpted into swirls and flowers, glossy enough to catch the firelight. It was beautiful, yes. But it was also *decoration*.

"This frosting's good," I said quietly.

He grinned, already carving off the top with his fork. "Best part."

"Sure," I said, smiling. "The best part. But eat only frosting and see what happens. You'll get the rush, but you'll stay hungry."

Richie pulled a face—one eye wide, the other squinted—giving me that boyish, exaggerated look he'd always used when we were playfully debating in college. He teased me saying "I sense some words of wisdom coming my way from my unofficial lifecoach here! "

I smiled, though my tone stayed calm, almost reflective. "You see, the frosting is what draws you in first, " I said, glancing at the slice between us, "like outer beauty does in life. It's the sweetness, the shine, the surface charm. You see it, you want it, you can't resist tasting it." I tapped my fork lightly against the spongy base. "But the cake underneath—that's where the real flavor lives. That's the substance, the depth, the part that actually fills you. Just like in relationships, what truly nourishes us isn't the appearance, but the personality, and the connection that grows from it. If all you ever do is lick the frosting and never taste the cake, you'll keep craving more and never feel satisfied."

For a moment, the noise of the group faded in the background. He fell quiet, fork suspended mid-air.

I went on gently, "I know how far you've come, how hard you've worked. But if you keep feeding yourself only what excites you in the moment, eventually nothing will excite you. Do you remember, back in college, sometimes all we ate was instant ramen, that too straight from the packet—and somehow even that tasted like heaven? You relished it like a delicacy, because you'd gone hungry all day. You would have devoured anything at that point. But when you've been munching all day, full to the gills, even this delicious cake—and no kidding this cake is really delicious—but even this would taste bland, dull, even uninteresting."

I could see the thought land in his eyes.

I let my gaze drift toward Lena, who sat a little apart, scrolling absently on her phone, bathed in the soft orange glow of the fire. "Right now you have a beautiful cake, but it's sitting untouched... unappreciated..." I added softly. "Don't let that hunger die, Richie. Don't let your palate be ruined by junk. Keep it refined. Relish what you have, savor every bite, let it nourish you."

Richie set his fork down slowly. There'd always been this thing between us, a way of talking about life like it was a game, half-serious, half-joking. But I could tell this one hit home.

Richie looked at me, and for the first time all night, his playful mask slipped. There was understanding in his eyes, a kind of clarity that needed no more words. He gave me a nod, then smeared a dab of frosting on my nose to break the tension. "Got it, Ma'am. I'll keep it in mind," he smiled, as if to remind me he hadn't lost his sense of humor.

The conversation drifted, the group's laughter rose and fell, and Richie went back to moving among his friends—pouring another drink, teasing someone about their old college crush, clapping a shoulder here and there. But somewhere in that easy flow, I noticed his focus shift. Bit by bit, his orbit narrowed until he gently slipped beside Lena. I caught the moment he said something that made her laugh, really laugh, not the polite chuckle she had given others all evening. Her phone slid into her lap, forgotten, as he leaned in close.

I sat back, the warmth of the fire on my face, a small smile tugging at my lips. I wasn't sure how long these two would last, but at least they made sense together. Each carried their own weight in the world, and together they seemed to balance the scales—the makings of a power couple. There's something deeply satisfying about seeing two people of equal value—equal caliber, equal league—find each other. It's the feeling of puzzle pieces sliding into place, of a river finally reaching the sea, of a compass needle finding north after spinning too long. Balance. Sustenance. A deeper satisfaction—the kind that lingers, even after the sugar rush fades.

****

Mountain Trek

Chapter 20: Deceptions

The days after Richie's party passed in a haze, but my mind kept circling back to that night. Strange, how after heartbreak you can sink so deep into yourself that nothing feels interesting anymore—food loses its flavor, music dulls, people blur. But sometimes all it takes is one evening, one push out the door, to remind you that life is too big, too dazzling, to waste on replaying the same memory of one person over and over.

That night had been more than just reconnecting with old friends. It had planted something in me. A new lens perhaps. A sharper way of looking at attraction: *we are always attracted to what we value.* Strength, wit, beauty or wealth. It doesn't matter what form it takes, our hunger turns toward it.

The drive is always sharper when we are hungry. But in the world we live in now, we never let ourselves feel that hunger. We snack all day long—a photo here, a reel there, a chat that goes nowhere. A video that fills a moment and is forgotten. Little bites of stimulation. If you keep grazing like that, where does the hunger come from? The hunger to go out, to really seek love, to build connection, to pursue value with your whole self? It doesn't. And so our superpowers—memory, language, empathy, creativity—sit idle gathering dust. Because we are never hungry enough to put them to use. Never desperate enough to cook a proper dinner when junk food is always at hand.

Perhaps that's why Richie, who was once such a romantic at heart, seemed so different now. In college he would tell me all he wanted was a girl to love, someone to make happy, someone whose smile could light up his whole world. He dreamed of holding hands, of being the kind of man who brought flowers just because. I used to tease him for sounding like a Nicholas Sparks novel, but he meant it. That tenderness was real. Which is why it jars me now, to see him surrounded by smiles and yet unable to give his full attention to the one woman he once would have died for. Somewhere along the way, that hunger in him—the hunger to love, to connect—got drowned out by the noise.

I zipped open my duffel bag and laid it flat on the bed. Hiking boots, water bladder, trail snacks. A stack of wool socks. A windbreaker. My mom had suggested the trip—"Go somewhere far, your mind needs a reset, let nature heal your heart," she'd said. And when the hiking group announced a weekend trek up Mount Rainier, I signed up before I could second-guess myself. I hadn't traveled anywhere after my breakup. Always postponing, telling myself I wasn't ready. But something shifted after that party. For the first time, I felt ready.

I paused, folding a thermal shirt, remembering Lena, beautiful enough to stop traffic, standing ignored, unimportant, reduced to little more than a showpiece. If she could be left waiting, what hope was there for me? For anyone? That thought had struck me like cold water on the face. Because I had blamed myself, over and over, for the moments my ex ignored me. The unreplied texts, the vague "I'm busy" excuses, the sense that he just wasn't that interested. Each time I thought it must mean I wasn't enough—wasn't pretty enough, young enough, fun enough. But then I saw Lena, the closest thing to a living Instagram filter, scrolling alone by the fire. It's strange how I found comfort in Lena's disappointment—as though her silence whispered to me, *"See? Maybe you were never the problem."* I felt my pain reflecting through her. Different stories, the same ache. And in that moment I stopped blaming myself. Maybe it wasn't me. Maybe the fault was deeper.

The truth was everywhere: men weren't trying anymore. No effort, no spark, no drive. They used to go to war for women. Now they barely send a text. The irony made me laugh aloud as I stuffed trail mix into a side pocket.

My phone buzzed earlier that evening. Richie. He wanted to explain. "I don't think Lena's right for me. She's...expensive. High upkeep." I'd let him talk, biting my tongue. I couldn't help but laugh at the irony of it. The very things Richie had once flaunted to win Lena over—the expensive dinners, the lavish gifts, the glittering grandeur he showcased—were now the very things he resented her for asking. Her desire for the very things that first got her attracted to him, suddenly became "too much upkeep." But who set those expectations in the first place? He did.

It's like a woman wooing a man by cooking him feasts at the start, then never lifting a spoon once she marries him. Or the guys who write *traveling* in their dating bios, only to invite you over to their apartment again and again. Or the people who proudly claim they're "so kind," yet never actually show that kindness to you. What's the use of a quality if it never makes its way into the relationship? Keep that kindness, that love of travel, that talent for cooking to yourself then.

When Richie went on and on about Lena's demands on the phone, I almost wanted to say—Richie, my mate, if you didn't want the fancy dinners and gifts to count, you should've made that clear from day one. If you wanted Lena to fall for just your charm and wit, then you should've relied on those alone. But no—you rolled out the red carpet, dangled the shiny things, put on the show. That was your strategy. So why sulk now? You can't hand out champagne in the lobby and then switch to tap water once people are seated. You set the stage, my friend—now keep performing.

But of course I didn't say any of that. There was no point. That relationship was done—and honestly, it was never built to last. I had tried at the party, nudging him, knocking a little sense his way, but he's on a roll with his success now. Time will teach him better than I ever could. I could already see the pattern forming: one of those shy schoolboys who, once they taste success, start hopping from woman to woman until they either tire out or grow old and settle down with someone half their age.

He's my friend, yes. But it is what it is. I couldn't help but smile wryly at the thought.

We put so much into impressing each other at the start—displaying our value, our qualities, our sparkle. But once the relationship actually begins, so many of those qualities vanish, tucked away as though they were just props for the audition. And when that happens, what's left feels like *deception*. Not outright lying, but an unspoken promise broken—as if you've been sold a dream that no one intends to keep.

I tucked a flashlight into the bag and sat on the edge of the bed for a moment, letting the thought settle. This is why the courting period matters so much. It's when you learn who a person really is—not just through their words, but through their actions. Love bombing is easy in the beginning. Anyone can say, *"You're the most beautiful woman I've ever laid eyes on.*" But it's only over time you discover whether he actually makes you feel that way. Can he drop everything when you call? Can he show up for you the way someone would for the most beautiful woman in the world? I laughed at the thought.

The problem is, we don't allow enough time for that anymore. We find attraction and leap straight into intimacy, skipping the bridge in between. Maybe that was Richie and Lena's mistake. Maybe it was mine too. The courting period has nearly disappeared. Yet it's the essential segue between attraction and relationship—the slow simmer, the patience, the joy of watching the romance unfold. Because once the relationship begins, expectations begin to pour and then you can't back out.

You can't just tempt and withdraw. You can't parade a cake and then hide it back in the fridge. You can't boast of a Porsche and then pick her up in a minivan. Relationships built on deceptions are always short-lived.

But then there's another school of thought, almost idealistic, that says relationships should be selfless, free of expectations. I know many who would sympathize with Richie, who would call his girlfriend demanding, unreasonable, even difficult. They'd say she shouldn't be expecting anything from him, shouldn't demand—that love should be for who he is, not for his luxury or lifestyle, but for his heart. It sounds noble in theory, yes. But is it practical? Can two people really survive without needs, without demands, without exchange? *Is it possible to be selfless in a relationship?* That's the question that lingered with me

Attraction is the first step in a relationship. I understand that. It is crucial, like the spark that lights the fire. But spark alone doesn't keep the fire burning. It must be something else that keeps it going. If a relationship starts with attraction, what *sustains* it after that? Is it loyalty? Honesty? Selflessness? That's the question gnawing at me now, the one I'll carry with me up the mountain.

I cinched the duffel straps tight, imagining the thin alpine air of Rainier, the breath of the pines, the crunch of gravel under boots. A place far enough from the chatter, from the feeds, from the endless snacking of the internet that dulls our hunger for real connection. Maybe there, I'd find some space to think.

Chapter 21: Avoidance

Seattle was already loud when I reached the bus stop that morning. Engines idled, people talked over one another, and the smell of coffee hung in the air. Pike Place Market was in full motion—fish flying, vendors shouting prices, tourists clustering with cameras and paper cups in hand. Everyone seemed to be going somewhere important, even if they didn't know exactly where that was.

I stood there with my backpack over one shoulder, watching it all happen. Someone bumped into me, brushed past without stopping, and muttered something closer to irritation than apology. A stranger asked for directions to the gum wall, and I pointed vaguely without really thinking. A flower vendor pressed a single daisy into my hand and smiled. "For luck," he said.

That's usually how life feels when you're deep inside it— constant movement, unexpected interactions, small moments of kindness mixed in with frustration. You don't get to choose the mix. You just keep moving forward and hope you notice the good when it shows up. I tucked the daisy into my bag and waited for the bus.

When the bus arrived, I climbed on with a small group of hikers. We were strangers, but bound by a shared direction. We traded surface-level stories and practical advice—the kind of conversation that fills space without demanding anything deeper. It felt comforting in its simplicity. At that point, simplicity was all I could manage.

Heartbreak has a way of making the world feel too crowded. After enough disappointment, even familiar faces begin to sound like noise. You lose the energy to engage, to explain yourself, to stay open. Everything feels like demand. What you want isn't connection—it's *space*. It's *distance*. Somewhere life can't reach you for a while.

Stepping back in those moments can look like self-care. And sometimes it is. Rest is necessary after effort. The body needs it. So does the heart.

But what we often call a *break* is sometimes something else entirely—a familiar coping mechanism disguised as healing. *Avoidance*.

Avoidance isn't rest. It isn't a clear, grounded choice made from exhaustion. It's *fear*. It's what happens when you no longer trust yourself to survive another rejection or loss. So instead of building resilience, you remove yourself from risk. You don't *recover*—you *retreat*. Not to *heal*, but to *hide*.

Rest is what you take after playing hard. You step off the field knowing you'll return. Avoidance is quitting the game altogether, because you're afraid to lose again. One restores you while the other teaches you how to stay gone.

The problem is how similar exhaustion and fear can feel. Both ask for distance. But only one prepares you to come back.

At the time, I couldn't tell which one I was choosing. I didn't know whether I was stepping back to gather myself—or stepping away with no intention of returning. I wasn't thinking about how I'd reconnect. I wasn't imagining my way back to people. I just wanted out.

As the bus pulled away from the city, everything began to thin out. Skyscrapers gave way to warehouses, warehouses to suburbs and suburbs to open fields. Traffic noise softened into the steady roll of tires. Stoplights vanished, as if rules no longer applied beyond a certain mile. The air changed too—less exhaust, more pine, with the crisp, clean bite of altitude. It felt like crossing an invisible boundary, the one where urgency starts to loosen its grip.

And then, suddenly—there it was.

Mount Rainier rose out of the horizon like a sleeping god cloaked in white, unmoving yet impossibly alive. The bus fell quiet, not because anyone asked for silence, but because awe doesn't require commentary. Some things speak directly to the nervous system. They remind you how small your worries are without dismissing them.

At the trailhead, we began together, moving through dense forest that smelled damp and alive. Birds startled and vanished. Someone pointed out a deer slipping quietly into the woods. Another hiker explained which berries were safe, which ones weren't. Small attempts at connection—but at the time, even that felt too much

As we climbed, the world fell away. The forests thinned. The trees gave way to smaller shrubs, wildflowers brushing our legs as butterflies hovered briefly before darting out of reach. Gradually, even those disappeared, until there wasn't much to see at all. Color drained from the landscape, replaced by gray stone and patches of snow. The air sharpened. My breathing grew louder, more deliberate. At some point, the voices behind me faded. When I looked back, the group had become distant figures scattered along the trail. I didn't wait.

Leaving them wasn't a decision born of impatience. It felt instinctive. Just as I had needed distance from relationships, I needed distance here as well. Space to walk at my own pace.

Space to listen without interruption. Space to stop carrying everyone else's expectations alongside my own.

The higher I climbed, the quieter everything became. Not just around me, but inside me. With each step, it felt as though I was setting something down—old conversations, unresolved disappointments, the heartbreak. The mountain didn't ask me to forget any of it. It simply refused to carry it for me.

Up there, there was no room for mental noise. I had to watch my footing, stay attentive, look for the trail. Focus was no longer an option but the demand of the terrain. And somehow, in concentrating so fully on the next step, the weight of everyday worries began to loosen. Problems that had felt overwhelming back home shrank into proper proportion. Not solved—just quieter, less urgent.

And finally—the summit. It wasn't loud or triumphant, just there: vast, unbothered and eternal. Snow stretched in every direction, unbroken and quiet. No birds. No movement. Just space. For a moment, it was just me surrounded by the snow. As time slipped by, I couldn't tell whether I was watching stillness or the stillness was watching me.

The others had likely stopped lower down to camp. I didn't mind. Maybe I was even grateful. I rolled out my tent, coaxed a flame to life, and cooked something simple. Soon, the sun began to sink. The light shifted slowly across the snow, changing colors as it disappeared. I didn't rush to capture it with my phone. I just watched.

Later, lying in my sleeping bag, I stared up at a sky filled with stars. The kind of sky you don't see when you're surrounded by streetlights and deadlines. For the first time in a long while, my thoughts didn't spiral. They settled.

My mother had been right. She'd told me to go, to get away, to breathe clean air and let nature do what time and therapy couldn't. "Let it reset you," she'd said. And now, with the cold pressing close and the constellations burning above me, I finally understood what she meant.

Alone, yes. But also at peace. Amidst the silence of the peaks, solitude didn't feel empty. It felt like medicine.

Chapter 22: Engagement

I woke up to silence.

The fire had long gone out, leaving only a black circle stamped into the snow. I unzipped the tent and stepped outside, coffee packet in hand. My stove hissed to life, steam curling upward into the stillness. The mountains stretched before me exactly as I had left them the night before—white, frozen and unchanging.

At first, I liked it. The stillness. The way nothing moved. It felt clean, stripped of noise, as if time itself had paused. But as I sipped my coffee and waited, something in me began to itch. I started feeling *isolated* and *alone*. I had expected to hear voices climbing up the trail, the shuffle of boots, the familiar chatter of my group. But no one came.

I scanned the ridges. Every direction looked the same. Snow, ridges and the sky. No trail markers. No footprints but my own. My thoughts started to nudge me: *How did I end up alone? Where is everybody? What if I took the wrong turn yesterday? What if they've forgotten about me?*

The silence that had soothed me last night now pressed in heavier, like a weight. Alone, it seemed less like serenity and more like *absence*. The mountain no longer felt like a companion. It felt indifferent. Cold and lifeless.

I missed my groupmates—their stories, their laughter, their company that added color to this experience. I remembered the journey up the mountain—dense forests buzzing with life, bursting with berries, butterflies, and the restless noise of wildlife. Every step felt like an adventure. The snow peak, by contrast, was serene, but it was also silent. Beautiful, but lifeless—eventless, a canvas with no colors, a calm that carried no story.

I looked at the snow and wondered, half with humor and half with dread: *What if I fall? What if I slip into a crevasse? Who would even know? Who would pull me out?* I looked at my phone again. It had no signal, of course. The screen mocked me with its empty bars as the fear of isolation began to engulf my heart.

In life, it isn't danger that frightens us most—it's the thought of facing it alone. The comfort comes from knowing that if something goes wrong, there will be people who notice, who reach for you, who help you stand again. That knowledge turns fear into something manageable. Without it, fear spirals.

The silence at the summit began to reflect the loneliness in my own heart. Ever since my breakup, I had felt suspended in space—not the beautiful kind where you imagine yourself floating among stars, but the kind no telescope ever captures: the dark stretches between galaxies. A vacuum. Empty. No sound, no touch, no life. That was this mountain. And perhaps that was how I had become too—isolated, distant, and cold.

The thought unsettled me. Because isn't that what happens when we avoid relationships? When life overwhelms us, when heartbreak breaks us, when disappointment crushes our soul? We retreat. We climb to our inner mountains, seeking calm, seeking safety. And at first it feels like medicine. But stay long enough and the medicine turns bitter. The silence deepens. The stillness becomes suffocating. We think we've found peace, but really, we've only found *absence*.

I bent down, scooped a fistful of snow, and held it in my palm. At first it bit into my skin with its cold sting, sharp enough to make me flinch. Then I pressed harder, crushing it, grinding the crystals against each other. The friction made a fragile warmth bloom in my hand. Slowly, the crystals began to melt, turning snow into water. I felt it trickle through my fingers, proof that even something frozen and lifeless could be changed by contact.

It felt like a revelation, as if the mountain itself had staged a lesson for me. Without touch, the snow remained locked in its form—cold, rigid and unmoving. But the moment I *engaged* with it, pressed against it, it transformed. The tiniest collision released heat, motion—and then, *ah*, change!

It struck me then—*isn't that what we are too?* Full of locked energy, waiting... silent and still, until someone presses close enough to melt us. Until *engagement* sets our energy into motion. Nothing releases energy without contact. Not a match, not a fire, not even us. Engagement is what creates the spark. Engagement is also what sustains that spark. Without it, we're like atoms that never collide—powerful, yes, but dormant.

If you think about it, life itself began with collision. Nothing in this universe comes alive in isolation. Stars are born from pressure. Fire needs a strike. Energy in the atoms stays locked until another atom collides with it. Even the heart— especially the heart—needs engagement to be moved, to experience feeling of every kind, to live up to its full potential.

We aren't meant to be mountains: beautiful, serene, untouched. We are meant to be marketplaces and forests— noisy, inconvenient, bursting with exchange. As children, we know this instinctively. We reach, we play, we collide without fear. It's only later—after disappointment teaches us caution— that we mistake withdrawal for wisdom. But the heart doesn't forget. It keeps craving connection, even when we deny it on the outside.

My eyes wandered back down the slope, searching for movement, for any sign of life. And suddenly I longed for the marketplace I had left behind—the fishmongers, the tourists, even the man who barked at me when he bumped my shoulder. Annoyances, yes. But alive. That bustle was messy, inconvenient, loud—but it was also connection. And in this frozen silence, I found myself missing it. In the presence of others, there were stories being made—and I was part of them. I missed the chaos because it reminded me I wasn't *alone*. The challenges, the noise, the unpredictability gave the journey depth. Without them, the beauty felt distant—something to observe rather than experience.

Because that's the truth of it, isn't it? Solitude gives us calm. But engagement—messy, noisy, chaotic engagement—is what gives us life.

Just as that thought landed, I heard my name carried on the wind. A voice. Faint at first, then louder. I turned, heart jolting, and saw one of my group mates climbing toward me, waving. A glimmer of motion against the white. A glimmer of hope.

And for the first time since waking, I exhaled.

.

Chapter 23: Friction

For a moment I thought I'd wandered into nothingness, swallowed by the blank slate of snow. Then, like a crack in ice, I saw a face. Human. Familiar. A rush of relief surged through me, the kind that warms you from the chest outward. Thank God, I thought, I haven't lost the trail after all. A face, any face, feels like salvation in the white wilderness.

It was Adam. One of the fellows from the group.

"Yes, you did take a wrong turn," he said with a half-smile. "Our group had chosen a different spot. They were looking for you, so they sent me."

I was surprised they'd chosen him. Adam hadn't spoken much to me since the start of the trek—just our names, a few pleasantries—but I understood immediately why he was the one they chose. Adam was no casual hiker. He was a seasoned climber, the kind of man who treated Mount Rainier as if it were his backyard.

By the time I rejoined the group, the weight I'd been carrying—the ache of feeling disconnected, isolated, alone—slipped off my shoulders. There's something about being with others that steadies you. Fear shrinks in company. In a group, the mountain doesn't seem quite so indifferent. Groups have their own magic, their own survival code: one person with a compass, another with medical know-how, someone else cracking jokes to keep morale alive. Together, weaknesses blur, strengths multiply. In life it's no different. With family, friends, a partner—we feel less alone. Less frightened. We lean into each other's skills, cover each other's blind spots. The climb, both literal and metaphorical, becomes easy. Becomes possible.

The second night we camped again. This time the tents went up more easily, like hands had already rehearsed their parts. Someone tied a stubborn knot, someone else lent a missing stake. Pieces of gear passed back and forth until no one lacked for anything. That's the beauty of connection: chores stop feeling like chores. Mundane tasks turn into small adventures when shared, and impossible challenges shrink into puzzles solvable with laughter and helping hands. Life, in those moments, feels lighter.

Still, I noticed Adam. He pitched his tent a little further from everyone else, a pocket of solitude at the edge of the group. Over the hours, I'd seen his pattern: quiet, almost aloof, yet unfailingly attentive to others' needs. The first to offer help, the last to speak of himself. By now, I knew pieces of everyone's life except his.

I found myself quietly amused by him. He wasn't just built like a mountain—tall, strong, muscular—he was one. Upright. Stoic. Unyielding. Maybe, like me, he had been living in avoidance too, keeping his distance from others, afraid of what vulnerability might ask of him. I understood that posture. It was one I'd worn myself.

That night, we sat around the fire. Flames licked the cold air, sparks vanishing into the vast dark sky. Someone cracked open beers—I hadn't thought climbers brought those, but apparently they do. The cans passed hand to hand, the conversation rolling easily. We talked about the mountain, about work back home, about small absurdities of daily life. Then, as fireside talks always seem to do, the topic drifted. Love.

One after another, people began sharing their verdicts on it. How love was doomed. How true love didn't exist anymore. How it had all become a matter of convenience.

Adam sat slightly apart, as always. Not isolated exactly, but orbiting outside the circle. He flicked small twigs into the fire, one after another, with the slow rhythm of a man passing time. His jaw was square, unreadable. His posture was upright, his gaze distant, as if he were present and absent at once. He looked more like part of the mountain than part of us.

Watching him, my curiosity grew. Earlier that day, I'd held snow in my palm, felt it burn cold until it melted. The mountain had taught me something simple but true: if you want to open something up, you have to engage with it. People, I suspected, were no different.

So I leaned forward, mischief in my voice. "I'm sure Adam can tell us a word or two about love," I said, in a playful voice. "He seems like the kind of guy with loads of experience." The sarcasm was deliberate, meant to draw him out, a pebble tossed in still water.

The mood was light, beers in, laughter easy. I was teasing, but beneath the joke was my favorite game. I've always been fascinated by unfolding the hidden sides of people. Nothing excites me more than peeling back the layers: nudging someone too rigid until they soften, or lifting someone too tender until they stand taller. We all carry different shades inside us, and I can't resist stirring the pot to see what surfaces.

Adam looked up, almost startled, as though I'd called on a man who hadn't raised his hand. "Me?" He pointed to himself, incredulous. "Love? No way. I stay away from it. Love invites too much drama."

The circle chuckled, but I kept my eyes on him. He was uncomfortable, shifting in his seat, and I recognized that sting—the same sharp bite I'd felt with the snow pressed against my skin. Engagement isn't always comfortable. Like friction, it can burn a little. But that's how you break the ice, how you crack the hard outer shell.

I leaned in again, teasing, "But love *is* drama. What's wrong with a little of it?" My voice lifted in a giggle, lighthearted, like I was tossing him a dare.

Maybe it was the beer, maybe the mountain air, maybe just the ache of being alone the night before, but I felt myself reaching out too, hand extended for connection. For once, the probing wasn't just for him, it was for me. I could feel my playful side surfacing again, a part of me I'd locked away these last few months. For the first time in a while, I didn't want to just observe. I wanted to be involved.

He hesitated at my question, as if weighing whether to say more, then let it slip away with a scoff and a shake of the head, the kind that said: don't even get me started.

I wasn't giving up that easily. So I push him a little further, to throw out a trigger he wouldn't be able to resist. "Are you saying women are full of drama?"

That did it! Now he was fully awake, ready to carry the conversation forward. "I mean... kind of. Forget a birthday and it's the end of the world. Don't text back right away and suddenly I'm accused of cheating. Women make a big deal out of everything. Relationships are... a lot of work."

"So what? You want lazy love?" I asked.

"Not lazy, but easy, simple love. Without the complications. I love you, you love me. That's it. Done. Why repeat it every day like a parrot? Why all the updates... where are you, what are you doing, why didn't you text? It's draining. Love should be divine. You are supposed to feel it in your heart. Not by words or flowers."

The group quieted. His voice had sharpened, as though my teasing had brushed against a bruise.

I smirked. "So you're fine keeping it all in your heart. But what about your partner? Maybe they need words. Expressions. The daily affirmations. Not saying 'I love you' every day is like eating once and claiming you'll never need food again. Or sleeping together once and deciding that's enough for life. Yet you go back for it, over and over, don't you?"

The circle broke into laughter. I had them on my side. The point had landed, and I knew it.

Adam flushed, jaw tight. He wasn't about to let this go. He had to win. Restless, he played his ace: the noble card, the holier-than-thou line. "You shouldn't need validation every day," he shot back, voice edged with righteousness. "Love is supposed to be selfless. But you wouldn't know that... and that's okay."

His words caught me off guard. For once, I had no comeback. My mouth opened, closed, a small *uhm... mhm...* escaping as I fumbled for something clever. Nothing came. He'd pinned me in the corner, and I hated to admit it, but he was sort of right.

The group leaned in, waiting for me to fire back, but I stayed quiet. That was when the old man spoke, his gray beard glowing in the firelight, eyes deep as a river. He carried the most experience among us, not just in years, but in wisdom. Age hadn't slowed him down; whether it was hiking the trail or sparring in conversation, he was always present, sharp and alive.

"Selfless love is a myth, Adam," his voice calm but certain, the way only someone who had seen much of life could manage "And silent love doesn't last."

Adam looked at him, startled.

"Love isn't only what you feel in your chest. It's how you show it. Love without expression dries up—like a river without rain, shrinking day by day until all that's left is dust."

Adam bristled. "But all those things—dates, flowers, constant words—they cheapen it. They make it shallow. Love should stay pure, felt in the heart, not performed." His voice was calmer now, less like he was sparring, more like he was honestly searching.

The old man shook his head. "But love is a performance—a dance. You don't just stand in the corner and watch while your partner moves alone. You join in, step for step, gesture for gesture. That's what makes it beautiful."

"Unless, of course, it's love from afar. A one-sided love, a crush, an admiration you never confess. Then it's fine if you keep it all in your heart. But to truly be in love, to live with that love, to share a life with someone—you have to show it. That's how love grows into a relationship. And relationship," he paused, letting the word settle, "isn't only giving, and it isn't only receiving. It's both. A balance. An exchange. That's what keeps it alive."

His gaze lingered on Adam. His sharp eyes moved over him slowly—taking in the rigid line of his shoulders, the tension in his jaw, the jacket, the wristband—catching the small details most would have overlooked. It was the kind of look that came from years of reading people, from seeing the stories they wore on their skin long before they ever spoke of it.

The old man's voice deepened. "You say you want it divine, untouched, silent—but even divinity has sound. Prayer has words. Music has notes. Love needs expression. Look at yourself..."

His hand lifted gently toward Adam's gear—the worn jacket, the knitted wristband, the careful patch stitched onto his pack. "That jacket—wasn't it a gift? That wristband—someone made it with care. Even that patch—someone mended what you tore. You didn't ask for these, yet you received them. Not feelings in the air. Not silent devotion. But actions. Effort. Love, made visible."

Adam's face softened. A small, crooked smile tugged at his mouth, and for the first time his voice carried something more than pride.

"The jacket?" he said, brushing the sleeve with his fingers. "My ex picked it out. She was half-crazy, but she had great fashion sense. Did most of my shopping, actually." A flicker of amusement crossed his face, but there was something wistful in it too, a trace of what he hadn't said.

He held up his wrist. "The band—my sister made it. She's crafty like that, always braiding or stitching something. I couldn't tell her no even if I tried."

Then his eyes slid to the pack beside him, a quiet laugh escaping. "And the patch? My mom sewed it. She knows I'll never let this old thing go—it's my favorite. So she keeps it alive for me."

The group fell silent, listening. The laugh lingered, but there was a shine in Adam's eyes now, emotion breaking through the armor. He wasn't debating anymore. He was remembering.

The old man studied him for a long moment, a faint smile touching his lips. "It shows, you know... the care they gave you. You may not crave flowers or words. But if she does, why not give them? And if you want something—her touch, her patience, her time—you have every right to ask. That's what love is. Not selfless. Not one-sided. But an exchange. A meeting of needs. Without that, it withers."

Adam stared into the flames, silent. His shoulders, usually rigid, sagged just slightly. For the first time, he looked less like a mountain and more like a man carrying one.

One by one, the group began to drift toward their tents, satisfied. The hike that morning had tested their bodies, and now the night had fed their minds. It was the kind of fullness only days in the wild can bring—exhaustion in the muscles, wisdom simmering in the heart.

I lingered by the fire, watching Adam across the flames. I was glad I had pushed him, even if it meant a little *friction* between us. Without it, his softer side would have stayed hidden. That's what we're afraid of these days—pressing, probing, causing friction. We fear the rub. The clash. But friction is what sets the wheels turning; without it, nothing moves, and we remain forever stalled at the same crossroads.

And I remembered what the snow had already tried to teach me: it takes touch to melt the shell. Even the strongest among us carry stories too heavy to share, until someone dares to draw them out, and in that daring, sets their world in motion again.

Chapter 24: Exchange

We broke camp that morning, tugging down tents and shaking the dew from nylon, the smell of damp earth clinging to our hands. I stood for a long moment before Mount Rainier, soaking in one last breath of sharp mountain air. Majestic. Unshaken. I'd never thought of a mountain as a teacher, but now I knew better. It would never be home, not really, but it could always be a refuge—a place to return to when life pressed too hard.

That's the cycle, isn't it? When life grows heavy, we reach for relief. When it lightens, we start craving challenge. Peace drifts into boredom, boredom sparks adventure, adventure quickens into thrill, and thrill hardens into tension—until we're aching for peace again. Life doesn't lie in one or the other. It lives in the motion, in the movement between the two. Much like a river that travels from the mountain to the sea and back again, giving form to life in the process.

The mountain had given me my calm, my stillness. But now it was time to go back to people, to connection. I wanted it—but I didn't want to repeat my mistakes. I was still searching for clarity, still chasing the answers I'd been looking for since my breakup. A manual, I thought—something as simple as the ones for driving or swimming: *How to be good at relationships?*

The old man had nudged me closer. Attraction may light the spark, but it's *exchange* that keeps the flame alive. And that's what we so often forget. We bind ourselves to the big vows and promises—be honest, be loyal, in sickness and in health. But what about the everyday? The small trades of patience, the words, the touch? Too often we're tired, worn thin by the constant grind of modern life. Or distracted by screens that fill the silence before longing can rise.

And so somewhere along the way, we began to idolize love—set it on a pedestal, too divine to touch. We made it too virtuous, too lofty. We said it should be selfless, above need, beyond validation. But if love is to survive the grind of daily life, it isn't built on grand vows or lofty ideals. It rests on something simpler: *the exchange*—the small, steady give-and-take—that keeps it alive.

When the bus pulled up, I lingered to catch one last look at Rainier, the peak cutting sharp against the sky. Then I climbed aboard. Adam was at the front, sitting alone. He'd been different since last night—lighter, easier. He'd helped me fold my tent in minutes, his big arms making quick work of what would have taken me all morning. We'd shared coffee, traded jokes, the beginnings of a rhythm. I nearly slid into the seat beside him. My mind flickered with possibilities—a phone number, a story unfolding, maybe something more.

But my eyes kept drifting toward the back, where the old man sat by the window, quiet as ever. Wisdom seemed to travel with him, as steady as his shadow. The old man's quiet gravity stood in sharp contrast to Adam's easy smile. I hovered there in the aisle, caught between the spark of desire in the front row and the steady flame of wisdom waiting in the back. I knew myself too well: I had leapt into love too quickly before, mistaking sparks for fire. And I was tired of failing without knowing why.

So this time I chose differently. I passed the front row, walked deeper down the aisle, and slipped into the seat beside the old man.

I turned toward him, my voice steady, almost eager. "Hey... how you doing?"

The bus rattled awake, gears grinding as we pulled away from the trailhead. Out the window, Mount Rainier slid behind the trees, still towering, still magnificent, like it was waving us off without moving an inch.

The old man dropped into his seat beside me with the same easy energy he'd had on the trail. He wasn't the kind to retreat into silence—he had hiked with the strongest of us, kept pace on the switchbacks, and always found a way to toss in a quip when the group chatter ran thin. It wasn't the hush of a classroom. It was closer to the way a grandfather tells stories— casual, vivid, with wisdom stitched in so lightly you almost don't notice you're learning.

He glanced at me with a half-smile, as if he already knew I'd chosen his company over Adam's. "Most women would've picked the young buck," he said with a grin. "So, what brings you to the old man's corner instead?"

I laughed, shaking my head. "Tempting as the front row was, I figured I'd get more out of this seat. Adam's good company, sure, but he's not about to hand me answers I've been chasing." I hesitated, my tone softening. "Truth is, I've been looking for something... clarity, maybe. And I get the feeling you've got more of that than anyone else on this bus."

He chuckled, shaking his head. "Clarity, huh? Careful what you wish for. Most people don't really want clarity. They want comfort. And comfort's easy. Clarity—" he tapped the seatback in front of him, "that usually stings first, then heals later."

I leaned in, lowering my voice. "You talked about exchange yesterday—it was beautiful. It made perfect sense. Relationships can't thrive without it. But then why has that exchange stopped in our generation?" I hesitated, words tumbling out faster now. "I was thinking about it last night... we hardly exchange anything anymore. We don't feel the need to—because, truth is, we don't really need each other for much at all. We've all become so—"

"Independent?". The old man's eyes lit with mischief as he finished for me.

"Exactly," I said, a rush of recognition warming me. My eyes met his—I knew he'd pull me somewhere deeper.

The old man leaned back, his eyes glinting as if the thought amused him. "Independent? No, no. Your generation is anything but independent. You've only shifted dependence somewhere else. Instead of leaning on your parents, your friends or your neighbors—you lean on screens and strangers who sell you things. And you call that freedom? It isn't. It's just dependence in disguise—the worse kind, actually."

He paused, his voice softening as it slipped into story, like memory breaking through. "Back in the day, if you needed a recipe, you asked your mother. If you needed help with a school project, you turned to your father. If you wanted to hear stories from history, you sat at your grandfather's feet. And it wasn't just children needing parents—parents needed children too. A hand in the kitchen, a bit of cleaning, a run to the pharmacy.

You couldn't survive on money alone; you needed people. There were no apps to summon help, no delivery services at your fingertips. If you asked your neighbor to help in the garden, maybe the next week they'd ask you to steady the ladder while they fixed the roof. Everyone brought something unique—some skill, some knowledge, some effort. And the only way to unlock that value was through engagement. You had to show up, interact, weave those exchanges into a relationship.

That wasn't dependence," he said quietly, "that was *interdependence*."

He gestured toward the window, where the trees blurred past in streaks of green. "That's how nature works too—through interdependence. Watch a garden long enough and you'll see it. A bee drifts from flower to flower, feeding her hive while keeping the blossoms alive. Birds scatter seeds. Fungi whisper beneath the soil, passing water and nutrients from one tree to another. Wolves keep the deer in check so the forest can breathe. Nothing survives alone. Everything thrives in an ecosystem. Everything is linked."

I nodded, caught in the pull of his words.

"We're no different. From birth, we need others. At first we need our parents—to feed us, to protect us, later to guide us, remind us who we are. And then the current reverses. Parents lean on children. Children become parents. The cycle continues. That's not weakness—it's the design."

He tapped the seatback in front of him, slow and deliberate. "But look at what's happening today. You don't ask your mother for recipes anymore—you ask the internet. You don't lean on neighbors—you hire someone online. You don't sit with your kids to mend what's broken—you let machines do it for you. It's convenient. It's Efficient. But it's also dangerous. Because when you stop depending on people, you strip love of one of its deepest forms: *value*."

"Nature reminds us: *everything has value*. Everything is both needed and needful. The bee helps the flower, the flower feeds the bee. The bird scatters seeds, the tree offers shelter. That interdependence is what keeps life alive. Families and communities work the same way. Romantic relationships do too. Real connection isn't found in grand vows or lofty ideals. *It's found in being useful to one another*—in giving something the other wants. In showing up. Doing what no app, no machine, no sum of money can do: listening with patience, offering comfort, fixing what's broken not only in the home, but also in the heart."

I let his words settle, then leaned back, almost thinking aloud. "That's it, isn't it? Relationships are built on value. Attraction begins with the value we *see* in one another. Connection grows from the value we *exchange* with one another. But when we stop depending on our relationships, we strip them of value. It's like saying, I don't need you—I'm fine on my own. And while that sounds noble, while independence has its virtues, it also drifts us apart. That's what's happening now."

"We don't need our parents, our friends, our neighbors for anything. Everything is handled by the market—by services, by apps, by an economy that turns every human need into a product. Time, attention, education, skills... even love, or at least the illusion of it, is available for sale."

I turned to him, searching. "But when did that shift happen? When did we forget people and start trusting products instead?"

The old man nodded, as though he had been waiting for that question. "It wasn't always this way. In early human communities, everyone played a part. Some grew food. Some made tools. Others hunted, or built, or raised children. And they all shared. They all depended on one another. Tribes and civilizations weren't sustained by lone wolves. They thrived because of exchange. They thrived because of trust.

"But dependence carried risk. What if someone didn't share fairly? What if someone hoarded? Out of those uncertainties came something that felt safer—*money*. Now, instead of depending on people, we could depend on currency. If you had enough of it, you didn't have to ask. You didn't have to engage. You could buy food, shelter, clothes, pleasure, even attention. Independence, bought at a price."

"But what have we really achieved? Now we depend on money instead of people. You no longer think, a farmer fed me. You think, I bought this. You don't see the weaver, the builder, the hands behind the work—you just see a transaction. And once you stop seeing value in people, you stop loving people. You start loving money instead. It's not entirely our fault—it's the way society has been designed."

"But here's the truth: you're still not independent. Once, women depended on their husbands for financial security. Today, many depend on their jobs. Once, we relied on our tribe. Today, we rely on systems and strangers. The core truth hasn't changed. You may not rely on a neighbor for food, but you rely on a paycheck. On your boss. On your next client. On your online store working. If any of those collapse—your entire structure crumbles. And that dependence is worse, because *if you lose money, you lose everything*."

The puzzle pieces clicked together in my mind. I turned to him, a smirk tugging at my lips. "You're right. We aren't independent at all. The focus has just shifted. Instead of depending on our people, we've become dependent on money. And perhaps that's why, we don't have relationships with people anymore... we have one long relationship with money."

The bus rumbled on. Pines gave way to bare fields, fields to warehouses, and warehouses to glass towers. The stillness of the mountains blurred in the window's reflection, replaced by billboards, traffic lights, and the restless rhythm of the city. Nature faded behind me, but the hike had given me the clarity I was searching for. Step by step, I had been piecing together the fragments of what makes a relationship last, what makes it feel whole and fulfilling.

****

Thanksgiving

Chapter 25: Homecoming

It had been several weeks since the hike. Summer had softened into fall, and the world itself seemed to take a long, wistful breath. There's something undeniably romantic about autumn—the crisp air, the way leaves burn into gold before surrendering, the melancholy of beauty fading right in front of you. But I carried my own caution. I had promised myself I wouldn't tumble recklessly into love again, not without the answers I was still chasing. Another heartbreak would crush me, and I wasn't sure I had the strength to rebuild twice.

I had pieced together much already—how attraction sparks, how attention sustains, how drive, value, exchange, and interdependence weave the fabric of a bond. I knew how connections were built. But one question lingered, the next piece of my puzzle: *how do you strengthen those connections?*

What makes exchange feel effortless with some people and forced with others? What differentiates an ordinary bond *from* a really strong bond?

I knew this answer wasn't hidden in libraries or buried in the minds of professors. It lived in the people I was already most connected to—because the strongest bonds I had were living proof that something had worked. My parents, my siblings, my childhood friends—the ones who had known me most of my life. If I could understand what made those connections so resilient, maybe I could learn to build that with someone new.

That's why, as Thanksgiving approached, my excitement grew. If there was anywhere to seek those answers, it was home.

Airports at Thanksgiving are a kind of madness. Crowded gates, restless lines, the annual migration of hearts trying to find their way back. My own journey carried me from the pacific northwestern skies back to subtropical air where palm trees leaned like familiar faces and the warm salt of the ocean folded into the breeze.

By the time I arrived at my parents' home, I was lulled by both nostalgia and exhaustion. The neighborhood looked just as it always had: wide lawns manicured like paintings, driveways lined with spotless cars, houses with porches that stood like invitations but belonged firmly to tradition. A place where life seemed steady, insulated, and proud of its traditions. Even though I visit nearly every holiday, each return still carries the same weight of childhood nostalgia.

After the long flight, after the hugs and small talk, after the heavy meal that tasted like memory itself, I surrendered to a deep nap—jet lag pulling me under like an undertow. By evening, restless and needing air, I stepped outside for a stroll. The moonlight pooled in patches along the sidewalks. Sprinklers ticked in the distance, a dog barked two streets over, and the palm trees overhead swayed like dark green sails against the night.

That's when I saw them—Noah and Liam. Two brothers I had grown up alongside, though the years had carried us down different paths. Noah was still the same—steady, open, immediately warm.

"Look who finally decided to come home," he teased, clapping me on the shoulder. "I was starting to think Seattle swallowed you whole."

I laughed. "Yeah, it tried, but I escaped! Needed a little sunshine before I turned into moss."

"That's fair. We don't export sunshine here, you know—you gotta come pick it up in person."

It felt easy with him, the way it always had. We traded stories for a moment, the kind that didn't need effort to unspool.

"So you and Sarah finally got engaged, ha?," I said, nudging him. "Didn't even send me a warning."

He grinned, rubbing the back of his neck, a little sheepishly proud. "Yeah, I popped the question over the Fourth, and you know Sarah—she doesn't do small. So we planned a barbecue for the whole block. Burgers, corn on the cob, the works. Ended up turning into a three-day thing—kids running wild, someone set off fireworks in the driveway. Felt like the whole neighborhood showed up. Total chaos—but the good kind."

I could picture it instantly. Noah belonged here—his roots tangled into the streets, the porches, the very heartbeat of the place.

Then there was Liam.

"Hey," he said flatly, as if politeness was all he owed me.

"Hey," I echoed. He had shown up for the holidays after years away. The kind of guy who, once he left town for the city, rarely found his way back.

His face looked sharper than I remembered, his posture different—city edges, where there had once been something softer. He wasn't the same boy I had grown up with—running through sprinklers, climbing fences, stealing bites of pie cooling on someone's window ledge. Something in him had drifted, and I could feel the distance in a single glance.

As we walked together, my mind filled in their story.

They had been raised under the same roof, in the same neighborhood, yet carried two entirely different spirits. Noah, two years younger, had always leaned toward home—toward tradition, toward small rituals that stitched the community together. He carried extra chairs for his grandparents without being asked. He led the parade of bikes on the Fourth of July. He was the kid who kept score at little league when nobody else volunteered.

Liam was restless from the start. He rolled his eyes at traditions, scoffed at parades, slipped away to places that felt foreign to him. He was always chasing diversity, sampling other ways of being, but never quite knowing where he belonged.

Noah loved the comfort of his culture, his people, the town that gave life its shape. Liam ridiculed those very things, as if the place that raised him was something to escape from rather than cherish.

And now, standing in the moonlight years later, I couldn't help but marvel at how two brothers from the same family could grow into such different men. Growing up, I was close to them both. But now—with one, I felt the same comfort, as if nothing had changed, and with the other—I felt as though I were meeting a stranger I had once known.

Chapter 26: Roots

There's something about small towns that lives under your skin. For me, this one always feels like a soft sweater I never outgrew. I know the cracks in the sidewalks, the way the church bell lags by a minute, the smell of cinnamon rolls drifting out of the bakery. I know which ice cream shop still gives extra sprinkles if you smile at the owner, which neighbor waves twice instead of once, which bar is generous with its pours when they recognize a familiar face. It's not just memory—it's muscle. Every corner holds a story, and every street feels like it knows my name.

Seattle, by contrast, was another planet when I first arrived. A city of transplants, everyone carving out a new life, everyone carrying an accent, a backstory, a different definition of home. The streets buzzed with possibility, but also with anonymity. Nobody cared that you were new, because everyone was new. It was thrilling, but lonely. Diverse in every way— cultures, cuisines, philosophies—but hard to stitch into a single fabric.

I remember struggling at first, watching people introduce themselves with job titles and ambitions instead of family names. Back here, you said who your parents were and people nodded—they knew you. There, no one knew me, and no one cared.

But even in Seattle, I never let myself drift too far. I carried my roots with me—not as baggage, but as compass. The rituals, the values, the small-town pulse I was raised on, they stayed in me like marrow. I made sure of it. I kept the phone calls alive:

checking in with my mom regularly, catching up with uncles and aunts, laughing with cousins. I sent flowers for birthdays, never missed a graduation if I could help it. I still remember taking a red-eye, skipping a meeting, just to see a cousin walk across a stage. Those things mattered more than any email waiting in my inbox.

It wasn't just staying in touch, it was staying engaged. Being present in their joys and sorrows. Listening to my grandfather's stories on the phone as if I were sitting in his library, sharing the milestones of my own life so they never felt left out of it. We often curse technology, and yes, it has its pitfalls. But in this one department, it's a gift. A lifeline. If you have the *will*, it allows you to stay connected to the people you love.

Sometimes I wonder about the future—maybe one day we'll step into teleporters and never really be away from anyone again. But even now, with phones, with FaceTime, with video calls that beam us into living rooms miles away, it's not so far from teleporting. You can collapse distance if you *choose* to.

And that's the key word—*choose*. Because everyone today preaches self-care: skin-care routines, morning routines, evening routines. But where's the *relationship-care routine*? Where are the reminders to call your mom, to check in on your siblings, to sit with your grandparents and ask them about their lives? Not just a polite visit, not a text to "stay in touch," but the real thing. Presence. *Engagement.* Letting them be part of your story and stepping into theirs. No one talks about this.

Noah and Liam had been a part of my story since as far back as I can remember—inseparable from the backdrop of my childhood. But over the years, especially as Liam stopped coming home for holidays, the orbit broke apart. Now, being back with both brothers, it felt like slipping into something we once were, like trying on an old coat pulled from the back of the closet. Not quite the same fit, but close enough to remember how it used to feel.

We decided to spend the entire day the way we once did as kids—running our old loop through town. Back then it was our ritual: start at the basketball courts, cut across Main Street for ice cream, then wander down to the lake before heading home at dusk. We did it every summer, every holiday break, until it felt less like an outing and more like muscle memory. The loop wasn't about the places themselves, but about how it tied us together—three kids with time to waste and nowhere else we needed to be.

This time, we piled into Noah's old pickup, a relic of our younger days—its cabin still holding the ghost of salt air, sunscreen, and a hint of gasoline that clung no matter how many times he cleaned it. Windows down, radio humming low, we drove through town like we had years ago, only now with bigger bodies and busier lives. It felt strange and familiar all at once—like tuning back into a song you haven't heard in years but still know every word to.

I remembered what Dr. Meyer said about long term memory—how it allows us to build and nurture our relationships across time. It's the thread that stitches the past to the present—and no matter how far you drift, one song, one scent, one familiar sight, a single touch of nostalgia can pull you right back to your people, just as it did for the three of us, reuniting after years apart.

Our first stop was the basketball court. The chain nets still rattled the same way, the blacktop still bore the cracks we used to trip over. Noah picked up a ball left behind and sank a shot from the free-throw line like it was nothing. I cheered, remembering how he had always been the one to beat. Liam laughed too, but in that slightly awkward way of someone stepping back into a place that used to be his.

From there we wandered to the ice cream shop. The smell hit us first—sweet, heavy, exactly the same. The owner looked up and immediately remembered Noah and me. He teased us about the sprinkles we used to beg for, the cones we'd try to balance on our bikes. But when his eyes landed on Liam, he squinted for a second before saying it had been a long time. We laughed it off, but I noticed Liam shift, just slightly, like the shop was part of a story he'd half-forgotten. For Noah and me, it was second nature; Noah still lived here, and I visited often, whenever I got a chance. We were still woven into its people and places. But for Liam, it felt almost foreign, unable to recall the last time he'd been here.

I watched Noah letting his ice cream melt in slow, sticky trails down his wrist. Then, with that same boyish mischief he'd never quite outgrown, he swiped it across my dress. I gasped and swatted at him, half laughing, half scandalized. "You didn't just—"

"Oh, I did," he said, grinning, that slow, infuriating grin.

Then in one quick move, he snatched my cone and held it aloft. I tried grabbing it, but he leaned back, teasing, keeping it just out of reach. I lunged twice, and each time his grin grew wider, as he held the cone high like a trophy. I finally rolled my eyes and shoved him toward the truck, and he wore that smug little victory grin all the way there. Liam trailed a few steps behind, smiling faintly but not joining in, as if the inside jokes belonged to another lifetime.

A moment later we were piled in, sun on our backs, music spilling out the windows as we bounced along the road. The lake was always the final stop.

Chapter 27: Scattered

The dock still creaked under our weight, the water spread out wide and silver, catching the light like a sheet of moving glass. We sat with our feet skimming the surface, skipping stones and counting ripples. For a little while, it felt whole again—the three of us, the loop, the truck waiting behind us like a bridge between then and now.

But as I watched Liam staring out at the horizon, I couldn't ignore the truth. Maybe that's why I struggled to connect with him after all these years. Not because he had moved away—I had too. But I never abandoned the things that tethered me. I left town, yes, but I carried it with me—the connections, the stories, the people—like cherished artifacts, reminders of who I am and where I come from.

Liam was different. Restless long before he ever packed a suitcase, he never seemed to treat this place as home. Always scanning outward, always chasing elsewhere. He hadn't just moved; he had moved on.

Change is the oldest story there is. People outgrow towns, stretch beyond the edges of their beginnings. We move because that's what survival asks of us: new places, new horizons and new light to grow in. Even plants, fixed as they seem, know how to wander. Seeds hitch rides on fur and fabric, burrs stubbornly clinging until they're carried miles from home. Fruits are eaten, seeds dropped far off, left to burrow into stranger soil. Dispersion is nature's way of saying: you can't all stay here. To remain crowded in one patch is to starve.

But movement itself isn't the problem. The danger is drifting without ever landing, scattering without sinking roots. That's when you stop knowing where you belong. And watching Liam that afternoon, I felt it. He had unmoored himself, like someone who had cut his ropes without finding another dock to tie to. He had let go of this place without ever finding another to hold him. And even now, I couldn't tell what he had changed into.

I thought of his digital trail, the scattered snapshots of his life I only knew through his socials. His Facebook updates read like postcards from nowhere: one week in Prague, the next in Denver, a summer on the road in an RV, majors switched as easily as shirts. Instagram was a blur of parties and new faces, friends who never lasted more than a frame. He looked like he belonged everywhere, yet somehow nowhere at all.

And it was the absences that cut the deepest. Never a steady girlfriend. Never the same companions appearing twice. Nothing steady that showed. Over time I realized I no longer knew what Liam stood for: what he believed in, what he loved, who he trusted. And without that, how do you find your way back to someone? Connection isn't just about affection; it's about *relatability*—an overlap of some kind, a *familiar ground* you can both stand on. Without it, connection slips through your fingers.

I remembered what Dr. Meyer told me about *empathy*: empathy doesn't vanish because people stop caring, it disappears when people stop being *relatable*. When lives scatter too far, when values and heartbeats no longer overlap, the bridge simply collapses.

That's the fragile truth about connection: unlike attraction, it isn't automatic. It's tended, built, guarded like a fire. And you do that by circling back, by engaging, by never letting go of those common threads—the shared activities, the shared interests, the shared topics. Because without this overlap, you lose *familiarity*. You stop being *relatable*. Conversations skim the surface. Gestures lose their weight. It happens all the time: in friendships, in families, even in marriages—the way things end silently, not because the love disappeared, but because the shared life did.

Back here in my hometown, relatability is stitched into everything. The same parades down Main Street, the same hymns in church, the same neighbor waving from her porch. It's perhaps why it's so much easier to weave strong connections here, in small towns. But watching Liam, I understood how easily that thread can fray once you let go.

And maybe that's what's happening to us now. We've become a generation scattered in every direction: careers, lifestyles, identities multiplying like tributaries of a river that eventually runs dry. We're spoiled for choice but starved for belonging. Told we can be anything, we try to be everything, and end up being nothing. We find a new self with every scroll, every playlist, and every outfit. Always sampling, but never staying.

In chasing novelty, we forget to belong: to places, to people, to anything at all. We float from interest to interest, city to city, face to face, without any anchor. We connect with everyone a little, but no one a lot. And then we wonder why affection feels thin, why conversations run shallow. The truth is, we've stretched ourselves too thin to hold onto anything deeply.

The modern age sold us individuality but stole from us the anchor of identity. Real identity isn't built in isolation; it's forged in community: in the meals shared, the stories repeated, the rituals kept alive. Without those, we don't just drift from others—we drift from ourselves.

The way back isn't complicated. It's quite simple. Instead of sampling, we must start choosing. We must choose our values. Choose our people. Not for likes or trends, but because they feel like ours. The ones we can relate to. The ones who root us. Let us belong, not to everything, but to the few that matter. To the ones that feel like home.

I stood back for a moment, watching the brothers framed against the lake as the sun began to set. The ripples from the skipping stones spread wide, circling back until they kissed the shore, as if the water itself refused to let go of what touched it. Overhead, a flock of birds shifted in formation, their wings flashing silver as they turned toward home. Even the wind carried a sense of return, rustling the reeds along the bank in a language I almost recognized.

For all our scattering, some things still find their way home—stones to shore, birds to nest, memories to places we belong. Standing there, I couldn't help but wonder if Liam would, too.

Chapter 28: Relatability

Thanksgiving has a way of pulling roots together. No matter where you scatter, you are expected to return, even if just for a meal. The holiday is more than turkey and pie; it is a ritual of remembering, of re-stitching old bonds. Around that table, families recount stories, laugh at half-forgotten jokes and revive traditions. Growing up together makes us relatable in a way nothing else can. You don't have to explain yourself to people who were there from the start. They already know.

Dinner was loud and messy and wonderfully warm. My parents' house overflowed with cousins, neighbors and friends. Plates passed hand to hand, laughter rose and fell like waves, and for a few hours, time itself seemed to collapse. The years away dissolved, and I was just a child again, stealing marshmallows from the sweet potatoes, listening to my uncles argue about football.

After the feast, as was tradition, I slipped away with Noah and Liam to their house. We'd done it since we were kids. Back then, we had our own Thanksgiving ritual: sneaking into the garage to play darts, the loser having to run a lap barefoot around the block while the others laughed and timed him with a broken wristwatch. It was silly, reckless, but it was ours. It was the kind of tradition that stitched us together, year after year through adolescence. And this time, we got to relive it all again—because the prodigal son, Liam, was back at last.

Yet as I watched him, I wondered if he was really back. He moved like a guest in his own home—polite, hesitant, unsure. His eyes scanned the room like he was looking for instructions.

When Sarah, Noah's girlfriend, handed out leftover pie, Noah already knew which cousin wanted extra whipped cream, which aunt was diabetic. I even remembered to set aside the corner slice for their father, because he liked the crust. Liam, though, looked surprised by every detail, as if he'd stumbled into someone else's house.

The truth landed heavy: I, the neighbor who had grown up beside them, knew more of their family ways than he did and he looked more like an outsider than me.

Still, we laughed some, told old stories, and teased each other. The conversation lifted the heaviness for a while. Later that night, I found Liam sitting alone in the den, shoulders slumped, the glow of his phone casting tired shadows across his face. He wasn't angry, just adrift—the kind of tender sadness that makes you realize someone needs a friend more than anything else.

I sat beside him. "You okay?"

He shrugged. "Yeah."

"You seem... I don't know. Disturbed. Did you and Noah fight?"

"No. Nothing like that." His voice was flat, tired.

"You know you can tell me anything right?" I said, attempting to remind him of the deep bond we used to share.

As kids, we shared everything: secrets whispered under blanket forts, dreams confessed in the dark, laughter that left us breathless. Years had scattered us into different worlds, but childhood bonds don't disappear like that. They lie buried, waiting. And in that moment, looking at him, I saw not the restless man but the boy I had trusted at ten. For the first time in years, he felt like that same friend again.

He paused. Then, voice cracked, he whispered, "Who am I, Sia?"

I turned to him fully.

"I don't know where I belong anymore. I spent so long trying to be different, trying to find myself out there... but now I just feel like I lost something along the way. I feel like I don't fit here anymore. But I didn't build anything that fits me either. It feels like I'm just... floating."

I didn't speak. Instead, I reached over, laid my hand gently on his shoulder, and slowly rubbed his back, steady and reassuring. Almost without thinking, my fingers drifted through his hair. I knew he didn't need words in this moment, just a gesture that said *I'm here, I'm present, I'm listening, and I feel you.*

After a while, I whispered, "Come with me", giving his arm a gentle tug. "Let's get some air."

We stepped into the night like we had a hundred times as kids, slipping away from the noise to talk about things that mattered. The moon was high. The November air was soft and breezy, typical of this little corner of the state. Palm trees lined the street like old sentries, their fronds dancing quietly in the wind.

I pointed to them. "Do you remember these?"

He nodded. "I used to pretend they were giants."

"They were small once. You could climb them. But look at them now—majestic, reaching for the sky."

He gazed up at the palm trees towering above us, regal and swaying.

"But you know what? They never left their roots. That's how they grew. They stayed connected to the ground that knew them. If we had cut one of these down and planted it in New York, would it have survived?"

He smiled faintly. "Probably not."

"No, it would've withered," I explained. "Because the sun would've been wrong. The air too harsh. It wouldn't have belonged there."

"Growing up doesn't mean breaking away," I said softly. "It means reaching farther... because you're anchored."

He closed his eyes and let out a breath he hadn't realized he was holding. We stood there in the still moonlight, the breeze whispering between the trees.

I looked at him, the thought forming as I spoke. "We spend so many years trying to find ourselves, chasing the next version of who we think we should be... and in the process, we forget who we were. We treat life like a *suitcase*—there's only so much room, so we keep tossing things out to make space for the next thing. Old friends for new ones. Old ideas for new ones. But Liam, we shouldn't live that way. Instead, we should treat life like a *bookshelf*."

He looked at me, curious.

"You keep adding new books as you grow—new experiences, new people, new knowledge. But you don't throw the old ones away. That's how you build a library. A library of connections, of stories, of legacy. Something worth passing on."

My eyes glistened as I spoke.

"But if you keep replacing the old books with new ones, always chasing novelty and discarding the past, you'll end up with just one book in your hand. Always just one. Never a library."

I put my hand lightly on his chest. "And Liam... there's space for many books in your library. You don't have to let go of what made you. Cherish it. Celebrate it. Only then will you truly connect—with friends, with family, with the world. If you keep forgetting the old faces, the old values, if you keep letting go of everything you once loved, if you keep running toward something new... one day, you'll wake up unable to relate to anything at all. The world will no longer feel like home, and everyone will look like a stranger."

Liam swallowed hard. In that moment, I could see his mind filled with memories long buried—the kind only silence and truth can unlock. Our childhood flooded back in color: running barefoot across hot pavement, building forts out of couch cushions, chocolate-smeared fingers, flashlight tags in the backyard, the smell of sunscreen and pool chlorine.

And then— A flash of a moment. He had been eight. It was a rainy afternoon, and he had drawn little faces on coconuts with a Sharpie. Stuck googly eyes on them, lined them on the porch like soldiers. One of them wore his dad's necktie and plastic sunglasses. He made me formally greet them all, bowing and offering them snacks.

Now, years later, that memory cracked open something in his chest. Then, without thinking, he said, "Remember when I stuck googly eyes on all the coconuts and made you talk to 'Captain Coconut'?"

"Oh yes, I do!" I said with a big, wide smile spreading across my face. "He was very sophisticated. He only spoke in riddles."

We both laughed, and the sound felt like coming home.

From the doorway, Noah chuckled too. He stepped forward slowly, no words, just an understanding in his eyes. He pulled Liam into a firm embrace. Liam held on tight. Then, without hesitation, both brothers pulled me in between them. I rested my arms lightly around their backs, as if afraid to break the moment—shoulder to shoulder, heart to heart—beneath the moon and the rustling palms. My childhood friend, not lost, but found again.

****

The Streets

Chapter 29: Addiction

I was fumbling through my purse, trying to dig out a few crumpled bills to pay for the coffee I'd just ordered at Starbucks. The holidays were officially over, and you could feel it in the air. The city had snapped back into its old motion, the heartbeat of the streets quickening again, as if someone had turned the volume back up. People seemed brighter though, their eyes still carrying a trace of the glow from turkey dinners, long naps, and renewed connections. Fed, recharged, they moved like soldiers returning from leave, ready to take on the world again.

Seattle looked sharp that morning, in the way only Seattle can. The sky was a wash of pearl-gray, stitched with streaks of silver light. The streets gleamed from a recent drizzle, sidewalks reflecting the city like broken mirrors. My car was in the repair shop, so I had to take the bus to work—an inconvenience, but also a chance to walk these streets, to be part of their restless energy.

It had been good to see the brothers over the holidays, especially Liam. Something between us deepened this visit, a closeness that surprised me. Liam had decided to extend his stay with his family for a few more weeks. The brothers had taken the boat out on the lake like the olden times. I saw the photos—smiles wide, the water glinting like liquid glass. It looked like fun, but more than that, it looked like Liam was slowly finding his way back, piecing together whatever parts of himself had scattered. That's the beauty of family: no matter how far you drift, it will always find a way to pull you home.

For me, it was a reminder. We have so many relationships in life that matter—family, friends, people who hold our history. But we often forget them. Instead, we build our whole existence around one relationship, one person who becomes the center of our universe. That's why heartbreak feels so catastrophic: when they vanish, it feels as though everything vanishes with them. And yet family never disappears. Even if we ignore them, they don't ignore us when we finally reach out. The bond is permanent, a kind of living archive of ourselves. Maybe *relatability* is the glue—it's why these ties hold so tight.

And perhaps that is what we should seek in love, too. Relatability—like attention, value, drive, and interdependence—plays a crucial role in determining the strength of our relationships. A good match, I think, is a delicate balance between someone you're attracted to and someone you can also relate to.

Dating apps, of course, claim to do the same. Their algorithms promise their own version of relatability—what they call *compatibility*—based on the movies we watch, the music we love, and the books we read. They try to match us through big and small details: hometowns, politics, food, travel, even down to the smallest quirks we share.

And yet, somehow, their formulas still fail to deliver true love. What they offer instead is a chain of disappointments. If compatibility on paper were enough, dating apps would be in the business of building lifelong marriages. Instead, you count yourself lucky if a match lasts longer than a month—or more than a single night. Luckier still if they don't ghost you before dessert.

And maybe we can't blame the apps entirely. Even relationships formed organically fail. I've seen it too often— couples who seem perfect for each other. They have attraction. They have relatability. They do everything right. And yet, somehow, even they grow tired. Even they fall apart. Why is that?

I thought I had found all the answers I was searching for— *what begins a relationship, what sustains it, what strengthens it*. And yet, something was still missing that held me back from diving into love.

Because from what I understood so far heartbreaks were inevitable. I had lived through it once and didn't want to endure it again. The pain is excruciating. And if even the most perfect of relationships eventually fade anyway, if love is bound to lose its shine, why sign up for that pain at all?

Unless, I could maybe find a way to avoid heartbreaks—if I could learn how to survive it, how not to be completely undone by it—maybe I could find the courage to fall in love again, to take my chances once more. But until then, I chose caution.

As I walked the streets of Seattle that day, I didn't know life was about to show me exactly that. Little did I know it was about to hand me a revelation—one I hadn't asked for, but one that would completely change how I saw love, pleasure, heartbreaks, and relationships.

A gust of wind snapped me back to the present as I turned onto Third Avenue. The street felt different now—edgy and fractured. A man hunched under a tent made of blue tarp. Another shuffled past me, his eyes unfocused, muttering to himself. Once, Seattle had felt like possibility, a city of glass towers and promise. Now sometimes it felt unrecognizable, a portrait smudged with homelessness, drugs, and an economy that had outgrown its own people. I kept walking, my eyes focused down on the sidewalk, careful of not drawing unwanted attention. My pace increased slightly as I walked down that block toward my office.

And then it happened.

A sudden tug at my side, a jolt, and before I could even register, my purse was gone—ripped from my shoulder. The man sprinted, his sneakers slapping against the wet pavement, darting past the tents and trash cans.

"Hey!" My voice cracked, more shock than rage. Adrenaline surged hot through my body as I lunged forward, chasing—my heart thundered in my ears, the world narrowing into the line of his back and the pounding of my own steps. People turned, startled. A horn blared. And just like that, the streets had pulled me fully into their story.

He ran along the sidewalk, every stride practiced and quick. I followed, my breath ragged, my mind a whirl of chaos: my phone, my cards, my ID—all gone if I stopped. My legs pushed me forward even as fear wrapped cold fingers around my throat.

"Stop him!" I shouted, though my voice sounded swallowed by the noise of buses, car horns, and the endless hum of downtown. Heads turned, but no one moved. People froze, watched, then carried on—as if a purse snatching were just another item on the daily program of city life.

He turned sharply, disappearing into a narrow alley littered with broken bottles and graffiti-scrawled walls. I chased, almost slipping on the slick sidewalk. For a moment I thought I saw victory—the purse swinging loosely in his hand, close enough I could imagine grabbing it back.

Then he glanced over his shoulder, smirked, and pushed harder, pulling farther ahead down the long alley.

I stopped, hands braced on my knees, catching my breath, chest heaving, a mix of rage and helplessness clawing at me. A police siren wailed faintly in the distance, but no one here looked like they expected help to come. And just when I had lost all hope, something unexpected happened.

"Hey!" A voice cut through the other end of the alley, just as my lungs began to fail me.

The thief stumbled, as if the sound alone had tripped him. A tall figure appeared at the corner ahead, intercepting with surprising speed. The next second was a blur—a firm grip, a twist of motion—and suddenly my purse was wrenched free. The thief bolted in the opposite direction, disappearing into the maze of tents without a backward glance.

The man walked toward me, holding up my bag like a prize. "Looking for this?"

Relief crashed over me like a wave. I rushed forward, practically snatching it back into my arms. "Oh my god—thank you! Thank you, thank you." I flipped it open with trembling fingers, checking: wallet, cards, phone—everything still there, like tiny miracles lined up in leather.

Then I looked at him properly. Recognition sparked, though I hesitated. "Wait... Rob?"

He laughed. "Finally. I thought you'd never get it."

My eyes widened. Rob—my old coworker. A few months back he had switched companies, just a few blocks away from mine now. While working together, we would often spend long hours debugging code and swapping sarcastic remarks over lunch. And here he was, saving my day in the middle of Third Avenue.

"I'm sorry," I stammered, embarrassed. "I didn't recognize you right away. It's just—you're clean-shaven now. You can't blame me. I've never actually seen the bottom half of your face before."

Rob chuckled, rubbing his jaw. "Fair. I'm experimenting with the look."

I grinned. "You guys always tease women for looking unrecognizable without makeup. Have you ever seen yourselves without facial hair? It's a whole different person!"

He smirked. "Touché. I'll take that one."

The tension of the chase melted into laughter, our words spilling into the air like a relief valve. Funny how emotions could flip so violently within minutes—terror to comedy and panic to ease.

We started walking back toward the main street. I shook my head, still rattled. "Never again. I'm never walking down that block again. This city…" I exhaled hard, frustration bubbling. "It's gone to the dogs. Drugs, tents, crime everywhere. Why don't they just lock up all the addicts?"

Rob glanced at me, his tone gentler now. "Sia, it's not that simple. Addiction isn't just a crime to punish—it's something deeper. The drugs or the people using them aren't the root problem. It's the nature of addiction itself."

I blinked at him, surprised. "That's not how I've ever thought about it. For me, addiction was always lumped in with crime. Rational solution—punishment."

He shook his head. "Temporary fixes never last. You treat the symptoms, but the disease always returns. Addiction is a growing problem—we're all becoming addicts in our own ways. Phones, food, work, validation... it just wears different faces."

His words hung in the air, heavier than the drizzle. I had always admired the way Rob thought—not just in black-and-white, but in all the gray spaces in between. At work, when everyone else patched problems on the surface, he'd drill down to the root cause. It made him not just effective, but oddly fun to work with—projects flowed smoother, ideas sparked, and I learned so much from the way he analyzed code like a story with layers.

Now, hearing him frame addiction that way—beyond crime, beyond drugs—I felt myself hooked.

I smiled faintly. "Well, you've got my attention. And I could use a new coffee, since I spilled mine chasing down my bag. Want to join?"

He grinned, mock-dramatic. "How could I possibly say no to coffee with you?" A wink.

We turned together toward the nearest shop, the city still buzzing and broken around us, yet suddenly it felt a little warmer.

Chapter 30: Rewards

We ducked into the café tucked inside the Amazon office building. The place felt less like a coffee shop and more like a refueling station in some corporate spaceship. Lines of people shuffled forward, ID badges dangling, faces pale under fluorescent lights. No one smiled. Their eyes were glued to laptops or phones, like pilots locked into their dashboards. Espresso shots hissed from the machine, a metronome to the grind.

I leaned closer to Rob, lowering my voice. "Tech jobs have become the new blue-collar jobs. Look at this—factory slaves in fleece jackets."

"Or minions with stock options", he responded with a smirk.

We both laughed, though the sight around us was anything but funny—people sprinting toward deadlines, emails buzzing in their pockets, meetings stacked like dominoes. Life, compressed into spreadsheets and pings.

"And the big companies," he said as we carried our coffees out, "they've built whole cities inside themselves. Cafes, gyms, salons, food courts—you never really need to leave."

"Exactly," I said. "Why bother with real life when you can just stay at work forever?"

We laughed again, the sound breaking the monotony of honks and bus brakes outside. Crossing the street, a cyclist nearly clipped us, cursing as he veered away. We found a bench by the curb, coffee warming our hands, traffic humming like background music.

"Well," I said, sipping, "that's why we need coffee. Fuel to keep the hamster wheel turning."

Rob tilted his cup, a half-smile playing on his lips "You know coffee's basically a drug, right?"

I narrowed my eyes. "Don't ruin this for me."

"Try skipping it one morning and see how you feel—tired, grumpy, maybe even with a headache. That's withdrawal."

I groaned. "Fine. But it's a stretch. I'm not going to mug someone's wallet if I don't get my latte."

He laughed. "True. Different scale. But the system behind it? Same as heroin."

I shot him a look. "Wow. So I'm basically a criminal in yoga pants?"

"Relax," he said, still laughing. "I love my coffee too. But think about it—coffee, wine, cigarettes, even the harder stuff— they all play the same trick. They light up your *reward system*."

"My what?"

"Your brain's built-in vending machine," he said, leaning back. "Imagine every time you felt good—pizza on a hungry night, your first kiss, a win on the tennis court—your brain pressed a button. Out came *dopamine, serotonin, endorphins, oxytocin*. Those chemicals made you feel happy—alive, comforted, connected. And your brain? It took notes. Stored the memory. Filed it under: *Do this again*."

I sipped, half-intrigued, half-defensive.

"That's why we all like different things," Rob continued. "Some people chase waterfalls, others chase roller coasters. Some lose themselves in books, others in video games. It's not random. It's conditioning. Your brain remembers what made you feel good once and tilts the compass back there. Doesn't matter if it's tennis or tequila—it whispers, *This worked.*"

"So you're saying I don't actually choose what I like?"

"Not as much as you think." He smiled, almost teasing. "Did you really choose everything you loved as a kid? Not really—you just went along with whatever came your way. Maybe someone handed you a book, and suddenly you were a Harry Potter fan. Maybe you flipped through channels, landed on *The Notebook*, and before you knew it, you were a hopeless romantic."

"So you're saying our brains have been in training since childhood, huh?" I said, trying to follow his point.

"Since before you even knew it. That's why it matters how kids are raised—the kind of things they're exposed to. When a child grows up knowing the joy of being loved, they seek that same feeling for the rest of their life. But if they've learned to find comfort in avoidance, they learn to live behind walls, even as adults. Similarly, a spark of joy in colors can shape an artist—just as a thrill in cruelty can shape something much, much darker. "

I let his words settle for a moment. "That makes sense. And perhaps what you are saying is true for kids. Because kids need guidance. But you can't use that same excuse for adults." I countered to make my point against drug use. "As adults we have choice. We can decide what we indulge in."

"I'll give you that. It's true—we decide for ourselves. But Sia, in this city life of deadlines, mortgages, and fraying connections, our choices shrink. And that's why many people are forced to settle for what comes easiest—screens, junk food, sex, alcohol, drugs. Quick hits of dopamine to feel alive "

"Are you saying one bad choice can create addiction?"

"Maybe not. But if you consistently find comfort in the same thing, over and over again—your brain starts to depend on it. It forgets there are other sources of pleasure and suddenly, the options disappear. You're no longer *choosing*; you're *chasing*."

His words lingered in the air.

"Want to hear something wild scientists discovered?", he asked

"Do I have a choice?"

"Not really." He leaned in, eyes gleaming. "They put rats in cages with two levers. One lever gave food. The other? Pure pleasure—direct stimulation of the reward center in their brains. Guess which one they chose."

"The food?" I guessed.

He shook his head. "Nope. They chose pleasure. They actually stopped eating, completely. Kept pressing the pleasure button until they died of starvation."

I wrinkled my nose. "That's horrifying."

"Yeah. But it shows you how the brain works. When reward pathways get hijacked—by sugar, by alcohol, by nicotine, by TikTok, even by toxic relationships—we can crave things that feel good but do bad. Over time, those cravings become habits.

Habits turn into identity. And once identity sets in? Well, then that becomes your destiny."

I was beginning to get his point. "If what you're saying is true, I can see how the real cause for addiction isn't just drugs, but the lack of fulfillment from the modern lifestyle."

I looked at him, then at the river of people rushing past—faces blank, coffees clutched, earbuds sealing them off. Suddenly the whole city felt like a giant rat cage, with everyone hammering their own invisible levers.

I took another sip of coffee, smiling faintly. "Okay, I'll admit it—you just ruined my latte. But in the most fascinating way."

Chapter 31: Tolerance

We drifted back into the current of the city, paper cups in hand. Seattle felt sharp-edged that afternoon—sirens echoing a few blocks away, a man slumped against the side of a building with a cardboard sign that read *Hungry, anything helps*. A woman in a puffer jacket stepped around him without looking down, her AirPods glowing white in the drizzle. My thoughts lingered on Rob's words as we walked—*addiction isn't always about chasing pleasure; sometimes it's about running from pain.*

I glanced at him. His insights were too good to walk away from, even though I knew I was supposed to be at the office. My curiosity kept tugging at me. Pleasure, dopamine, sex, drugs—they were all starting to blur into one web in my mind. Puzzle pieces I hadn't connected before suddenly felt like they might fit together if I just kept asking the right questions.

"So tell me," I asked as we stopped at a crosswalk. "Where does the problem actually start? If you find pleasure in drugs—that's fine, you can keep doing it as you please. But then how do people end up ruining their lives with it?"

Rob didn't hesitate. "Tolerance."

"Tolerance?" I repeated curiously.

"Yes", he went on, voice steady, like he'd been thinking about this for years. "Think of your first drink. One glass, and you're buzzing. But drink every day, and one glass won't touch you. You need more. The same with cigarettes, drugs, even coffee. The body starts adapting with time. It builds *tolerance*."

He paused to let it land and then gestured toward the slumped man with cardboard. "That's what tolerance does. The first hit feels like heaven. Pure lightning in your veins. But the body adapts fast. The next hit doesn't measure up. You need more, and then more again. You keep chasing the ghost of that first high, but you never catch it. That's why addiction is the worst kind of demon. It doesn't just take from you—it convinces you to hand yourself over, piece by piece. Before you know it you have lost everything - your house, your job, your family, your friends, even your dignity."

A chill went through me, sharper than the mist. "So this is how addiction ruins people," I said, the words leaving me with a sharp realization. "Porn, drugs, sex, alcohol—all different forms of addictions. They all ruin our lives in different ways."

He glanced at me, a grim smile tugging at his mouth. "You forgot *love*. People ruin their lives for that too."

I laughed at first, then caught the heaviness in his eyes. He wasn't entirely joking. The ache behind his eyes was familiar—the same shadow I'd been carrying.

"You mean to say *love is an addiction?*"

"Oh, very much so," he said. "The chemicals your brain releases when you see someone you're attracted to—it's not so different from what drugs trigger. Dopamine, serotonin, oxytocin... sometimes the overlap is uncanny. When you dissect it that way, it makes love seem nothing like the fairytales, but... simply as getting high on drugs."

I shook my head. "No. Love *is* different. Love is the natural way we find happiness. Drugs are artificial."

"I know, I know," he said, softer now. "You are right, love is natural and probably the rightful, intended way we were meant to experience pleasure. I'm not saying love isn't real. All I'm saying, it isn't magic the way some people think of it. It's chemistry. That's why it feels so powerful, and why losing it feels like *withdrawal*."

I thought about my own heartbreak—the nausea, the sleepless nights, the bone-deep ache. I had always tried to tell myself it was just in my head, that I should move on. But here was the brutal truth: it wasn't just in my head. *Heartbreak lives in the body too.*

"Okay," I said after a moment. "Then answer me this. If love feels so good—if it's giving us this incredible high—then why do people break up? Why let it fade? Wouldn't it make more sense to keep it alive?"

"Again, the same reason—*tolerance*," he replied almost instantly.

I stopped walking for a moment. His reply lit up my eyes, as if I'd stumbled on the missing piece I had been searching for. "So do we get tolerant to everything? *Even love?*"

Rob nodded slowly. "*Especially love.*"

We passed a bakery window; the smell of chocolate drifted out. He pointed at it. "Take chocolate cake. Everyone loves it. First bite—ecstasy. But eat it for breakfast, lunch, dinner? Every day? Eventually it makes you sick. Not because the cake changed. Because you did."

I laughed softly. "So you're telling me marriage is chocolate cake?"

He smiled. "In a way. The same body you fell for, the same jokes that had you in stiches—they lose their edge when they're on repeat. The thrill fades. Not because they stopped being attractive or funny, but because your brain got used to them. That's adaptation. We normalize even the best things. It's unfortunate, but it's also the truth."

Chapter 32: Love

And just like that—thinking about the parallels between love and drugs—my memory rewound to the day I first met the man I loved, the one whose absence I was still struggling to get over. The moment lives in me not as a fact, but as sensation, as if my bloodstream had been spiked with something euphoric.

It was about a year back. I had rushed into the café, walking briskly, my mind knotted around the presentation I still had to rehearse. A quick bite was all I wanted—something to fill me up before the meeting. It was then when I first saw him.

He sat at the table closest to the counter, a laptop open before him. His posture was casual, yet his presence was impossible to ignore. As I stepped up to place my order, he looked up. Our eyes met, and he rose to greet me—as if he had been waiting for me all along.

The world slowed. I swear it wasn't imagination—it truly felt as though time stuttered. The footsteps blurred into the background, hum of voices muffled, the hiss of the espresso machine fading into silence. For a few charged seconds, there was only him, rising into the light. He stood, light pouring across his shoulders as though the sun itself had chosen him as its stage. He was the most handsome man I had ever seen—tall, broad-shouldered, dressed in a light blazer and tailored pants that traced the lines of his muscular frame perfectly. His hair shimmered faintly, the kind of blond that makes you wonder if the sun follows him everywhere. His eyes so blue they almost seemed out of place in the gray city.

He smiled faintly as he reached his hand out toward me. It should have been a handshake. But when my hand slid into his, it felt like he was inviting me into a dance. The moment our fingers touched, a current shot through me. My chest buzzed as though every nerve had been lit, the same rush you get from your first sip of champagne on an empty stomach, or the first inhale of something forbidden—heavenly, intoxicating and impossible to resist.

My eyes locked on his. His on mine. Neither of us broke away. We just smiled—helplessly, childishly, as if we had been caught in some cosmic joke.

I sank into the chair across from him, still holding his hand, too lost to notice or care that none of this made sense. We exchanged names.

He had assumed that I was his client, the one he was waiting for, but he didn't pull back when he realized otherwise. Instead, he leaned in, asking, "How are you doing today, Sia?"

I melted into the sound as he spoke my name. His voice was deep and authoritative, yet it carried a warmth that made me feel suspended in some golden haze—the kind of high that makes you want to stare into nothing, smiling at everything and overwhelmed by a happiness too big for your body to contain.

He offered to grab me the croissant I'd come for, and I let him, though the truth was I couldn't have stood if I tried. My legs refused to move, not from exhaustion, but because staying there with him seemed like the most important thing in the world.

I watched him walk toward the counter and then back toward me with the order. His tousled hair moved with the faint breeze as he stepped closer, his eyes alive with emotions—deep, wild, and untamed, like the restless sea. His sculpted frame leaned slightly forward as he offered the croissant, as if he were about to feed me himself. The scent of his cologne drifted in the air, rich and dizzying. For a second, the world was right—everything felt aligned. People seemed happier, colors brighter, even the air easier to breathe. *This is how life is supposed to feel.* Everything around me shimmered with a glow, as though the world itself had taken a deep breath and exhaled joy. Although I have never done it myself, but from what I hear, it was much like someone had injected heroin in my veins.

We laughed when he finally explained the mix-up, how he thought I was his client. We both amused at the absurdity of it. I knew I had to leave—I had a meeting to prepare for—but I stalled. I asked him the time, hoping he might ask me to stay. He didn't, and so I reluctantly stood. Just as I turned and was about to leave, he called out, "Hey, I do taxes, by the way. If you ever need help, here's my card."

That simple card felt like more than paper—it was proof that this wasn't ending here. My heart soared as I took it from him, smiling in a way that felt like a promise.

The rest of the day unraveled like a dream slipping away. My presentation was a disaster—I faltered, forgot entire slides, stared at the screen until a coworker nudged me back. My manager spoke sternly afterward, reminding me of the stakes, his tone laced with disappointment. Normally, that would have crushed me. I'd built my identity on excellence—aced assignments in school, delivered flawless projects at work, prided myself on discipline and precision. But that day, nothing could touch me. I floated out of the office light as air, giddy, high on something no reprimand could touch. Even if they had fired me that day, I would have skipped home humming to the trees, twirling in the park, dancing with the wind.

That was the level of intoxication.

For months after the breakup, I blamed myself. For letting him reorder my priorities. For missing dinners with friends so I could see him. For skipping work to pick him up at the airport. For rearranging meetings to match his schedule. For carving myself smaller to make more space for him. I thought I was reckless, naïve, even weak.

But now with this new understanding of *love and addiction*, I see it completely differently. It wasn't my weakness that made me do all of that—it wasn't me—it was the effect of love itself.

Love is a drug. One hell of a drug. One of the strongest known to humanity. It floods your brain with dopamine, serotonin, oxytocin, making you feel blissfully whole. It makes you reprioritize not because you're foolish, but because you're high.

Recognizing that truth lifted something off my chest. I didn't need to keep punishing myself for the choices I made back then. Everyone has their indulgences: football, novels, cigarettes, heavy meals, hours lost in their phone. Mine was love. And yes, it made me vulnerable, but it also made me human.

For the longest time, I carried only shame. I was engulfed in regret—ashamed for falling for him, embarrassed to admit how weak I had been, how easily I let him take me for granted. I refused to talk about him. I dodged questions, changed the subject whenever friends or family asked about him. I was too humiliated to even speak his name.

For the first time, I allowed myself to say his name without shame. *Victor*. That was his name. I could speak it now, not with regret, but with clarity. Because now I understood what was really happening inside me. The chemical storm—the dopamine, the serotonin, the oxytocin—the surge that blinded me to logic and reason. My brain was only doing what every brain does when caught in the surge of pleasure. I hadn't been broken. I had been human.

And knowing that changes everything. That knowledge empowered me. My mind was no longer a mystery box. I knew why I felt what I felt, and I finally felt in control.

And for that freedom—for that rare clarity and understanding—I had no one to thank but Rob, my former coworker turned unexpected teacher, who opened the door and showed me the truth. His words, his insights, had given me back control over the one thing I thought I'd lost forever: my own mind.

I turned to him and embarrassed him with a tight hug. "Thank you, thank you, thank you so much".

Chapter 33: Pleasure

I stood hugging Rob in the middle of the sidewalk, cars rushing past, strangers throwing curious glances as they swerved around us. I didn't care. The relief was too overwhelming, too satisfying. For the first time, I understood—it wasn't me. The problem lies elsewhere. Love and drugs worked on the same circuitry, clouding judgment, making us reckless. And just like you can't blame yourself for saying stupid things after too many glasses of wine, I didn't have to keep blaming myself for what I had done in love. Silly, reckless, yes—but not a verdict on who I really was.

That thought alone felt like freedom. I squeezed him tighter, almost choking him, but he didn't complain. Maybe he even enjoyed the surge of affection.

"You've already thanked me a dozen times for getting your purse back," he said, muffled in my shoulder.

"It's not for that," I replied, finally pulling back. "It's for enlightening me."

He grinned, tugged at his collar with mock arrogance. "Stick around me long enough, and you'll always be enlightened."

I gave him a playful smack on the arm. "Okay, don't fly too high. Stay on the ground."

The moment softened into laughter, the tension finally ebbing from me. As we walked again, I asked, "So, what were you saying the solution was?"

He looked puzzled. "Solution?"

"You said addiction needs a lasting solution. You've convinced me drugs aren't the problem, nor are the people—it's the nature of addiction itself coupled with the soulless city lives that we live. I am convinced. So tell me... what's the solution?"

He laughed, shaking his head. "I never said I have the solution. I said we need to find one. A lasting one."

I nodded, though a trace of disappointment tugged at me. He had helped me see the problem in a way I never had before, but even he didn't hold the final key. Still, I felt a quiet gratitude. Sometimes seeing the outline of a problem is the first step toward finding its solution.

We were nearing his workplace now. Glass and steel rose into the drizzle, a corporate fortress of mirrored windows, revolving doors spitting out men and women in lanyards, clutching laptops and coffees like armor. Delivery trucks idled at the curb, horns blared in the distance, and the city pressed forward in its endless loop of urgency.

"Before you go, can I ask you something?" I said softly, slowing my pace.

He glanced at me. "Sure, Sia. Anything."

"And you'll answer with complete honesty?"

He raised a brow. "I always try to. Don't think I've ever lied to you. Besides—" his eyes twinkled—"you have that way of seeing through people. Even if I did, you'd catch me."

We both smiled, but my voice turned serious again. "So tell me... have you ever tried drugs? The real ones. The kind people sell their lives for. How does it feel?"

For a second he hesitated, eyes flicking away as though weighing whether to confess. I looked at him steadily, my silence begging: *Please, Rob. Just tell me the truth.*

Finally he exhaled. "Yes. Once. Just once." He emphasized the words. "It was back in college. I was reckless. And I don't recommend it. People make it sound like the most blissful experience of their lives—and sure, the pleasure was intense. But honestly, nothing I hadn't felt in other ways."

I blinked, surprised. "Like what?"

He thought for a moment, then smiled faintly. "I've felt that kind of surge—at concerts, when the beat hit just right and the crowd moved as one. In movies that left me buzzing for hours. Once, during a ceremony at a temple, when the air vibrated with chanting and devotion rose like bliss. I've felt the same euphoria at churches, when the choir rises and everyone feels lifted. I've felt that in skydiving, too—the rush, the freefall, the scream that's half terror, half joy. Even when my boss once praised me in front of the entire office, I felt that rush, the same high. Winning a big hand in a casino. Falling in love."

His eyes softened on those last words, and I knew exactly what he meant.

"The thing with pleasure," he continued, "is that it's *relative*. Imagine you're starving, shivering in the snow without a coat. I bring you inside, wrap you in a blanket, set you by the fire, hand you a bowl of warm soup. In that moment, wouldn't it feel like heaven? Now take the same soup, same fire, same blanket—just an ordinary Tuesday night at home. Nice, sure, but not the same. Same experience. Vastly different pleasure."

I nodded slowly, letting it sink in. He was right. Pleasure wasn't absolute—it was relative to context, timing, deprivation and relief.

"That's why it's tricky to explain," he said. "Someone with a miserable childhood, carrying trauma and loneliness, might feel euphoria from a needle far beyond anything I ever did in college. But me? It wasn't life-changing. Just a high. Life has moments that can feel the same—without the needle."

I paused, then smiled at him with more warmth than I had expected. His *honesty* drew me closer than any shared joke ever could. *Secrets always bind.* Confessions carve out a kind of intimacy words alone can't reach.

"Okay," I said, giving him one last hug. "Now go. You're getting late. I don't want to steal all your time." I nudged him playfully toward the street.

"It was lovely seeing you," he called, jogging across to his building.

I stood for a moment, watching him disappear through the revolving doors, then turned back toward my own office a few blocks away. At the intersection, I saw the same man slumped with a cardboard sign in his lap, unmoved, as if no time had passed at all.

And as I looked at him, a thought rose uninvited: *Nature has a strange way of balancing things. Whatever gives you an extraordinary surge of pleasure will, in its leaving, deliver an equal measure of pain.*

Chapter 34: Shortcuts

He couldn't have been older than thirty, maybe even younger. Perfectly capable hands, a body that could still work, still build, still earn. Yet there he was, slumped against the cold wall, a cardboard sign sliding down his knees. A man who perhaps had a job, a family, maybe a wife—now hollowed out, selling his life away for another hit.

It struck me then: what a tragedy it is to waste the one gift we're given. Out of billions of species, billions of organisms clawing for survival, only we are given this peculiar privilege—to not only live, but to *feel* so intensely. To savor music, laughter, a lover's touch, the comfort of soup on a winter night. And yet addiction, cruel and unrelenting, can strip all of that away.

Looking at him, I was pulled into a mirror of myself after the breakup. No, I hadn't collapsed into the streets, but inside I was no different. He begged for money, craving another dose. I begged my phone for a text, a call, a sign. Every few minutes I'd check—refresh, check, stare. Did he call? Did he post? Did he feel the same pain? Each time the answer was silence, and each time the disappointment hit harder, like the crash after a binge.

The symptoms were eerily alike. Sleepless nights that blurred into foggy days. Restless cravings, the shaking need for just one more fix—one more glimpse of his name lighting up my screen. The pounding headaches of unmet desire. The nausea of hope curdling into despair. Withdrawal isn't always from chemicals. *Sometimes it's from people too.*

For days after the breakup, I sat blank at the office, unproductive, uninspired. When I was high on love, work had slipped away because I was too happy to care. Now, it was the opposite—I was too sad to want to care. Two extremes, equally paralyzing. *Too much of anything renders you useless.*

But that's what addiction does—it swings you like a pendulum between *pain* and *pleasure*, never letting you settle in the middle. One moment it's a needle's high, the next a hollow crash. A rush of sugar one moment, a bitter emptiness the next. The glow of a first date one moment, the pain of being ghosted the other. We do not live on steady ground anymore—only spikes and drops. *We don't sit with pain long enough to heal it*; we leap toward the next hit of pleasure. We don't rebuild when something breaks; we simply buy a new one. We don't mend torn friendships; we replace people as if they, too, were disposable. Because that's easy. That's available. That's the shortcut.

That's when it clicked: people aren't addicted to drugs. They're addicted to *shortcuts*.

Pleasure itself isn't the enemy. Pleasure is what drives us to live. It's the brain's way of rewarding us for doing what ensures our survival: hunting, eating, mating, connecting, creating. It tells us to keep going. But somewhere along the way, we stopped working for it. We found ways to hack the system.

So now, instead of eating a fruit directly, we crush it into sugar and gorge on candy. That is because we have become too lazy to chew on an apple or even go look for real food. Sugar is a shortcut to calories, the shortcut to pleasure.

Instead of building with our hands, we tap a screen and have it delivered—because effort feels outdated and we want things served on a platter.

Instead of earning someone's love with patience, we swipe right and expect intimacy to arrive on demand—because we no longer have the patience to wait.

Instead of nurturing marriages, we scroll through strangers' profiles—because replacing feels easier than repairing.

Instead of speaking to our partners, we confide in our phones—because phones don't question back.

Instead of the slow dance of courtship, we stream instant gratification—because porn never says no.

Instead of letting wounds heal with time, we pop pills— because we've forgotten that healing is supposed to hurt before it feels better.

It's all shortcuts. Easy, instant, but hollow.

And shortcuts never last. The sugar rush crashes, it doesn't nourish you like an apple would. The excitement of shopping ends the second you rip open the package; it never gives you the satisfaction of building something yourself. Once the porn clip ends, you're still left alone, craving a real embrace. The thrill of the hookup is over, the moment the stranger leaves your room. It's a simple truth—the way you get something is the way you lose it. The faster they come, the sooner they go. And once it's over, what lingers isn't fulfillment—it's emptiness.

Shortcuts never work—not in life, not in love, not anywhere. Gambling proves it best. Gamblers are always broke. That's the thing about making money through shortcuts: money not earned through hours of effort slips away faster than it comes. Real wealth is built through paychecks—steady exchanges of hard work for reward. You give them your time, your energy, your skill; they give you something valuable back in return. And that's how relationships work too. Because that's how I had actually built all the real relationships in my life.

And Victor? Well, he felt like this jackpot I stumbled into—thrilling and blinding in one moment, fleeting in the next. What I mistook for a soulmate was really a shortcut to pleasure wrapped in desire, charm and validation. I rushed into it, too eager to put labels, too quick to give in, too fast to burn.

That's what we do these days. We don't chase connection; we chase pleasure—fleeting bursts of happiness, validation and instant gratifications. We chase body counts and one-night stands. But none of it lasts. Like a fire that flares too hot, it burns out quickly. We keep craving more, but it slips away, *like a deer darting into the woods* the moment you reach for it.

Because that's the curse of chasing pleasure: *it never chases you back*. You chase the high, but the high doesn't chase you. Drugs don't chase you back. Lust doesn't chase you back. And neither did Victor.

So what do we do? Do we just denounce pleasure?

No, not at all. The secret lies in finding pleasure through *reciprocation*, instead of *instant gratification*. Reciprocation, simply put, is a more established and sustained form of exchange between two people. It teaches you to give and receive, not by demanding, but by learning about each other and forming *interdependence*.

And once it does, there's no need to chase anymore. Pleasure flows naturally. The other person is drawn to you as you are drawn to them, effortlessly, like gravity. *That isn't addiction. That is connection.*

But to build such a connection, you can't remain centered only on yourself. Real bonds grow through recognizing and tending to each other's needs. This isn't about feeding your own appetite; it's about nourishing another person too. And by practicing reciprocation, you discover that pleasure doesn't live only in *receiving*—it lives in *giving* too.

Giving brings more than just pleasure. It brings respect. It brings confidence. It brings fulfillment. Because in bringing happiness into someone else's life, you proved that you matter. But when you only take—when you only think about yourself, when you only chase what gives you happiness—you remain in pursuit forever. You may taste brief moments of pleasure, but never that respect, that confidence and that fulfillment which only comes through *giving*.

Finding pleasure in giving rather than simply receiving is monumental. That is the secret to loving without ever breaking. The thing that finally frees you from the fear of heartbreak. Because now even if they don't always give back, you still feel whole.

I looked at the man holding the cardboard sign again and wondered how he had thrown away his life *chasing those fleeting moments of pleasure*—and how that chase had slowly hardened into addiction. So many options still open to him. He could rebuild, work, reconnect, even find love. But that's the thing with addiction—*it clouds judgment*. It tricks the brain into forgetting that joy can come from anywhere else. Just as I had forgotten, after the breakup, that my life was still full of options. So many ways to revive my bonds, reconnect with both my people and my passions: swimming, travel, books. Conversations. Laughter. Family. Friends. The very things that had once been my sources of joy and pleasure.

But then slowly, with effort, I retrained my mind to find joy in those places again. To stop chasing shortcuts and choose the *longer route* instead. To learn patience. To practice restraint.

To relearn how to wait—and how to sit with pain. That was the solution—not punishment, not shame, but simply reminding the brain where real pleasure lives.

Addiction doesn't make criminals. It makes captives. And captives need release. For the first time, I no longer saw addicts as criminals, but as people who had been carried away chasing pleasure—who grew weak, lost self-control, and gave in to shortcuts instead of walking the longer road. As that understanding settled in, my empathy returned.

I reached into my purse and pulled out my little notebook, tore a page, scribbled a number: the local rehab center. I bent down and handed it to him. "Call this," I said softly.

And at that time, his eyes lifted. A flicker of something—was it hope?—lit there.

As I crossed the street toward my office building, a funny thought struck me: if my purse hadn't been stolen, I might have never walked these streets long enough to uncover these new insights into love and addiction. I might have never truly forgiven myself for being reckless in love. And in that moment, my anger at the city—its chaos, its decline—melted away. In its place, something else bloomed.

Seattle had given me back my perspective. And with it, my love for the city returned.

****

A Hollywood Story

Chapter 35: Teamwork

The sun was already cutting sharp angles across the Hollywood Hills as our rental SUV wound its way up Mulholland Drive. I sat in the passenger seat, taking in the postcard details I'd only ever seen in movies: tall Italian cypress lining the road like sentinels, hills shimmering with sunlit villas and wide terraces, the Hollywood sign stretching across the hillside like a billboard from another era.

Behind me, the team traded jokes in the backseat, their laughter rising above the low hum of the engine.

I was working with Amazon Studios' visual effects team— the unseen bridge between storytelling and technology. For our latest project, four of us had flown down from Seattle to L.A. the night before and checked into a sleek hotel off Sunset, the kind with soft-lit lobbies, marble counters, and water bottles waiting on the nightstand. None of us slept much. There was too much anticipation about the morning ahead.

Today was the reason we were here: a pre-production meeting with *Harold Bennett*, a director whose name alone made the flight worth it.

"I still can't believe we're working with him," I said, eyes on the skyline. "He made *Ashes of Tomorrow*. That desert chase scene? Legendary."

From the back, our lead designer leaned forward between the seats. "Wait—he also did *Eclipse Run*, right? The rooftop motorcycle stunt?"

"Yep. That's him."

"Okay," he said, grinning. "Now I'm officially starstruck."

Our systems engineer smirked. "Amazon making movies still blows my mind. We started by selling paperbacks. Now we're stitching code into cinema. What's next—theme parks?"

"More like tax breaks," someone said, laughing. "Movies aren't just stories. They shape culture. And when you've got Amazon's money behind you, even a flop pays off in influence."

We laughed—the kind that admits he wasn't entirely wrong.

The car slowed as we turned onto a tree-lined drive. The studio sat tucked back from the street, the sort of place that drew attention without asking for it. Its power was in its understatement: clean white walls, tinted glass, and a discreet brass plaque with Bennett's name.

Inside, the lobby told the rest of the story—framed posters of blockbusters stretching back two decades, awards arranged like chess pieces on a shelf, black-and-white photos of him shaking hands with stars whose names you didn't just recognize, you'd grown up with.

A receptionist greeted us, clipped badges to our jackets, and waved us through security. We were guided down quiet hallways with the smooth efficiency of people used to moving important meetings along.

The conference room was spacious but lived-in, its walls lined with mood boards, concept sketches, and rows of taped stills. Bennett sat at the head of the table, relaxed but commanding, as if he'd been doing this his entire life. Beside him, the cinematographer flipped through a thick binder of storyboards, sleeves rolled up.

After introductions, Bennett leaned forward and tapped a sketch of a night sequence.

"In this forest chase scene," he said, "I want digital fireflies glowing around the characters—flickering dynamically as they move."

I glanced at our engineer, then back at him. "To preview that in real time, we'll need to use our live rendering engine. I can set up a small pipeline to composite a rough version in-camera. It'll be placeholder effects at first, but you'll be able to see the timing and movement before we lock the final VFX."

Our designer nodded, chiming in. "And we can dial the glow intensity on the fly. If you want it to feel more dreamlike or more menacing, we can adjust right there in the scene."

The cinematographer leaned back, considering. "That's perfect. If we can see how the light plays across faces during rehearsal, I can design the shots around it instead of guessing in post."

Bennett smiled faintly, the sort of smile that told you you'd just bought the team more trust—and more responsibility. The meeting had officially begun.

The hours that followed blurred in the way the best work sessions do—heated discussions, overlapping voices, sparks of debate that sharpened into ideas. This was the part I loved most: collaboration alive in the room, creativity bouncing between people, not screens. *Work relationships* were born this way—through shared problem-solving, through pushing and pulling at each other's visions until something better emerged. These were the bonds that outlasted projects.

I glanced at Bennett. He must be well in his seventies now, hair silver, his frame not as straight as it once had been, but his passion was untouched. He had directed through five decades of shifting trends, guided stars who had long since aged out of the spotlight. Yet he remained—steady, burning, like a North Star that endured through every storm.

He flipped a page and tapped a sketch of a garden scene, softer this time. "Now, the romantic sequence," he said, his voice dropping to something more reflective. "I see them walking under moonlight. When they finally kiss, I want a shimmer around them—light trailing gently, like stardust catching in the air."

I nodded. "That can be done. But, if you ask me, romantic scenes feel strongest without effects. The raw emotion on an actor's face...no computer, no AI, can replicate that."

The air shifted. My teammates froze. I seemed to have ventured beyond my scope—said something that wasn't mine to say.

Bennett's eyes narrowed. "You're going to tell me about emotions? About acting?" His voice carried a low edge, controlled but unmistakably irritated.

I held my ground, steady but respectful. "I only meant it as an audience member. Romance feels strongest when it's unadorned."

That lit the fuse. His voice rose, sharp with disbelief. "Do you know how long I've been doing this? I've worked with the greatest actors alive, directed love stories that made audiences cry in their seats. And you—fresh off a plane from Seattle—want to lecture me about authenticity?"

I was taken aback by his tone but kept my expression professional, refusing to lose composure "I thought you'd like a suggestion. But if you want stardust, you'll get stardust—exactly the way you pictured it."

The room went still, my teammates staring down at their notes, pretending to be invisible.

The meeting limped toward its end, and when the others hurried out, grateful for the escape, I lingered, sliding papers into my bag, uneasy with the weight of what had just happened.

Bennett walked over, slower now, his tone quieter. "You know, I've worked with a lot of tech people. But never once have I had one give me creative advice."

I met his gaze, managing a faint smile. "I don't see myself as just an engineer. I have my own head. My own voice."

For a moment, I thought I'd stepped too far again. But his expression softened, a flicker of something like respect.

"You know," he said, "I've been rethinking your point about that kiss. Maybe you're right. Maybe it doesn't need stardust at all. A kiss should stand on its own. Hell, the last thing two people need in that moment is glitter." He chuckled, a dry, genuine laugh that lifted the air.

As he spoke, my eyes drifted to the wall. A photograph hung there—sepia-toned, glossy, a snapshot from another age. *Sophia Maren*, the Hollywood darling of the '80s, stood arm-in-arm with rock star *Rafe Donovan*. My mother had talked about them endlessly, how they were the sensation of her generation, a couple who seemed to belong not just to themselves, but to the public imagination.

I nodded toward the photo. "Did you work with them?"

Bennett followed my gaze and smiled. "Sophia? She's like family to me. We've known each other for decades."

"Is she still making films?"

He shook his head. "No. She's living her life now."

"My mom is a huge fan," I said. "She'd be over the moon if I could bring home a photo or an autograph."

Bennett thought for a moment, then leaned back, a glimmer of mischief in his eyes. "You know what? I like you. And I want to make up for our little tussle. I go overboard sometimes. When I have an image in my head, I cling to it. But that's something I'm learning to change."

He lowered his voice, conspiratorial. "You want Sophia's autograph? Guess what? It's your lucky day. She's throwing a house party tonight. And I've got a plus one still open... "

Chapter 36: Forever

Hollywood has always been in the business of selling us *fairytales*. Cinderella sweeping into a ball. Beauty kissing the Beast and breaking his curse. Julia Roberts climbing the fire escape in *Pretty Woman*. Meg Ryan waiting in the Empire State Building in *Sleepless in Seattle*. Disney, romantic comedies, blockbusters—they all end the same way: *happily ever after*.

But does "happily ever after" even exist in Hollywood itself? Every morning the headlines tell a different story: a breakup, a divorce, a new affair, a scandalous link-up. Even the couples who look perfectly matched—those golden pairs who seem made for each other in every way: looks, values, status, age, compatibility—eventually unravel.

I still remember how my heart sank when Brad Pitt and Angelina Jolie split. They were the couple I looked up to, idealized, romanticized. I wanted what they had. And when they broke apart, I felt oddly unmoored—like if they couldn't make it, who could? Were all couples doomed to end? Or, if they stayed together, was it only through force and compulsion?

Because love, as I was starting to understand, doesn't just grow—*it grows tolerance*. The same face, the same smile, the same familiar eyes that once lit you up no longer evoke the same feelings after a while. The "honeymoon phase," as everyone calls it, slips away like sand through fingers, leaving behind something heavier, more deliberate. A forced promise. A vow. Obligation disguised as romance.

Maybe that's why we invented marriage vows in the first place. Because without them, desire would wither. The words become a contract, a reminder, a boundary line meant to hold us when passion fails. But I always found vows unsettling. I never wanted to stay with someone just because I promised to. I wanted to stay because we both still wanted to. Because we both still desired to.

And that raised the real question: *what keeps desire alive?* If love inevitably grows tolerance—just as you can't eat chocolate cake every day without it losing its thrill—then what hope does marriage have? Even if you found the most delicious cake in the city, could you really eat it daily with the same excitement, the same pleasure? Or would it become routine, something you consumed out of habit, laziness, or fear of unsubscribing from the plan?

I thought about my own relationship with Victor. Seeing him across a café once felt like a jolt of heroin straight into my veins. But the same face, as charming as it was, became over time more like a glass of wine, then just a sip, then finally ordinary water. His voice, which once sounded like music, softened into a dull hum and, in the worst moments, noise. He hadn't changed, but my tolerance had. And perhaps his had too.

At first he couldn't stop staring at me, couldn't stop complimenting, couldn't wait to see me or to set up dates. Slowly, the dates thinned. Weekly dinners became monthly check-ins, until even those vanished. He used to crave my voice—then he stopped answering calls. What began as us texting every minute of the day dwindled to once or twice, and even then it felt more like a formality than a conversation.

I could point out a hundred ways he could have been better. But that wasn't the point. *Even if he had been perfect,*

the truth is the honeymoon phase would still have ended.
Because how do you keep an exchange entertaining and alive
day after day? The same jokes, the same smile, the same
gestures—they eventually dull. Even the sweetest things lose
flavor when repeated too often. Cakes, alcohol, drugs, even
porn—they all build tolerance. And so, unfortunately, does love.

That's the tragedy. And it's not really a *modern curse*
either. I suspect even Adam and Eve might have grown tired of
each other eventually. Which leaves the question: why does
Hollywood keep selling us these impossible fairytales? Why do
we keep buying the idea of "forever" as if it were guaranteed?
Does happily ever after really exist?

I sat with those thoughts swirling, heavy and unresolved,
while I waited for the limo to arrive.

Even then, part of me couldn't believe Bennett had actually
invited me. At first I thought he was joking, dangling the idea
just to watch me squirm. A little revenge for our clash earlier in
the day—the kind where you hype someone up only to enjoy the
thud when they fall back to earth. I laughed it off at first, half-
ready to call his bluff.

Then he told me plainly - "Be ready at five. My limo will
pick you up."

That's when it hit me—he wasn't teasing. He had actually
invited me to Sophia's party. And with that realization, my
excitement knew no bounds.

My teammates were just as stunned; one joked, "If fighting
with him gets you to Sophia's party, I'm doing it in the next
meeting." We all laughed, but inside I knew it wasn't the
disagreement alone that earned me the invitation. It was the
fact that I had spoken my mind without fear. He was probably
used to being surrounded by people who buttered him up,

nodding politely at everything he said. But I have never been the one to hide behind the mask of politeness or professional distance. I speak from the heart. Always have. And maybe that was what he liked. And perhaps that is why he invited me.

And I am so glad he did—because as thrilled as I was at the thought of meeting Sophia, I was just as eager for a private conversation with Bennett himself—away from storyboards and production notes. Maybe he could offer a map I had yet to find.

I wanted a blueprint for a "happily ever after", and if anyone had been married to the idea of "happily ever after," it was Harold Bennett—he'd had made a career of crafting those endings—romances that lodged themselves in audiences' chests and lingered long after the credits rolled. He'd directed classics; he'd watched stars rise and fade; he'd seen what worked on film and, perhaps, what worked in life. If the man who made so many endings possible believed in something beyond vows and scripts, I wanted to know it.

So I said yes without overthinking it. This felt like a chance to learn something practical, straight from the horse's mouth: not a trick or a line from a script, but the kind of lived wisdom that might steer me away from repeating old mistakes. Tonight didn't feel like glitter and gossip. It felt like an appointment with possibility.

The limo slid to the curb, and the chauffeur swung the door open. Inside, Bennett sat with the ease of someone long accustomed to being chauffeured through Hollywood nights. He greeted me warmly, motioned to the seat beside him, and offered a glass of champagne.

It all felt dreamlike—the soft leather, the city lights, the legend sitting next to me. But even as I lifted the glass, I kept reminding myself: don't waste this. This was more than a ride to a party. It was a chance to ask the questions I'd been carrying, the ones I hoped he might finally answer.

Chapter 37: Romance

The limo slid into traffic, gliding past the glowing billboards and neon signs of Hollywood Boulevard. Outside the tinted glass, tourists crowded along the Walk of Fame, pointing at the stars inlaid on the sidewalk, pausing to snap photos with their favorite names in terrazzo and brass. Street performers in capes and costumes posed for dollars under the throb of electronic music spilling from souvenir shops. For a stretch, it felt as if we were riding through Hollywood's self-portrait: larger-than-life, glittering, and faintly unreal.

I caught sight of a poster plastered across a theater marquee—two lovers locked in a cinematic embrace—and I couldn't help myself. "It's ironic," I said, almost idly. "Hollywood tells the best love stories. Yet the real ones here rarely seem to last beyond a night."

Bennett raised an eyebrow, playful, not offended. The look said: *You're not wrong, but are you judging us?*

I smiled. "I don't mean just Hollywood. It's everywhere. Love stories don't last very long anymore. They didn't always back in the day either—but now even less so."

He swirled the champagne in his glass. "That's why people go to the movies," he said. "To live inside a fantasy, even for two hours. To taste what they don't get in real life."

I leaned in, playful but probing. "So the great director of Hollywood romances is telling me lasting love doesn't exist? It's all but an illusion? And you're just a magician, dazzling us with smoke and mirrors?"

For a moment his face softened, touched by memory. Then he laughed—a genuine, amused laugh that seemed to surprise even him. "You know what? You won't believe this. Sophia once asked me that exact same question. Almost word for word. It feels like déjà vu. Some questions are *timeless*."

His reaction startled me. Clearly, this was not a throwaway topic for him. He had thought about it, carried it, maybe even wrestled with it. I kept my eyes on him. "So...what did you tell her?"

He swirled the champagne in his glass, then leaned back. "You know what," he said, "let me tell you a story. Sophia's story. Sophia and Rafe."

The moment the words left his mouth, I felt my heart quicken. To hear him speak of them—not as gossip or myth, but as someone who had *been there*—was electrifying.

His tone shifted, becoming more like a narrator than a director, and the hum of the limo seemed to fade as his words filled the space. "It was the 1980s, and Sophia was Hollywood's golden flame. Rafe Donovan was chaos in leather—a rock god with a voice that could rattle stadiums. When they met, it was wildfire."

As he spoke, the scene unfurled in my mind like film on a reel. The Sunset Strip blazing with marquees, paparazzi bulbs exploding like fireworks, guitars wailing in smoke-choked clubs. It was as if he were projecting it onto the night outside the limo window.

Sophia Maren was radiant, untouchable, the woman whose smile could hush an entire room. Regal, magnetic, endlessly chased. Off-screen, she carried a mystery people wrote profiles about without ever really knowing her.

"Rafe," Bennett said with a half-smirk, "was the opposite. Loud. Reckless. Electric. He'd walk into a place like the world already belonged to him." I saw him as Bennett spoke—shirt unbuttoned, leather jacket hanging loose, whiskey in one hand, guitar strap biting into his shoulder like a scar. Women screamed until their throats broke; men copied his swagger and never pulled it off.

"They met at a party," Bennett continued. "Of course they did. The kind of party where nobody wore a watch, air thick with smoke and champagne, every laugh sounded rehearsed." I could picture her in sequins, her hair falling in glossy waves, wearing that faint expression of boredom beautiful women sometimes get. He crossed the room, offered her a drink and a grin that was all recklessness, and she laughed.

That was the spark.

From then on, they were *them*. Magazine covers. Tabloid spreads. Posters taped to teenagers' bedroom walls. America's obsession. "They made love look cinematic," Bennett said, almost wistfully, "but they weren't acting."

I imagined them everywhere—her hand looped through his arm on red carpets, his Corvette idling outside her building with music blasting loud enough to rattle the glass, their nights spent in rooftop bars where champagne frothed endlessly, in hotel suites overflowing with flowers sent by strangers who believed in their fairytale.

And their private moments were even better. They danced barefoot across kitchen tiles to the hiss of cassette tapes. They scribbled notes on scripts and guitar cases. He scrawled lyrics for her on the backs of set lists. She left lipstick kisses on his stage jackets before he disappeared on tour.

Bennett tipped his glass, watching the bubbles climb "It was stardust and champagne," he said. "Breathless. Intoxicating. Both of them—indulging, reveling, consuming. For a while, it felt endless."

But then his expression changed, his eyes clouding as he turned to the window, staring into the blur of passing headlights as though it were a screen replaying the past.

"By the twelfth month," he said, "the colors began to dull. I saw it on set—the way her lines faltered, the way the words no longer belonged to her."

I saw her as he described it—Sophia on set, dressed for a love scene. Her co-star touched her face, said his line, and she gave hers—but something caught. Something felt false. Not the line, but the sentiment. She'd said it a hundred times before, on-screen and off.

You make me feel like I've found home.

Bennett's jaw tightened. "But home? She didn't have a home. Not yet. Her condo still looked like a hotel suite. Rafe's place was always a party house. She couldn't even remember the last time they'd spoken without music in the background."

I felt my chest tighten as he went on—picturing her sitting in her trailer, staring into the mirror, wondering if this was how it always went. Maybe romance fades. Maybe the honeymoon is meant to die down. Maybe no couple, not even the brightest, is built for longevity.

"Rafe felt it too," Bennett said. "He still loved her smile, her warmth. But the thrill wasn't new anymore. And without the thrill—" he paused, his voice lowering—"it wasn't much at all. They weren't unhappy. Just... unmoved."

The limo's silence pressed in, his story filling every inch of it.

"Over time," Bennett said, "I began to notice it. Not in the tabloids, not on the red carpets—on sets, quietly, between takes. I saw it before anybody else did." He turned the stem of his glass slowly between his fingers, eyes still locked on the dark window. "She wasn't acting anymore. The tears were hers"

He let the words hang there, heavy. Then, softer: "One afternoon, after a take that landed wrong, I went to her trailer. And this is when she asked me the same question as you just did—about lasting love. Perhaps she was wrestling with the same thoughts as you are."

"I did not answer right away, instead I asked her to come to my house for dinner. To bring Rafe along. I told her I wanted to share something with them—perhaps an idea for a new film, something that might matter to her."

I leaned closer, caught in the pull of his memory. "And did they?" I asked quietly.

The limo curved deeper into the Hollywood Hills, where the houses spread farther apart. It was the part of the city built not for spectacle, but for peace.

Bennett glanced out the window, a knowing smile tugging at his mouth. "Oh—we're almost here," he said. "You might have to ask Sophia to finish the story."

I blinked, confused, as though he'd handed the narrative off mid-sentence. My eyes must have betrayed it, because he chuckled softly. Sophia was going to tell me *her* story? The thought left me half-thrilled, half-disappointed. Part of me wished the ride were longer, that I could have kept listening to him spool out the past like a film.

The limo turned through a set of discreet iron gates and rolled up a winding drive. There was no sprawling palace, no blinding glamour, none of the ostentation common to celebs. Instead, space stretched wide, framed by old oaks and gentle slopes. A vineyard spread in disciplined rows, its leaves gilded by the last gold of sunset.

The house itself was warm and unpretentious—stucco walls touched by ivy, terracotta roofs, wide verandas that opened to the air. It seemed less like a star's fortress and more like a retreat, a place chosen for breathing and belonging.

The party was the same—no pounding music, no paparazzi swarming the gate. Instead, laughter drifted easily across the garden, the sound of glasses clinking somewhere near the terrace. As the car pulled closer, the view opened up behind the house: the Hollywood Hills spilling away into the distance, rooftops scattered like toys, the sky painted in streaks of tangerine and violet.

It was almost too fitting. This was how I would have imagined a couple like them choosing to live out their later years—not in glitter, but in a calm perch above it all, with beauty and peace spread at their feet.

As we stepped inside, she appeared—Sophia Maren.

She looked every bit as radiant as the photographs promised, but in person there was more. Time seemed to have paused around her. The same smile, the same aura, the same unshaken glamour. She carried the kind of presence that emptied words from your mouth, leaving you caught in her orbit, staring longer than was polite.

She greeted Bennett first with an embrace, then turned toward me as he introduced me. "This is my colleague from Seattle," he said. "She's leading the VFX on my new project."

Sophia folded me into a warm hug. Her perfume lingered, light and elegant. "Lovely to meet you."

I managed only, "Big fan."

Bennett laughed. "You know what she asked me in the limo on the way here? The same thing you asked me thirty years ago. Déjà vu."

Sophia's eyes flickered with memory, her face softening as though she'd slipped back in time. "The first time you invited us over," she murmured. "Yes...I still remember it. Clear as glass. I asked you, *does lasting love exist, or are you just a magician?*"

The words startled me. Two women—different decades, different stories, different worlds—yet bound by the same question.

She looked at me again, differently this time. "Really?" she whispered, as though marveling at the echo. Then she smiled, slipped her hand into mine, and said, "Come with me."

I let her lead me through the crowd, surprised at how quickly the connection had formed. Behind us, Bennett stood watching, a small smile playing on his lips, as if he had known all along this would happen.

Chapter 38: Creation

Sophia's hand slipped into mine, and just like that, she treated me less like a stranger and more like an old friend she'd been waiting to see. As we passed through the crowd, she introduced me to guests in quick, easy gestures, her arm brushing mine, her laughter spilling like it belonged to both of us. This is the thing about women, I thought—how we connect instantly when we recognize something familiar. A pain. A memory. Even the same unanswered questions.

She guided me onto the terrace, where the evening air carried the faint perfume of jasmine and the hills stretched out in twilight hues. The chatter of the party softened behind us, replaced by a stillness that felt almost conspiratorial.

"You know," she began, resting her hand lightly on the railing, "I still remember the night Harold invited Rafe and me to dinner. He told us it was to read a script for a movie. But little did we know, he was going to write the script for *our* story. But at the time, we didn't know any better." Her tone slipped into something almost conspiratorial, as if sharing a secret.

I listened carefully as she picked up the story right from where Benett had left me hanging.

"Until then, he'd only been my director.", she continued, "Brilliant, yes. But a friend? Not yet. That night was different. He had this uncanny eye—you couldn't hide from him. He could read the ache in your heart before you even admitted it to yourself."

I could tell the memory held weight for her—the way she recalled it with such precision, every detail sharp, as if she had replayed it many times over. It was one of those nights a person carries like a hinge, where life swings into a new direction.

"During those days," Sophia went on, "I was carrying the same question you are now. Does lasting love exist? Or was it all just an illusion? Rafe and I could feel it—our love slipping, the thrill fading, even though we still wanted our forever story."

Her voice dipped lower, almost confessional. "That night over dinner, Harold asked us something so simple it actually startled me:

What have you two built together?"

She paused, her eyes searching mine, and I could feel how deeply the question had lived in her.

"At first I didn't understand. We thought love was about giving—attention, affection, laughter. But he explained that giving isn't enough. Anyone can give a kiss, anyone can give a night. That doesn't last. What lasts is what you create together. What exists in the world because of your love that didn't exist before?"

Her voice softened, but her gaze stayed steady on me.

"Great loves are built, not just felt. They transform you. They multiply. They create not just fun moments but lasting memories—family, children, meaning. A life you can call your own. A legacy that you can pass on. Without that, even the brightest passion fades. That was the lesson he gave us—and it changed everything."

I felt a chill ripple through me, realizing she wasn't just telling me a story. She was passing a truth along, like a flame carried from one generation to the next.

Sophia turned back toward the hills, the sunset dimming into violet. "That night, Rafe and I left Harold's house in silence. We didn't even turn the radio on in the car. His question kept echoing—*what have you built together?*—and we both knew the answer."

I pictured it as she spoke: the two of them driving through the city lights, his hand tangled with hers, both staring out the window, both suddenly aware of the hollowness between them.

"At my apartment," she went on, "we poured two small glasses of port and just sat in the kitchen. I remember the clock ticking too loudly, the silence too heavy. Finally, we both realized he was right. We had built nothing. We had only *consumed* each other: our time, our energies, our souls. His words had quite an effect on Rafe too. For once, he didn't try to charm his way out of it. He admitted he'd been afraid of foundations—commitment, attachments, afraid that settling down would mean losing himself."

Her voice softened, carrying both the ache and the tenderness of the memory. "I told him maybe foundations don't trap you. Maybe they just hold you in place so that you can build."

She smiled faintly, recalling the shift. "That was when he looked at me—not with the old thrill, but with something steadier. And he said, *Do you want to see the world with me? Not tomorrow, not someday—now. Let's create something to remember.*"

I leaned in, breath caught. "And did you say?"

Her eyes gleamed with the reflection of the terrace lights. "Yes! I said yes! We packed bags that very same night. Paris, Rome, Barcelona—we wrote our new script together. For the first time, we weren't just consuming moments. We were building them. Building us."

I stood there, heart quickening, knowing she had just handed me what I had been searching for—the key I hadn't found in books, or films, or my own faltering attempts at love.

"Lasting love isn't an illusion, Sia. It's real—so long as you two are willing to keep *creating*, to keep growing, day after day. What you create together binds you like a glue. Your growth lets you bring something fresh to the table everyday: that's how it stays alive."

Her words settled between us, warm and steady, like embers that refused to fade. For her, it was memory. For me, it was revelation.

Sophia gave my hand a gentle squeeze before slipping back toward the guests. She moved with the same warmth she had shown me, laughing easily as she disappeared into the current of the party. I stayed behind on the terrace, watching the sunset as the city glittered below. Her words replayed in my mind, not just as a story of the past but as something living, meant for me. *Love isn't about consuming. It's about creating.*

Chapter 39: Vineyards

As I stood there watching the city lights, a flood of thoughts crossed my head—putting pieces of the puzzle together, the pieces I had collected bit by bit over the last few months. Perhaps now I would be able to see the full picture.

It is true that reciprocation sustains a relationship—but reciprocation alone is never enough. You can trade warmth, touch, laughter, even time, but that kind of harmony only lasts as long as both people keep giving. The moment one person grows tired, distracted, or simply stops, the whole thing collapses.

The real secret to lasting love isn't in the exchange. It's in what you *do* with that exchange.

When your partner gives you something—attention, affection, a joke, a kiss, a piece of themselves—you have a choice. You can consume it in the moment, let it fade like wine on the tongue, feed your ego, stroke your pride, flatter your vanity. Or you can choose differently. You can take that exchange and turn it into confidence, into motivation, into momentum that carries you forward. Into fuel that helps you grow, that inspires you to create. And that choice, more than anything, determines the trajectory of your relationship.

Love, I realized, is a lot like a sweet fruit. Someone hands you one, sweet and small, and you devour it. The moment is gone. Or—you plant it into the soil. You water it, protect it. And in time, it becomes a tree. That tree doesn't just give back the single fruit you were given—it multiplies. It becomes abundance.

But when you never plant, when you only consume, all you're left with is the sweetness of now. Another bite, another moment—until one day, there's nothing left. Love collapses, not because of betrayal or cruelty, but because it's been depleted.

I exhaled, staring at the lights flickering across the Hollywood Hills. Wasn't that exactly what had happened to me—with Victor? With all those dizzying beginnings that ended in silence? We had consumed until there was nothing left to taste.

The relationships that had lasted in my life—family, friendships, mentors—hadn't been built on instant sparks. They had been cultivated. My bond with my mother and siblings took decades of shared rituals and unspoken care. My friendship with Liam and Noah was etched into holidays, long drives, the same old jokes repeated until they became tradition. With my professor, it was hours of conversation, trust slowly growing from the steady exchange of ideas. With Richie, it was the proximity of college—late nights wrestling with assignments, bleary-eyed lectures. With Rob, it was the time spent troubleshooting code, brainstorming, finding solutions. Even now, those relationships lived in that same rhythm.

Each of these ties had been planted, watered, tested by time. Like vineyards, they had taken seasons to bear fruit. And because they had been grown, not just consumed, they carried a richness—playfulness, concern, resilience—that no instant spark could ever replicate.

I looked out at the vineyards stretching below, neat rows carved into the hillside. Without it, the hills would be bare, stripped of the very soul that made them what they were. Their beauty transformed this very place. But these vineyards hadn't sprung up overnight. They were built on patience—years of tending, pruning and waiting. And so now, these vineyards belonged to this land alone. No one could shift it or take it elsewhere.

These vineyards reveal the true process of creation. Creation isn't just hoarding or collecting. Creation is transformative. A seed becomes a tree. A spark becomes a flame. But it needs tending. It's never passive. Creation needs engagement. Friction. Persistence. *The way milk, churned with care, becomes butter—something richer, longer-lasting, able to weather time.*

Even the smallest acts could carry that energy of creation. Cooking dinner, for instance. At first, it's just a meal: chopping, stirring, eating, gone. But if you laugh while cooking, turn mistakes into stories, invent a recipe that belongs only to you two—then you've built something greater than food. You've made a memory. A habit. A ritual.

That's how relationships grow: not through stored-up gestures or transactional trades, but through transformation. Through creating something neither person could have made alone.

I pictured it then—inside jokes that no one else would ever understand, the customs that stack over time like bricks into a home: Sunday morning coffee runs, songs that become soundtracks, words that turn into mantras. A family you've nurtured together, transforming you from wide-eyed lovers into spouses, and then into parents. Children who bind your souls and carry your legacy forward. Or perhaps simply a life so uniquely yours that no one else could ever replicate it.

That's what makes love *irreplaceable*. Not just the person beside you, not just their body or their presence, but the *world* you've built together. That world is what no one else can replicate. And once you've built that, *love stops being a transaction. It becomes expansion.*

Chapter 40: Mindsets

I stepped down from the terrace and wandered into the house. At first glance, it was elegant but unassuming—no glossy, magazine-perfect showcase, but a home heavy with memory. Every wall, every shelf seemed alive with stories, as though the years themselves had been carefully framed and preserved.

Photographs led the way: Wedding photos framed in gold, her veil caught mid-sway, his smile unguarded and boyish. Travel shots from Paris, Milan, Kyoto—moments caught mid-laughter on cobblestoned streets, dinners under fig trees, sunsets splintering into gold across foreign skies. Achievements too: awards polished to a gleam, letters from fans folded into leather-bound books, songs recorded, scripts annotated with fading ink—proof of careers built not just on talent, but on persistence

In the corner sat a piano, its lacquer worn soft from years of use. I imagined her fingers brushing the keys in the stillness of night, him leaning against the doorway, humming. In the kitchen, I pictured their laughter over burnt toast and lopsided cakes, how those imperfections had become private jokes. Upstairs, footsteps of children had once rattled the hallways; now it was the grandchildren, darting between legs, filling the house with shrieks and the thump of small feet.

Every object had its story. A chipped teacup from their first Sunday morning as newlyweds. A candle bought during a power outage that became the centerpiece of an impromptu picnic in the living room. A rock from the beach where Rafe had slipped a ring onto her finger. Each relic whispered the same refrain: *we made this.*

I paused, struck by the depth of it. All this while, I'd believed that *tolerance was a curse*—especially when it came to love. It was the enemy of passion, the reason everything eventually fades. Too much of the same dulled sweetness—like cake that turns bland when eaten daily, wine that no longer buzzes after the first glass, cigarettes that lose their edge, a job that wearies when the desk never changes. And marriage—I thought obeyed the same law. That you grew tired. That passion burned itself out. And all that remains is ash.

But standing there, inside the house they had built, I understood—*the problem was never tolerance, the problem was the mindset.*

If you live with a *consumption mindset*, tolerance will suffocate you. Because consumption feeds on novelty. It devours and demands more. The same sweetness that once thrilled you will no longer satisfy. And then you look elsewhere, chasing a new thrill, convincing yourself that the love has died.

But with a *creation mindset*, tolerance becomes a gift. It refuses to let you stay complacent. It insists you stretch, expand and evolve. It pushes you out of comfort zones and into discovery—different shades of personality, new set of skills, fresh interests, deeper connections. It asks you to surprise your partner, to offer new flowers instead of the same bouquet, new expressions instead of tired phrases, new firewood every day to keep the flame alive.

That is the paradox of tolerance: for the consumer, it's a curse; for the creator, it's the very force that pushes you to grow.

The thought lingered for a moment before the noise of the party pulled me back. The air in the room shifted then—a hush, a swell of anticipation. Heads turned toward the staircase.

Sophia and Rafe descended together, hand in hand, their steps slow but steady. It was their thirtieth wedding anniversary, and yet they moved as though no time had passed. Their children gathered near, their grandchildren clustered around the cake waiting below—three tiers dressed in ivory and silver.

Rafe leaned close, whispered something only she could hear, and Sophia tipped her head back and laughed. Not politely. Not out of habit. But with the full-bodied joy of someone still being surprised by the person she had chosen decades ago. Still laughing. Still holding. Still *together*.

I thought to myself Life can be so unpredictable sometimes. All this while I was looking for a fairytale, wondering if they were real or just an illusion crafted by Hollywood. And now here I stood, in the very midst of Hollywood hills, witnessing a fairytale, a happily ever after, unfolding right in front of my own eyes. Was it a dream, was it real life? I could not tell at the moment!

****

The Monastery

Chapter 41: Knowledge

From my seat by the window, the Himalayas rose like another planet, jagged and untamed, their peaks lit by the first strike of the sun. Gold clung to the ridges as if the mountains themselves had been crowned, while valleys below drowned in deep blue shadows. It was the kind of sight that demanded silence—not admiration exactly, but surrender.

The air hostess leaned over with a quiet smile, balancing a tray in her hands. "Wine?" she asked softly. I accepted, though I barely tasted it. The gesture itself felt like a reminder of the world I had just left behind—a world where we try to soothe every discomfort with something to sip, something to scroll, something to distract. I set the glass down and turned again to the window—to the vastness of the Himalayas.

It had been *a year* since Hollywood. A year since Sophia and Rafe had made me believe again—not in stories, but in the kind of love that endures beyond scripts and spotlights. They helped me put together the final pieces to the puzzle of *lasting relationships*. Healed me, even. I came home ready to search for my own fairytale, my forever. And so I did.

I threw myself into it, not holding back, not making excuses. I replied to every message, met every stranger who showed interest, leaned into flirty texts and late-night calls. I never said I was too busy for drinks, for dinners, for one more chance at connection. I looked everywhere—local bars, work, old friends I'd once felt sparks with, the endless scroll of apps and meetups. I gave it a full year. I told myself if love existed, I would find it. And yet, every attempt dissolved into disappointment.

This is the trouble with knowledge: it heals, but it also sharpens. It raises your standards in ways you can't reverse. I had learned too much about *attraction, reciprocity,* and the *creation* process that relationships require. I could no longer be fooled by labels or swept away by grand gestures. I wanted maturity, someone who could meet me where I stood, someone who would build with me. And suddenly, the world felt empty.

Knowledge, I realized, isolates you. Once you see clearly, you can no longer pretend. You catch people's intentions almost immediately—what they want, what they don't, what they'll never give. You see when they're chasing only pleasure, when they have no desire to reciprocate, when they are unwilling to take care of your needs, your longing for attention, your desire for something steady. And so you walk away before the illusion can even start. You don't get those fleeting moments of bliss anymore, those brief nights of believing you've found your fairytale. Wisdom steals even that. The tragedy of being wise is that you don't even get to enjoy the lie. You see through the act right away, and you turn back, leaving with silence where once there would have been a few bright moments of dreaming.

And ignorance, for all its cruelty, at least lends you that momentary pleasure. When you don't know better, you can believe someone's story for a while. You can convince yourself it's real. You can taste the sweetness of the illusion before the truth sets in. But once you know, there's no going back. Knowledge is both a gift and a burden. It makes you stronger, but it makes your pool smaller. It makes you wiser, but it makes you lonelier.

I thought of the choices I had now. To keep searching endlessly—pouring time and hope into faces that blurred together. To settle for someone I didn't love—a compromise that would eat at me slowly every day. Or to end up alone, building a life where the absence of love would echo in every silent moment. And none of them felt like answers.

The city had made those choices harder to bear. The endless cycle of dates and disappointments. The constant reminders—Sophia and Rafe's perfect love, their ease with each other, was proof of what might never be mine. Maybe love like theirs was only for the rare few, the lucky handful. Maybe the rest of us were just drifting from one person to the next, hoping something would stick. And when it did, we called it love. We called it marriage. But I didn't want something that merely stuck. Which meant maybe I'd have nothing. And that was terrifying.

So when my hiking group planned this trip, I was ready without hesitation. I needed to get away, to be somewhere far from the noise, somewhere where silence didn't feel like failure. Maybe here, in the Himalayas, I could find something else—a thought, an idea, a mantra to carry with me. A truth I could cling to when the longing returned. Something strong enough to keep me peaceful, content, steady—not restless, not endlessly waiting for love to arrive.

The plane dipped lower, circling into the valley. Below, a town appeared, pressed into the lap of the mountains. Stone and wood houses clung to the slopes, smoke lifting from chimneys into the thin morning air. Bright strips of cloth fluttered from rooftops, their colors alive against the gray. A silver river cut through the valley, winding with the patience of centuries. From above, the place looked timeless, a pocket of life stitched carefully into the silence of the peaks.

I tightened my grip on the armrest, my heart already shifting toward what lay ahead. The trek. The silence. The peace. Perhaps the mountains would not hand me love, but maybe they could give me something else: *a way to live without it*. And with that thought, I felt the first flicker of anticipation—the sense that the journey was only just beginning.

The wheels touched the runway with a jolt, pulling me back into the present. Outside, the valley town stood quiet beneath the watch of the golden peaks, smoke rising steadily into the sky. For a moment it felt as if the mountains themselves were waiting, patient and unmoving, daring me to search for my answer among them—*Can you find happiness without a life partner? Can single be whole?*

Chapter 42: Desire

We stepped off the plane into a different world. Each breath tasted clean, as though it had been filtered through stone and snow. The airport was hardly more than a long hall of stone and glass, with faded signs in a language I didn't know and a single conveyor belt that creaked slowly to life. Outside, a line of jeeps waited, their paint chipped from years of mountain dust, their roofs lashed with ropes for luggage. Drivers leaned casually against the doors, as if time ran slower here.

Our group piled in, and the jeep rumbled forward, tires crunching over gravel before finding the winding road that snaked up the valley. The ride was jarring, every bump a reminder of how far we were from city smoothness. Outside the window, the town slipped past—narrow streets lined with stone houses, women carrying baskets of wood, children chasing one another with laughter that echoed against the hills. Donkeys moved steadily under the weight of supplies, bells around their necks clinking with every step.

As we climbed higher, the road curved sharply, and then I saw it: the monastery. It rose from the ridge like a vision, red and orange flags rippling from its highest points, catching the wind like flames against the sky. Bells swung slowly, their deep chimes rolling out over the valley. From a distance, it didn't look like a building so much as a place suspended between heaven and earth, a temple tethered to the mountain itself.

Inside the gates, it was another world. Monks in saffron robes moved quietly about their tasks—sweeping the courtyard, tending to goats in a small pen, carrying buckets of water from a stone well. Others sat in the shade grinding herbs into powders, or repairing prayer wheels with hands worn but steady. No one rushed, no one raised their voice. Life unfolded here in a rhythm so different from the frantic tempo of the city that it felt almost staged, like I had stumbled into a dream of simplicity. And yet it was real. A hundred small acts, all performed in harmony, each monk part of a single organism. *Interdependent*, connected and respectful. They worked as if they were not individuals but pieces of one whole.

Our rooms were plain, carved simply into the monastery's old stone. My cell held a wooden bed with a thin mattress, a single blanket, a clay lamp, and a window that framed the mountains like a painting. No luxury, no excess, and yet I felt oddly complete. Everything I needed was here—and nothing more.

It struck me then: *those who learn to live with less never feel a shortage; those who live in excess never feel enough.* Desire is a strange creature. The more you feed it, the hungrier it becomes. Even the richest man on earth is never satisfied, always reaching for more. But if you practice restraint, if you slowly reduce your wants, you shrink desire itself. It is not deprivation; it is *discipline*. One less bite each day until your body forgets to ask for more. One less indulgence until the craving quiets. Desire is elastic—it can stretch without end, but it can also be trained to shrink.

I remembered something my mom used to tell me: *sleep, anger, and hunger expand the more one indulges, and shrink the more one restrains.* And suddenly, it made sense. This softening of desire wasn't the same numbness that comes after overeating or the haze that follows a night of indulgence. This wasn't the shallow calm of a mind dulled by scrolling or drugs. Those are brief respites born of excess, where you silence desire only because you've smothered it. But soon it returns, stronger than before, demanding even more.

What restraint does is different. It doesn't mute desire for a moment—it shrinks its size. Like a stomach that slowly contracts when you stop overfeeding it, longing too can diminish when you stop indulging it. And perhaps that was the lesson of this place: to find contentment not in what was abundant, but in what was *enough*.

And I realized, looking out through the small square window of my room at the red flags snapping in the wind, that this was exactly what I needed.

The monastery hadn't been our first choice. All the hotels in town were booked solid, and the monastery was the only option left. At first, it felt like a compromise, but standing there within its gates, I realized it was something better—an opportunity that had slipped in through the back door of inconvenience. Adversity, it seemed, had handed us a gift.

My fellow trekkers, though, seemed to miss the luxuries they'd half-expected. Perhaps a spa to soak away the flight, a mini bar hidden in the corner, a pool shimmering under the sun. One even wandered through the courtyard as if a gym might reveal itself between the stone walls. Their disappointment carried its own humor—the contrast between what they imagined and what awaited us here. For me, the absence of those things felt like a kind of relief.

Lunch was served not long after. We sat cross-legged on the floor in a simple pavilion—a stone floor beneath us, wooden beams above, the sides open to the mountain air, the meal ladled onto broad leaves placed before us. Rice, lentils, a thin vegetable stew. Nothing elaborate, but when you've traveled since dawn, hunger does half the seasoning. We ate with our hands, licking every last bite from the leaf until it shone.

Someone joked it was the best meal they'd had in days, and everyone laughed, because hunger makes a liar of us all.

After lunch, my companions drifted to their rooms, some eager to nap, others just tired from the journey. I, on the other hand, felt restless. The sound of bells echoed faintly through the air, low and rhythmic, almost as if they were calling. I followed them through narrow stone corridors until they led me to an open terrace at the edge of the monastery.

Beyond it, the Himalayas stretched wide and unbroken, while rows of monks sat cross-legged on woven mats, their saffron robes glowing against the stone. The hum of "Om" filled the space, not loud, but steady—a vibration you felt in your chest more than heard with your ears. At the front, seated slightly higher, was the head monk—the Guru. His presence was quiet yet commanding, the way still water commands attention.

His face was weathered yet serene, his eyes bright behind round glasses, his hands folded loosely in his lap. There was no force in his presence, no demand, yet he seemed to anchor the entire gathering—as if the chant itself took its rhythm from the stillness of his being.

I wasn't sure if it was a class or a session, or simply a way of life being lived in front of me. There was no sense of beginning or end. The monks were not performing meditation; they were inhabiting it. Still, I wanted to join. Slowly, careful not to disturb, I slipped onto a mat at the back.

At first I tried to follow their rhythm, closing my eyes, letting the sound wash over me. But my mind betrayed me after a few minutes into it. I thought about what my groupmates were doing. I imagined my phone chiming somewhere in my bag. I opened one eye. That was when the head monk's voice reached me.

"Focus, child. Focus inward."

Chapter 43: Focus

I flushed, suddenly self-conscious. I shut my eyes again, determined to try. Minutes passed. Again, my mind slipped its leash—a stray thought here, a worry there. My eyes flickered open without permission. This time, the monk beckoned.

"Come here, child."

I hesitated, then rose and moved to the front, seating myself before him. He studied me with calm curiosity, his gaze steady but kind.

"Tell me, dear," he asked, "why do you think we meditate?"

The question felt like a trap, as if I'd been put on the spot. My mind scrambled, unsure of the right answer. "To find peace?" I said at last, though it sounded more like a question I was throwing back at him.

He chuckled softly, shaking his head. "No, no, my child. That is the mistake everyone makes. They think we meditate to find peace. But the truth is, the purpose of meditation is not peace—it is *joy*. Remember this: *there is no peace without joy.*"

The words struck like a stone dropped into deep water, rippling through me. I had never thought of it that way.

"Tell me," he continued, "what do you enjoy doing most? Where do you find joy?"

I thought hard, trying to answer as honestly as I could. "Tennis," I said finally. "The fun of the game, chasing the ball, the thrill of outwitting an opponent." Then another image surfaced. "Swimming too. The rhythm of the strokes, the way the water holds you on all sides." I paused. "And sometimes just watching sunsets on the beach, lying in the sand, watching the waves roll in—that endless calm of staring into the horizon."

He nodded. "Good. Now, what is common between them?"

I averted my eyes, as though I might find the answer somewhere else. But I couldn't see it.

After a pause, he answered himself. "In each, your mind stops *wandering*. You are in the game. You are in the water. You are with the beauty. For those moments, you are not elsewhere. And when the mind stops wandering, joy appears."

His words landed like a revelation. All this time I had thought meditation was about peace, spirituality, silence— something serious, something solemn. Never once had I equated it with joy.

He smiled at my expression, then said simply, "The human mind is *restless*. Always moving. Always thinking. Always elsewhere. Even when you sit still, your mind wanders. Even when you sleep, your mind dreams. Does it ever rest?"

I nodded in agreement, because it was true. My mind was always busy, rehearsing regrets of the past—things I couldn't change. Or worrying about the present, even when those worries had no relevance to my immediate actions. And if everything was fine in the present, I worried about the future, things that hadn't even happened yet.

He continued, "A deer only fears when it sees a tiger. But humans? We *imagine* tigers. We imagine them creeping toward us at every moment."

I smirked and shook my head at the strange *paradox of imagination*. Nature has blessed us with this wonderful gift—our greatest strength—yet the same gift so often turns into a curse. We suffer problems that aren't even real. Why? Because we imagine it in our heads. We worry about things that have never happened, and perhaps never will. But we spin these endless what ifs in our heads: *What if I lose my job? What if he leaves me? What if this, what if that?* And in doing so, we unintentionally invite anxiety into our lives when, all this while, it was still resting quietly somewhere far away.

And just like that anxiety creeps into our lives. Perhaps ever more so quickly in our modern life, because our mind has forgotten how to be idle. In waiting rooms we pull out our phones. Stuck in traffic, we either daydream or simply worry. Talking to people, our thoughts drift elsewhere. Even when watching a movie, it's hard to focus sometimes—always snacking, checking phones, distracted by something else. The truth is, our minds rarely sit still anymore.

"Our minds," he said, "are no longer under our control. They are chasing desire, hoping joy lies just around the corner. But when joy comes, it vanishes in an instant. Then the chase begins again."

He paused. "Meditation, my dear, is the art of ending that chase."

The chanting behind us rose and fell like a tide. He let the sound carry his words before continuing. The prayer flags overhead fluttered in the breeze, their colors flashing briefly against the pale mountain sky. I sat there, absorbing every ounce of wisdom he offered in that moment.

Then he asked me another question, "Now tell me, what do you not enjoy doing at all? Something you never look forward to, but are still forced into?"

I didn't need to think long. The first flash of annoyance came immediately. "Definitely sitting in traffic. That's the worst part of city life. No one can look forward to it."

The guru only smiled, his eyes glinting with quiet amusement. "Are you sure?"

I nodded firmly. Nothing could change my mind on this—traffic was misery.

"Very well," he said. "Imagine yourself sitting in your car. The line ahead of you inching forward, every stop and start testing your patience. Your mind restless, thinking, *Why aren't they moving? What's going on? I'm late.* All that usual chatter"

He paused, letting me sit in the scene. My jaw tightened; I knew it too well.

"Now," he continued, "imagine the very same traffic, the very same crawl of cars. But instead of sitting in it, you are watching it from above—from a bridge, from the top of a building. The cars move in the same slow pace, but from up there, it feels different. Which view makes you more relaxed?"

The answer rose without effort. "From the top," I said quietly.

He laughed warmly. "This is the trick, my child. *Perspective.* When you let yourself be trapped by things outside your control, you suffer. But when you rise above, see the world from a *higher perspective*, the same situation loses its teeth. It becomes smaller, less urgent, even harmless."

I looked at him following these words closely. "Higher perspective?", I repeated, not sure what exactly he meant by that.

"Yes. Think of life itself from a higher perspective: *At the end, none of it matters.* We all live, we all die. We are like drops lifted from the ocean, suspended for a brief moment, before it must return to the water. However high a drop may rise, it always falls back. So why worry? Why stress? Why cling on to thoughts—when you can simply let it pass?"

A bell rang from somewhere deeper in the monastery, its vibration carrying his words through the air, resonating in my chest. A higher perspective—perhaps that was what I had come seeking in these mountains. But meditation was hard. It was tough to let go of your thoughts. Each time I tried, distractions yanked me away from focus.

He looked at me with patient eyes as though reading my thoughts. "Focus does not come overnight. It is a discipline. Like any other skill, it requires training. That is what we do here. Day by day, breath by breath, we train the mind. Each day your focus will grow stronger, and with it, joy will return. Work, painting, cooking—even the smallest task—will become as joyful as watching the sunset at the sea."

A chill ran through me. I knew I had come to the right place.

He smiled softly, then closed his eyes, returning to meditation as naturally as one returns to breath. His voice slipped into the low hum of *om* around us, dissolving into the chant like a drop returning to water.

I felt the vibrations encircle me in their steady swell, his words echoing within me. *Joy is not in chasing. It is in focusing.*

With that thought, I closed my eyes again—this time not gripping my mind tight, but letting go, letting my thoughts drift free—like birds released from a cage, into the mountain air.

Chapter 44: Joy

The mountain air wrapped around me like a blanket, the chant still echoing faintly in my chest as I made my way back to my room. The door closed softly behind me, sealing me into a space of bare walls and silence. Yet the stillness was deceptive. Inside me, the monk's words stirred like embers refusing to go out: *Joy is not in chasing. It is in focusing.*

Does focus really bring joy? I wasn't yet convinced. Was it truth, or simply the sweet cadence of spiritual jargon, the kind that lingers in the air but dissolves in real life? I had to find out. That was the way my mind worked—always double-checking, re-verifying. If something was truly universal, every search, every angle of inquiry, should point to the same conclusion. Only then could I trust it.

So I turned to the only oracle I knew: my search tabs. Page after page, study after study, I read until my doubt cleared. The monk had not been speaking in riddles. He was right. Research shows that people report no wandering thoughts during the very moments they enjoy most. The moments that make life feel alive, worth living, are the ones when we are fully present, when the mind is tethered and still.

Think of a football match, the final seconds ticking away, your team about to win, the very last kick suspended in the air—in that instant you don't think of anything else—no bills, no deadlines, no fears of tomorrow. You are nothing but breath and heartbeat, wholly alive. Your whole being vibrates in the present. Or those hours when you slip into the *flow state* at work, absorbed so deeply in a project that time itself disappears. And what about *physical intimacy*? Studies reveal the mind wanders least when we are intimate with our partners. No wonder those moments feel so consuming, so unforgettable. No wonder we crave them: they are the few moments when the mind finally sits still.

But when the mind is restless, the opposite happens. Waiting in a doctor's office, the hands of the clock seem frozen. Waiting for a package to arrive, for results to be announced, for the weekend to begin—time slows to a crawl. Yet when the weekend finally arrives, it vanishes in a blink, precisely because you are engaged, your mind is steady and your focus is clear.

I thought of the days that had stretched endlessly, unbearably. After the breakup, every hour felt swollen with waiting. Waiting for a text, a call, a word. Those days dragged like years. And yet the moments with my lover—however fleeting—had felt light, intoxicating and joyful. Not because he had solved any of my problems, but because for those moments, my restless mind had stilled.

I thought of the past year I had spent chasing my fairytale, my forever person. The search had left me anxious. Each date carried its own anticipation, each possibility its own weight, and each disappointment struck harder than the last. Together they drained me, stripping joy from my days. When we are so busy looking, we often forget living.

But here, within the monastery walls, I felt alive again. My focus anchored in the present, I could finally take in each moment as it came. Even in meditation, once I was able to find my focus, time moved like a breeze through open windows. The anxious thoughts, the irrelevant worries I had carried for months—they dissolved, slipping away as though the mountain air itself had lifted them. Meditation hadn't just calmed me. It had unburdened me.

Isn't this what happens with *a glass of wine*? We feel merry, light, even joyous, not because our world has changed, but because our anxious thoughts loosen their grip. They quiet the mind long enough to make us laugh, dance, forget our problems. The same with any kind of *drugs*—for a moment, they mute the noise, allowing the user to fall wholly into the present. For a moment, simply staring at a wall can feel enjoyable. The resemblance between a *meditative* state and a *medicated* one struck me—uncanny, almost identical. Both can deliver joy, both still the mind. But the difference was sharp. One borrows from outside, the other brings joy from within. One makes you *dependent*. The other sets you *free*.

Our brains are naturally capable of finding joy in whatever we do—painting, swimming, music, dancing—so long as we are fully in it. But we forget. We believe the keys to our happiness rest with someone else, and unless they unlock the door, we are doomed to sadness.

That is simply not true. The people and things we cling to— they are only triggers. The source is always within. Once we recognize that, we stop being dependent on the triggers, and start finding joy not just in people or moments, but in life itself.

Chapter 45: Distractions

I stood near the window in my room, the Himalayas spread before me like a dark, endless silhouette. The peaks glowed faintly under the night sky, as if the stars themselves had been scattered across their ridges. There was a stillness in it, a silence so vast it felt eternal—an ancient reminder that joy had always lived within, unshaken by the noise of the world.

And then, the spell broke. A buzz in my pocket. A notification flashing on my phone. The mountain night gave way to the glow of a screen, and I looked down. A glowing screen stared back at me, demanding attention.

It made me wonder something frightening. How do we find joy in the modern world—a world full of *distractions*? A world where our lives are constantly triggered by glowing screens—phones, apps, social feeds, endless alerts—all designed to keep us distracted. We've become so dependent on them that we can't even enjoy a good moment without reaching for one. Even in the middle of our best memories, we interrupt ourselves—snap a photo, post it online—convincing ourselves it will elevate the joy, when in reality it does the opposite.

Think of couples at dinner. Two people sitting across from each other, plates steaming, a perfect chance to connect. And yet, instead of soaking each other in, they're both scrolling. The precious minutes that could have deepened intimacy evaporate into the glow of their phones. Or imagine this: you're with the most loving partner, the one you've prayed for—but then, in a careless moment, your eyes land on the hot stranger on your screen. Suddenly, your mind wanders. She's just pixels, nothing real, nothing attainable, but she steals from what *is* real, what *is* already yours. That's the tragedy of modern life. We're constantly distracted by possibilities instead of focused on the miracle in front of us.

The fear of missing out has spoiled our joy. Too many options—that's our curse. We rarely feel satisfied, because every decision carries the shadow of what else we could've chosen. A different car. A bigger house. A newer partner. And so we second-guess everything. Less, it turns out, is more. A cluttered house brings stress; a cluttered mind does the same. Fewer choices, fewer distractions—that's where clarity lies.

I remembered nights wasting away on Netflix, endlessly scrolling, wanting to watch everything but settling on nothing. That's modern life in a nutshell. We want it all, and in the wanting, we enjoy nothing.

Options feed desire. Focus starves it. And maybe that's why dating feels so complicated now. Every face on an app, every swipe left or right, unknowingly inflates our appetite. We want more, we want different, we want novelty—and even switching partners every month doesn't fill the void.

It wasn't always this way. Once, choices were limited. You met someone at school, at work, in your neighborhood, and that was it. The pool was small. And because it was small, people valued what they had. Today, options are infinite, which ironically means we value almost nothing.

The curse of endless choice is that it blinds us to the value of what is right in front of us. And this is the lesson of focus. *Focus breeds appreciation. Focus teaches gratitude.* When we're present, we stop looking elsewhere. We see our partner, our family, our work, our home, and in that focus we find joy.

It is so important to stay focused because the truth is that life itself is limited. Limited energy, limited time, limited space. When we cram it with distractions, we leave no room for what matters. That's why we feel lost, why we feel disconnected.

I stepped outside into the courtyard and lifted my eyes to the sky. The night stretched endlessly above me. Stars blazed with a clarity I had never seen in the city. Every constellation sharp, even the faint light of distant planets. In the city, pollution and noise blur them into obscurity. Here, they shone as they always had, waiting only for the air to clear.

And I thought—this is what technology has done to us. It has clouded our skies. The stars of our lives—our families, our friends, our connections—are still there, but their light has been dimmed, drowned by smoke and noise.

The thought lingered, like the last vibration of the temple bell that carried on the wind.

Chapter 46: Peace

The next morning, as my group strapped on their boots and prepared for the week-long trek into the peaks, I lingered. I told them I wasn't feeling well—a light excuse, softened by a smile. Solitude, I had already tasted atop Mount Rainier, standing in the snow's white silence. That wasn't what I sought now. What I wanted was different: not the isolation of the peaks, but the presence of joy. Not escape, but *peace*. And I knew exactly where to find it—not high above, but here in the valley, within these monastery walls.

The days that followed unfolded slowly, like pages turned by hand. Life in the monastery had its own pace, steady as the ringing of the bells. At dawn, the monks walked barefoot through the courtyard, their saffron robes brushing against stone, their breaths visible in the crisp air. I joined them sometimes, though no one ever asked me to. They moved with such intention that even the simplest act—sweeping leaves, carrying water, lighting lamps—felt like prayer.

Meals were plain, always the same: rice, lentils, vegetables cut into small pieces. Served without garnish or ceremony. We sat in the open pavilion, eating in silence. At first I missed the comfort of flavor, the indulgence of choice. But scarcity makes everything precious. By the third day, I realized I no longer wished for more. Each bite filled me enough, and enough had become everything. *Gratitude came easily when there was nothing to compare it to.*

I learned how little I actually needed. A wooden bed with a thin blanket. A single candle at night. A wash of cold water in the morning. What I once would have called "bare minimum" began to feel abundant. I thought of my life back home—closets spilling with clothes, shelves filled with things I had forgotten I owned. Here, there was none of that. And strangely, I felt no shortage.

Each morning I sat in meditation, not always perfectly still, but better than the day before. My mind wandered less. The stream of thoughts that once raced—work deadlines, old wounds, unanswered messages—slowed until they passed by like clouds. Some days I failed completely, unable to anchor myself. But even then, I noticed something subtle: the failure didn't sting. I no longer measured myself against perfection. Even trying had its own kind of peace.

One afternoon, I helped a group of monks in the garden. Together we pulled weeds, our hands in the soil, our backs bent under the sun. No words were exchanged, yet there was no silence either. A harmony pulsed between us, the kind that comes when many people act as one. When the task was finished, I looked at the neat rows of earth and felt a pride I couldn't remember feeling in years. Not the pride of accomplishment, but of belonging.

Another evening, I followed the sound of the prayer bell to the rooftop. The valley spread wide beneath me, villages no larger than toys, rivers winding like threads of silver. The monks sat cross-legged, chanting in Sanskrit, the sound weaving itself into the mountain air. I closed my eyes and listened. The words were foreign, but the rhythm was not. It was the same pulse I had found in my own body when I finally stopped fighting my thoughts.

Over those days, something began to shift. Desire, once so loud in me, shrank to a whisper. I no longer thought of what I didn't have. I no longer ached for a message that never came.

Even my longing for a fairytale, for a soulmate, softened. I still wanted love, but not with the same hunger. It no longer felt like a wound, but a possibility—something to be welcomed if it came, not chased if it didn't.

The turning point arrived one afternoon in the refectory. A tray of fruit had been set out, rare in its sweetness compared to our usual meals. My first instinct was to reach for more—to hoard, to indulge, to take before it was gone. That reflex of wanting, of grasping, rose quickly, almost automatic. But then I caught myself. *I let the impulse pass*, taking only one piece. I ate it slowly, tasting every bite as though it were the only fruit in the world. And in that simple act, I felt a joy deeper than greed could have ever given me.

The monastery had not given me new possessions or answers, but something far greater: *the capacity to be present*. To be grateful. To find joy in what already was.

And I realized, perhaps that was the real miracle. That joy didn't arrive in grand gestures or perfect endings. It was already here, waiting quietly in the rice, the silence, the brush of a broom against stone.

Chapter 47: Abundance

When my trekking group returned days later, they looked like survivors of another world. Dust clung to their boots, their cheeks were windburned, their laughter loud and raw from the thin air of the high passes. They spilled stories over dinner—frozen rivers, aching climbs, the exhaustion that melted into triumph when they reached the summit. Their eyes sparkled with the wildness of it, their bodies still humming with the pride of endurance.

I listened, smiling at their adventures, grateful for their joy. But I felt no envy. If anything, I sensed I had not missed a thing. While they had conquered peaks, I had uncovered something quieter but far rarer. What I had gained could not be measured in photographs or tales—it was the most precious jewel of our time: *peace.*

Departure came too quickly. My bag lay open on the wooden bed, its contents sparse, its weight lighter than when I'd arrived. I folded each piece slowly, aware that what I was really packing away were the days themselves—the vibrations of bells, the quiet meals, the patience of the garden, the stillness of meditation.

As tradition held, every guest went to bid farewell to the head monk. One by one, my companions stepped forward, bowing low, receiving his blessings for the journey home. When it was my turn, I bowed deeply, my palms pressed together. My voice trembled with both humility and hope.

"Bless me," I whispered, "so that I can be a good person."

The monk's eyes lingered on me, and in that pause I sensed he had chosen to offer more than a blessing—perhaps some farewell words. He had observed me these days—the halting attempts at meditation, the small acts of restraint, the curiosity that tugged me back again and again to sit, to listen, to learn. I felt honored, almost privileged, that he considered me ready for parting wisdom. My hands folded tighter in respect, waiting.

At last, he spoke.

"If you ask a hundred people what it means to be good," he said softly, "you will hear a hundred different answers—honest, loyal, kind, loving. And all these are noble things. But in truth, what we call a good person is simply someone who is *pleasant*. Pleasant in behavior. Pleasant in words. Pleasant in thought."

His voice was calm, unhurried, like water flowing over stone.

"And what makes a person pleasant?" he continued. "It is not a virtue on its own, but the outcome of your *state of being*. When you are well rested, when your belly is full, when your heart feels safe and protected—you are pleasant. When you are starved, weary or troubled—you are not."

"To be pleasant is not about effort, it is about *fulfillment*. The more fulfilled you are, the more warmth you give. The less fulfilled, the more you take away. So if you wish to be good, do not chase virtue directly. Live a life that fulfills you. Let desire shrink until abundance appears all around you. From that abundance, sharing becomes natural. From that fulfillment, pleasantness blooms."

He smiled faintly. "Everyone today wishes to be righteous. But what the world needs, my child, is more people who are simply pleasant. So here, I bless you—to be a pleasant person. *May you find fulfillment wherever you go. May you find abundance wherever you go, and may that abundance spill into others."*

I bowed again, overcome with gratitude. His words felt like more than a blessing—they were a compass. A steady truth to carry back into the clamor of the world. Abundance, fulfillment, pleasantness—these were not lofty ideals, but simple states of being. And they were mine to choose, to cultivate, to live.

As I stepped away, I knew this was the gift I would take with me—more enduring than peaks climbed, more precious than any treasure: the blessing of fulfillment, the wisdom that joy is not found in chasing, but in being.

Fulfillment and abundance, I realized, can be reached by *two paths*. One is through fulfilling desire; the other, through controlling it. One by *indulgence*, the other by *restraint*. One by *engaging* with the world, the other by *detaching* from it.

Back in the Hollywood Hills, I had seen a perfect picture of the *first path* in Sophia and Rafe. They had chosen to *engage*—to attend to their desires, to focus *outward*. Their attraction for each other was radiant, not only sustaining them but inspiring those around them. They exchanged value, fueled one another's dreams, and co-created a life that stretched beyond themselves—a home, a family, children, grandchildren. Abundance surrounded them in laughter, in stories, in the little rituals of daily life. They had built something beautiful by leaning into love, not resisting it.

Here in the monastery, I had witnessed the *other path*—a life of *detachment*. A deliberate refusal to chase desire, to grasp at every passing temptation. Instead, the monks practiced restraint, patience and discipline. They turned *inward*, focusing not on the exchange of energy with others but on the cultivation of their own stillness. Their joy sprang from within, requiring no one and nothing else to sustain it. *What they found was not creation, but peace. Not expansion, but contentment.*

Two paths, so different, and yet both valid. *One springs from engagement and leads to creation. The other springs from detachment and leads to peace. One multiplies life outward, the other quiets it inward. Both, in their own ways, lead to fulfillment.*

Finally, I felt I had the philosophy I could cling on to for the rest of my life. There was no single formula for joy, no universal law of abundance. What mattered was knowing there were two roads—and that both were open to me. If life gave me love, a partner, a chance to build and co-create, I could walk that path with confidence. And if life gave me disappointment, solitude, or heartbreak, I would not be lost. I could walk the other path—the quieter one—and still find joy, still find abundance, still find peace.

Whatever the future held, I now knew I was not helpless. Whether in Hollywood or the Himalayas, in the arms of another or in the silence of my own company, I had a way forward.

And that thought itself was the treasure I had come here to find.

Chapter 48: Balance

When it came time to leave, the gates of the monastery stood open. Beyond them, the world stretched wide—roads winding back to towns and airports, to cities and their endless noise. I hesitated, standing between two worlds. Behind me, the stillness I had learned to love. Ahead of me, the uncertainty of life waiting to test me again.

Could I hold on to the higher perspective when the traffic surged, the deadlines returned, and technology seduced me back with its luminous glow? The monastery had made it easy—meals appeared without choice, days followed a steady pace, and every sound, every face, felt purposeful. But out there, life would roar back in full volume: notifications blinking, clocks ticking, choices multiplying like a buffet designed to feed every craving.

Stepping beyond the monastery walls felt daunting. But I couldn't stay forever—I had a flight to catch and a life to rejoin, whether it was ready for me or not. As I took the plane back home, the blessing of the monk echoed within me like the temple bell still ringing from a distance: May you find fulfillment wherever you go. May you find abundance wherever you go.

The city greeted me not with silence, but with sirens. Traffic lights blinked like restless eyes, horns stabbed through the air, and billboards glowed with promises of everything I did not need. Yet even in the noise, something in me felt different. I walked slower. I breathed deeper. I caught myself smiling at the smallest things. The world hadn't changed, but I had.

The real test came that evening, behind the wheel.

I found myself inching through traffic, brake lights stretching ahead like a red river. My hand tightened on the wheel, irritation rising in me like an old reflex. So much for inner peace. And then I remembered the guru's words: Look from above. Hold the higher perspective.

So I tried. I pictured myself not behind the wheel, but above it all—the cars moving slowly through the city like ants, the lights blinking in the dark, my own small figure a flicker in a vast design. And suddenly the weight of it fell away. What did this moment matter in the sweep of space and time? We were all just brief sparks in an endless sky, a bleep in the great silence of the universe. The thought calmed me. My mind sat still, even while the car barely moved.

And just then, a horn blared behind me, sharp as a slap. The light had turned green and I hadn't moved an inch. I jolted forward, heart pounding, realizing: of course. You cannot drive a car from high up. To reach home, you must descend into the grit—watch the lights, notice the lanes, stay alert to every honk and crosswalk.

I laughed at myself. There I was, trying to achieve nirvana on the I-5, and nearly causing a pile-up in the process.

But beneath the laughter, something clicked. Stress and vigilance were not enemies of peace. They were what kept us safe, what kept us careful. Without them, we'd drift through red lights, ignore the lanes, let harm come our way. The monastery had taught me to rise above. The city was teaching me that the ground matters too.

The secret, I realized, was balance. Not the monastery or the city. Not calm or stress. Not the higher perspective or the ground reality. Balance was in holding both—at the same time.

The car ahead cut into my lane; I braked, irritated for a moment, then let it go. A pedestrian wandered too slowly across the crosswalk; I tapped the horn, sharp enough to alert, but without anger. Small moments, but the practice was there: attached to the action, detached from the outcome. Give your best. Then let go.

The road began to clear. The cars thinned, the traffic opened, and I drove forward with a strange ease, as if the path itself had been waiting for me to stop fighting it.

A song came on the radio—something upbeat, almost ridiculous after the heaviness of the last hour. I turned it up. Loud. And for no reason at all, I started laughing. At the traffic, at the honking, at myself trying to find enlightenment between lane changes on a Tuesday evening.

Maybe that was the balance I had been missing all along. I had spent so many months before the monastery weighed down by everything I was learning—about attention, about value, about exchange—turning every interaction into an equation, measuring every relationship against a formula. The knowledge had become its own kind of cage. And the monastery had swung me to the other extreme—let go of everything, detach, float above.

But life isn't lived at either extreme. Balance isn't a place you arrive at—it's a practice. You find it, lose it, and find it again, like keeping your footing on a boat that never stops rocking. Not every moment has to be analyzed, and not every moment has to be released. Some moments are just meant to be lived—messy, unplanned, imperfect. The secret is not to treat life as an arena, where you fight to win, but as a stage, where you joyfully perform—a game, fierce but fun, like a competitive match of football where the friction is part of the play.

This, I thought, tapping the steering wheel to the beat, is how you bring balance into relationships too. The couples who last aren't the ones who never fight—they're the ones who fight over the last scoop of ice cream, argue about who's better with directions, clash over something stupid on a road trip—and still find laughter waiting at the end. To argue without breaking. To clash without shattering. To fight, and still hear the music playing underneath.

By the time I reached home, I turned off the engine but didn't get out. Just sat there for a moment, hands still on the wheel, the silence of the parked car ringing louder than the traffic had.

I realized how many years I'd spent suffocating under the weight of expectations—my own and everyone else's. Every friendship, every connection measured on a scale: Is this person giving me enough? Am I getting back what I put in? And when the scale tipped, I'd pull away, hurt, convinced the other person didn't care enough. That silent tally had been its own kind of prison. It hadn't protected me. It had isolated me.

Now, something had loosened. Not into carelessness, but into ease. What if the moment was its own destination, and the journey its own reward? If the world is a stage, why fear tears, heartbreak, or rejection? After all, what makes a great play great? Balance. The joy and the sorrow, the triumph and the loss—all of it woven together. A story with only happiness is boring. A story with only pain is unbearable. But a story that holds them all? That's the one you remember forever.

Smiling, I unlocked my phone. I scrolled to Rhea's name— my best friend from high school, the one life and hesitation had slowly drifted away from me. I found a picture of mine from the Himalayas, still saved in my gallery, my face half-lit by mountain light.

I didn't overthink it. I didn't calculate whether she'd reply, or wonder if too much time had passed, or brace myself for silence. I just did it.

Attached, I typed a simple line: "Guess where this is?" And I pressed send.

****

Pillow Talk

Chapter 49: Sharing

A few months slipped by, the seasons tilting toward winter. Life resumed at its usual pace. The Himalayas had not isolated me. If anything, they had untangled me. I still went to dinners, saw friends, met new people. But now, the weight of reciprocity—that silent tally of who gave how much, who tried harder—no longer sat on my shoulders. I stopped caring whether others matched my effort. The moments of engagement themselves became enough: a laugh across a café table, a long walk under winter skies, an unexpected exchange of ideas. Whether any of it unfolded into a fairytale no longer felt like my concern. The moment was its own destination, and the journey its own reward.

Living like this opened doors I'd left closed. People I had hesitated to text, old friends I had assumed were lost, began to resurface. And to my surprise, most of them reconnected with warmth. Hesitation, I realized, isn't one-sided. Often, we're both waiting for the other to reach out, each mistaking the first move for weakness. But when the connection is real, the first move is a gift for both. Everybody wins.

The best of these reconnections was *Rhea*. She and I had lived almost parallel lives. We grew up in the same town, walked the same high-school halls, applied to colleges together, and moved cities side by side. Although we weren't especially close in high school—more classmates than confidantes—our bond tightened once college began. It often happens that way with people from your own hometown; a kind of *familiarity* draws you together in a new place, turning shared origins into real friendship.

For a time we were inseparable—cafeteria lunches, college parties, nights spent binge-watching chick flicks and whispering about crushes. Two peas in a pod.

But then, as often happens, a man entered the picture. Rhea started dating, and our twosome became a triangle. Movie nights turned into couples' nights, and I, the ever-smiling third wheel, watched our inside jokes and pillow talks fade. By the time we graduated and found jobs in different fields, our weekly meetups became monthly, then vanished altogether. We both probably felt the sting of the other's silence, but in the quiet battle of egos, no one tried.

When I finally sent her that text—a selfie framed by snow peaks and prayer flags—she called me within hours. We spoke for an hour straight, and it felt as though no time had passed at all. Since then, we'd been meeting again: holiday shopping sprees under glowing mall garlands, steaming cups of hot chocolate, snapshots with a mall Santa for no reason other than nostalgia. Sunday brunches that stretched into afternoons. Early morning runs when the city was still a mist of breath and frost.

Jake, her boyfriend—now fiancé—had been with her since college. I assumed their trajectory was fixed, inevitable. But during our renewed closeness, I began to notice cracks. A hesitation in her voice when I asked about wedding plans. A quick change of subject whenever I pressed about their weekends. A quiet zoning-out when his name came up. I never pushed. I trusted she'd open up when she was ready.

And then one evening, she did. She told me they were splitting up.

My heart sank. I couldn't believe it. All those years together, all those shared memories—her entire twenties poured into this relationship. Her emotional energy invested like coins carefully placed in a bank, only for the bank to default, leaving her empty-handed. Victor and I had lasted only a few months—not really a life built, but more like a missed possibility, and even that loss had bruised me so deeply. But hers was not just a heartbreak—it was an erasure of years.

The thing with women—especially when they love deeply— is that they often isolate themselves without realizing it, building their world around the man they love. "You're my world," "You're all I need," sound beautiful in books and films, but in reality it's like moving all your savings into one account. When that account vanishes, you don't just trip; you fall right out the window, long and hard.

I wanted to be there for her, truly there—Sharing her pain, lifting her spirits. Heartbreak steals your dopamine the way low blood sugar drains energy from your body, and the only cure is a rush of comfort. So we planned an old-fashioned sleepover. Ice cream, rom-coms, candles, cake—all the emergency rations of the broken-hearted. The only time calories don't count.

That night, snow fell softly outside her window—a rare Seattle hush. Inside, fairy lights twinkled across the glass. The fireplace crackled. It was like we had built a cocoon against the world. We sprawled across her bed facing each other, like the old days. She laughed through tears at one of my jokes about heartbreak diets ("Netflix, ice cream, and tissues—the three major food groups"), and for a moment, her shoulders softened.

Chapter 50: Gossip

The fairy lights glowed softly against the window, their shimmer blending with the faint white of snow outside. Seattle rarely looked like this—the fire in the hearth, the hush of the streets, the flakes sparkling against the glass. It felt as if even the weather had chosen to go silent, to listen as we whispered our hearts out, pillow-to-pillow, like we once did in our college dorm. And then like so many nights before, our conversation drifted naturally, almost inevitably, to boys.

I had known her long enough to remember her beginnings—how in high school she seemed so effortlessly magnetic. She wasn't the loudest in the cafeteria or the star of the pep rallies, but people noticed her anyway. She had that unforced ease—a way of tucking her hair behind her ear, a confidence in the way she moved through hallways—that made boys curious and girls a little envious. Even teachers lingered a beat longer when she spoke, as though her opinion carried more weight than the average sixteen-year-old's.

But beneath it, I had also seen the lessons that life had taught her under the surface, the ones she never asked to learn.

"Do you remember Chad Radcliff?" she asked with a half-smile, as if testing whether I could summon the ghost of her first heartbreak. Of course, I remembered. Everyone did. Chad was a senior, two years older, already jaded in a way that felt cool. He had that confident slouch boys develop when they're told too often that they're handsome and not often enough that they should be kind. He wore the same pair of ripped jeans almost every day, smelled like peppermint gum and cologne from CVS, and made everyone feel like they were on the verge of something unforgettable.

Rhea was flattered he even noticed her.

Her first kiss was in the back hallway behind the gym, where the vending machines buzzed and smelled like bleach. She laughed nervously afterward, unsure what it meant, but he smirked like it didn't need explaining. That was how things went with Chad—he never said much, but you were supposed to know what he meant anyway.

They started "hanging out," though no one ever used that word. It was just rides home, late-night texts, and the occasional stolen moment behind locked doors. There were no titles. No milestones. No conversations about feelings.

And Rhea didn't ask for any.

Because she knew what kind of girl Chad liked: the "chill" ones. The ones who didn't start drama. The ones who laughed at his jokes and rolled their eyes when he was mean. The ones who didn't cry if he didn't text back for two days. The ones who didn't ask where he'd been, or why he smelled like someone else's perfume.

So she became that girl. *The chill girl.*

The girl who said, *"It's fine."* Who texted back, *"No worries!"* Who swallowed her questions and smiled too easily. Who called him "complicated" when what she really meant was *inconsiderate.*

And he rewarded her for it.

He'd put his arm around her in public sometimes. Let her wear his hoodie. Compliment her when she wasn't wearing makeup. Each small gesture felt monumental, like unlocking a new level of a game she didn't understand but was determined to win.

But deep down, Rhea always had this quiet ache. A low-level anxiety that hummed beneath her skin. A need to know: *Do I matter to you? Or just right now?*

She never asked. Because chill girls don't ask.

And Chad made sure she knew that. Anytime she came close to wanting more, he'd pull away—*"You're not getting weird on me, are you?"* Anytime she got upset, he'd joke—*"I liked you better before you got so emo."* And if she ever dared question his behavior, he'd sigh and say, *"God, you're not like one of those needy girls, right?"*

She learned quickly: the price of keeping him around was pretending she didn't have needs.

Because that's the thing about boys like Chad. They want your affection, your laughter, your admiration—but none of your *expectations*. They want to be desired without being *responsible*. To be adored without being *accountable*.

And so, Rhea held her tongue. Smiled through the silence. Shrunk her feelings to fit inside his comfort zone.

And when it finally ended—without explanation, without closure—she didn't fall apart. She just internalized it. Filed it away as "what love feels like." Quiet. Uncertain. Asymmetrical.

"I never told anyone how small I'd felt.", she said softly, reflecting back at her time with Chad. "How lonely it was to be the girl who was always 'easy to be around'. How exhausting it was to constantly perform detachment, just to stay close to someone who never really offered anything real." Her voice cracked with emotions.

She explained how from that point forward, every man she dated got a version of that same girl. The one who knew how to be low-maintenance. The one who gave more than she asked for. The one who made sure he was never uncomfortable—even if she was.

Because men had taught her, asking for clarity was neediness. That vulnerability was unattractive. That accountability was optional.

So Rhea became what the world said was desirable: *Chill*.

She didn't just learn it—she perfected it.

And so, years later, when she met Jake—her now ex fiance, she carried that same lesson forward.

Chapter 51: Pain

Rhea never meant to fall for Jake. Not in the usual way she fell for Chad or any other guy. It was quieter than that—like fog rolling in. A gradual blur between casual and meaningful, with just enough light to keep walking forward.

They met at a rooftop bar. She hadn't even wanted to go—I had practically dragged her there. A party she meant to skip, a night she planned to forget. And yet there he was, wearing a worn leather jacket and that grin people mistake for depth. The usual casanova type. He had a way of listening that made her feel interesting. As if he were cataloging her details—her favorite brand of tea, her distaste for cilantro, the way she looked away when she was about to say something true.

Their first kiss tasted like white wine and possibility. He texted the next day—nothing poetic, just "last night was fun"—but it was enough to keep the story alive.

Jake wasn't a bad person. And that's exactly what made it harder. He wasn't your usual douchebag like Chad, carrying narcissism on his shoulders. If anything he was the opposite—kind, gentle, even considerate. And perhaps that's why Rhea let herself fall for him, believing he might be different.

Jake never lied. Never pretended to be something he wasn't. He showed up, made her laugh, held her hand in public. But he also disappeared when it mattered. Cancelled plans. Left her unread messages hanging for hours, sometimes days. He'd pop back in with a "sorry, this week's been insane" and she'd forgive him before he even asked.

The chemistry between them was great. He'd rest his head on her chest, eyes closed, like he belonged there. And maybe in those moments, he did. But that didn't help. Once the clothes were back on, he was already retreating into himself. His phone buzzing with notifications. His mind somewhere else.

Rhea told herself she was fine with it. But the truth sat heavier than she admitted: she wanted more. Not just physical closeness, not just the casual intimacy of shared meals and tired jokes. She wanted to be chosen. Deliberately. Fully.

And so she tried harder. Laughing more. Caring more. I remember how she would wear the lipstick he once complimented. Sending flirty pictures when he hadn't even asked. Turning herself into the kind of woman he might not forget so easily.

But still, she waited.

Waited for him to put a ring on her. Waited for a promise for the future. Waited for the moment he'd say: *I don't want anyone else.* That moment never came. At least, not for a long time.

But then a year or so back, something changed. Jake lost his job. He moved in with Rhea. Soon after, he proposed. I remember seeing their engagement post on Facebook and feeling genuinely happy for her. At the time, I wasn't sure how much of the proposal had to do with his financial instability, but I didn't question it then. People usually flock to their loved ones at times of distress. I thought that is what Jake did too.

But today, listening to Rhea pour her heart out, sharing every detail of their relationship—how she was the one to always put in all the work—I couldn't help but feel the ick at the timing of that proposal.

"So what really happened?" I asked, gently. "You guys got engaged, moved in together... when did things start to go wrong?"

Her laugh was dry, almost bitter. "Let's just say things were never really right."

She told me how she'd catch him chatting with random women online—exchanging photos, subscribing to sites he shouldn't have. She convinced herself it wasn't *infidelity*, not technically. Told herself that men look, that eyes wander, that it was harmless. At least he wasn't acting on it.

Her voice wavered, then steadied again. "But then that night..."

I saw her jaw clench as the memory broke through.

"He canceled dinner plans—said he was working late on some project. It had become a habit by then, him canceling last minute. I felt the sting but swallowed it like always. And then my phone lit up. A story posted by common friend—Jake at some bar, some friends, some girl sitting way too close. At first, I brushed it off. But then I realized... it was the same girl he'd been messaging."

Her words hung in the air, raw and final. That was the moment. The moment the denial cracked. He wasn't just lurking online anymore. He wasn't just scrolling through half-naked women on screens. He was meeting them. The promise wasn't enough. The ring meant nothing

Her tears came then—fast, unguarded. And I realized I hadn't seen her cry like this through any breakup before. This wasn't just heartbreak. This was betrayal. This was her whole future collapsing in on itself.

I let her cry, knowing that tears aren't painful in themselves—they're simply an outlet for pain to escape. When they finally come, they carry the weight of hurt along with them. The body has its own ways of healing, and crying is one of the oldest, most *natural remedies* we know. Tears don't just fall; they release hormones that ease emotional and physical pain, lower stress, and steady the mind. In the silence between sobs, something inside her began to realign.

And then, as suddenly as they came, the tears stopped. Her face softened into something calmer, more resolved. She unlocked her phone, found his name, and deleted his number—not out of rage, but clarity. Not to punish him, but to forgive herself for waiting so long.

Because somewhere along the way, she had shrunk herself. Put his comfort before her own. Bent until she was easier to hold, easier to leave.

And she was done being easy to leave.

Outside, snow pressed softly against the window. Inside, the fairy lights shimmered, catching the wet shine of her eyes. She turned to me, her voice quiet but steady—"Why has love turned into a transaction?"

Chapter 52: Insights

The fire in the hearth had burned low, embers glowing faintly red, shadows stretching long across the room. I bent down and placed another log on the grate, sparks jumping as it caught. The warmth flared again, soft light filling the space. We both knew we weren't going to bed yet.

The tears had settled now, emotions easing the way clouds clear after a storm. There's always that stillness that follows—the kind that feels almost sacred. Confession does that: the release of worst fears, the breaking open of vulnerabilities, the rawness of admitting truth. It feels unbearable while it pours out, but afterward, there is calm, like sunlight slipping through after rain.

It wasn't about Jake anymore. Not really. Nor about any particular person. What lingered was a bigger question—one that seemed to gnaw at her as she stared into the fire.

"Love has turned into transaction, hasn't it? I give intimacy, he gives attention. I give patience, he gives presence. But somehow I was the one who always ended up paying more." she sighed.

Her words pierced me because they weren't just hers—they were ours. How many times had we bartered pieces of ourselves just to keep someone around? How many times had we mistaken compromise for connection? How many times had we settled for crumbs and convinced ourselves it was love?

Yes, it is true that love thrives on exchange. But not just any exchange—it has to be a *balanced exchange*. Without balance, it turns into barter, where one side often holds more leverage, more power. And in that, love stops being love. It becomes a losing trade, one where you are pressed into giving more—far more—than you ever receive.

This was the pattern Rhea was finally starting to see.

She had spent years giving—her time, her touch, her presence—waiting for men to turn toward her. To truly see her for who she is—her value, her desires, her needs. And over and over again, what she met was the same thin line of affection: just enough to keep her from leaving, never enough to make her stay by choice.

And for the first time, she realized something.

It wasn't the men. The problem was the world they lived in.

A world that gave men like Jake endless options, and gave women like Rhea endless hope. A world that handed men agency and handed women patience. A world where men seeking *casual encounters* could find them in seconds, while women seeking *commitment* had to wait—indefinitely.

Her words echoed in me. Listening to her, I thought of how effortless the world had made it for men like Jake. He never had to choose. Why would he, when the world kept offering him a never-ending stream of comfort? Instagram's highlight reels. OnlyFans if he wanted to see more. Porn sites with fantasies tailored to him. A Tinder date on Wednesday, a late-night Snap on Friday. He never had to feel lonely, never had to wait. Everything was available. Easy. The world was designed to please him. And so, Jake never chose.

But Rhea? What she longed for—something rooted, steady, something that didn't vanish by morning—*couldn't be bought.* It had to be given. Freely. And only by someone who truly wanted to give it.

Rhea sighed, her voice low but certain. "You know how many times I've been told to just relax? To not be so intense? To just go with the flow?" She paused, shaking her head. "But the flow always seems to go in one direction—*away from what I want.*"

I listened, realizing the truth in her words.

She leaned back on the pillow, eyes fixed somewhere past the ceiling. "Men aren't asked to prove themselves anymore, you know. They don't have to court, or fight for affection, or commit to anything real. *The chase is gone.*"

She paused, her voice tightening just a little. "And it's not just for single women like me, either. Even in marriages, I've seen it. Friends who tell me their husbands don't try anymore—no dates, no surprises, no effort."

She was right. The chase was gone. The efforts had disappeared. It had been replaced by... algorithms, convenience, dopamine hits. Everything's too easy now. Why would they bother choosing?"

And the women?

Still waiting. Still hoping to be chosen. Still trying to be "chill" enough, sexy enough, interesting enough, easy enough.

We remembered what we'd known from history, read in books, seen in films—not with nostalgia, but with a kind of wondering curiosity. What had been true only a few decades ago now felt like something from a thousand years past. Back when men made gestures—real ones. When love wasn't effortless; it was effort.

Men used to build houses—literally. They'd take jobs they didn't love. Move across states. Stand outside windows with boomboxes. Write letters from war. Save for rings. Meet families. Ask for blessings. Promise forever.

Even the average men—the ones with messy cars and rough hands—would show up cleaned, flowers in hand, shoes shined. They'd say, *I want you,* and then prove it with something real. A plan. A sacrifice. A vow.

They didn't expect love just because they existed. They earned it.

But somewhere, that changed.

Now, the same men who spent hours researching flat-screen TVs couldn't be bothered to define a relationship. Effort was "too much." Exclusivity was "too soon." Marriage was a punchline. Vulnerability was "drama."

Rhea wasn't angry anymore. She was just tired.

Tired of pretending scraps were enough. Tired of acting fine with crumbs of affection. Tired of a world that rewarded detachment over devotion.

She wanted to believe *balance* could return. That someday, women could hold power again—not through manipulation or performance, but through *value*. Through a culture that saw love not as weakness, but as something worth fighting for.

But she wasn't sure how.

"How do you bring balance," she asked finally, her voice breaking the silence, "to a world that no longer asks men to rise to the occasion? How do women reclaim power in relationships when everything they want—*devotion, effort, permanence*—depends on a man's willingness to give it?"

Then she turned to me, her eyes steady, searching. Her voice lowered, almost trembling. "*What would it take for men to want to try again?*"

The fire cracked softly in response, throwing sparks into the air. Neither of us spoke. Neither of us had an answer.

I lay there, staring at the ceiling, turning her questions over in my mind. The monastery had taught me to let go—to stop keeping score, to release expectations, to find peace within myself regardless of what others did or didn't give. And it had worked. That surrender had softened me, opened me, brought me closer to people like Rhea in ways I never could have managed before.

But listening to her tonight—hearing what she endured, what she forgave, what she lost—I couldn't help wondering: is letting go really enough? Is it enough to find peace within ourselves while the world outside keeps taking from us? Is inner calm an answer—or is it just a way of making the unfairness easier to bear?

Because Rhea didn't need to meditate more. She needed Jake to be held accountable. She needed consequences for broken promises. She needed a world that didn't reward men for doing the bare minimum while women bent themselves into pretzels trying to be enough.

I didn't have the answer. But for the first time since the monastery, I felt the question pulling at me again—not as the old obsessive scorekeeping, but as something deeper. Something that wouldn't let me sleep.

The silence settled not as emptiness, but as something full—of shared questions, of unspoken grief, of the quiet bond only women can form in the aftermath of love lost.

At some point, our words ran out, our bodies sinking into the warmth of blankets and the faint glow of the fire. Outside, snow kept falling, steady and sure, wrapping the city in a thick white blanket. The streets emptied, the world slowed. And inside that room, between the fading embers and the hush of the winds, we drifted into sleep—two friends carried by the same current of exhaustion and hope, held for the night in the stillness of winter.

****

The Greek Goddess

Chapter 53: Horizons

The air in Greece tasted different. It carried salt and heat, softened by the faint perfume of citrus trees and sun-warmed stone. By the time we had dropped our bags at the resort, the four of us were already laughing like we had been set loose from something heavy. Rhea's smile hadn't come easy in weeks, but here, under a sky stretched impossibly blue, it began to return.

I had learned something along the years: travel heals in ways time alone cannot. When the heart feels heavy, distance lightens it. When questions have no answers, new places make them less unbearable. It had always worked for me, and I believed it would work for Rhea too.

She needed more than comfort in the moment—she needed a horizon, a sense that tomorrow still held something for her. So I suggested we plan a girls' trip. Somewhere fun. Somewhere drenched in sun, where the waters shimmered blue, the skies stretched clear, and the walls themselves told stories older than sorrow—the kind of place where history and beauty breathe in the same air. The first image that came to me was Greece, and once it came, it wouldn't leave. Within days we circled on it, the four of us—Rhea, myself, and two of our closest friends— plotting itineraries like teenagers planning their first adventure.

The days leading up to departure carried a hum of anticipation. Work carried on, life went on, but beneath it all was that steady current: the thought of slipping into another world, swapping emails for a rendezvous with the Aegean.

Excitement became its own kind of balm. For once, we weren't circling the same questions that had weighed on us for months. The doubts, the heartbreak, the late-night what-ifs—they all quieted under the brightness of what lay ahead. Planning flights, browsing photos of whitewashed villages, picturing the blue domes and sunlit waters—we filled our days with laughter and lists, small details that made it real. And in that anticipation, we felt light again, like girls with an entire horizon waiting for us, forgetting, if only for a while, the heaviness we had come from.

So often, what makes life feel unbearable isn't the weight of our circumstances, but the fear that they will never change. We do not suffer because of the cage itself, but because we see no door—no opening, no escape. It is the illusion of permanence that makes us feel trapped.

It is easy to move through life when there is something to look forward to. Perhaps this is why children brim with happiness, why teenagers pulse with enthusiasm—their lives stretch before them in wide, unbroken roads: college, love, careers, endless possibilities. But as we grow older, that excitement often fades. Not because life becomes less enjoyable—in fact we may even have everything we ever wanted: wealth, status, family, comforts—but because, in having them, we stop seeing what lies ahead. The horizon narrows. And without a horizon, joy shrinks.

That is why it is vital never to let life stagnate. To always keep it moving along a growth path, each year offering something to strive toward, some new peak to climb. A dream.

An ambition. A lighthouse in the midst of the ocean—its beam cutting through darkness, pulling you forward even when the waters feel endless. With such a beacon, enthusiasm never dies. You wake with purpose. You row even when the storm rages. Because when you have a *why*, you can always figure out the *hows*.

And perhaps that is what we were really searching for in this trip to Greece—not perfect answers, not neat solutions, but a hint of hope and a flicker of excitement. A glimpse of something bright enough to remind us to keep moving forward, to live not just in emptiness but with anticipation, the kind that makes life feel alive again.

And so we packed our bags and landed in Athens, our little girl gang stepping off the plane with sunglasses, hats, scarves fluttering in the breeze, luggage in hand. Greece welcomed us with skies clear as glass and a sun that turned even the stone walls honey-gold. The scent of salt and citrus lingered in the air. Our resort perched on a hill overlooking the sea— whitewashed walls, blue shutters, bougainvillea spilling over balconies in cascades of fuchsia. It felt like stepping into a postcard, except the laughter was ours.

We had hardly unpacked our bags before the pool called to us. The Aegean glimmered in the distance. The resort itself seemed designed to trap you in luxury—white loungers, umbrellas fluttering, trays of cocktails carried past like offerings. By late afternoon we were sprawled across our chairs, wide-brimmed hats tilted against the sun, drinks sweating beads of condensation in our hands.

Around us, the hotel settled into a low hum of leisure— couples entwined on loungers, bronzed bodies stretched beneath the umbrellas and the gentle murmur of voices slipping between laughter and the clink of glassware.

Chapter 54: Courtship

It felt like one of those suspended afternoons when time seemed to slow, every detail heightened, every glance charged. And then, breaking the stillness of the pool, came a splash— followed by a ripple of laughter. A group of young men slowly drifted in the pool, their laughter carrying across the water. Every so often, one would dive in with exaggerated strokes, muscles slicing through the turquoise. Another leaned back against the edge, cracking a joke loud enough for us to catch. It wasn't overdone—not chest-beating bravado, but subtler. A display, yes, but calibrated for the audience.

We noticed. Of course we noticed. Eyes flicked, glances traded, our group rippled with muffled giggles and whispered commentary. A well-timed splash earned a smirk, a casual flex sent a raised brow across our row of loungers. It was the oldest dance in the world, dressed up in swim trunks and mirrored shades.

Once they realized they had our attention, they took it a notch higher.

Their movements weren't subtle anymore—they were expansive, deliberate, almost performative. The way they dove under and surfaced, tossing their hair back, shaking droplets from their faces, it was less about cooling off and more about showing off. They laughed louder, their voices carrying across the pool, bodies cutting through the water with a kind of practiced ease. Shoulders flexed as they hoisted themselves onto the edge, droplets sliding down firm lines of muscle, then plunging back in with a force that sent ripples racing outward.

One raised his glass mid-laugh, angling it toward us as though in a silent toast, his grin almost daring us to look away.

They moved with the swagger of men who knew they were being watched, like actors aware of their audience, like peacocks unfurling their feathers in a bright, unapologetic show.

It wasn't swimming anymore. It was seduction by spectacle.

And there was nothing wrong with that. After all, the peacock doesn't get his mate by a strike of chance—but in the ritual of this spectacle. He fans his feathers—not as decoration, but as proof of his worth. He strides with pride because he knows what he carries. Those feathers are not ornaments; they are the slow work of evolution, earned over time. A man who knows he has something to offer—strength, intellect, character—feels the same drive, a deep sense of purpose in showing it.

And we women, sitting there, laughing and teasing as we watched—we were the peahen. The peahen too carries equal pride knowing she is the chooser. Her approval means something. She knows she is desired and that her attention holds value.

This is how the world is built—by design, not by flaw. Men must prove their worth through effort: by displaying strength, resilience, intelligence, or character. Women, by contrast, hold value intrinsically—through their beauty, their virtues, and their singular ability to nurture and create life within themselves. The entire animal kingdom turns on this principle, and humans are no exception.

A man often spends his life striving to increment his value. He labors, competes, takes risks, and ventures outward into the unknown, hoping that his work will make him more desirable. He is restless, eager to expand, to conquer, to show that he can shoulder the weight of survival and provide more than the next man. His worth must be earned, again and again.

A woman, however, is charged with preserving her value. Her task is not less demanding, only different. She must guard her choices carefully, because one mistake can cost her dearly. While men throw themselves into the fray, women weigh, analyze, and observe. Patience becomes her strength. Restraint her strategy. She is not reckless with her value, because she knows that bad choices can compromise it.

This is the principle at the core. Yet it is important to remember that the outer details are fluid. A woman can build and expand her value through effort just as a man can learn to guard and preserve his. These are not rigid laws, but broader truths, archetypes written into nature. The specifics shift across time and culture, yet the underlying dance remains the same—effort meeting wisdom, offering meeting choice.

And that afternoon by the pool, it was all there before us—sunlit bravado on one side, amused appraisal on the other. The timeless ritual of courtship, replayed in laughter, splashes, and glances across the water.

It struck me then: this is how courtship is meant to be—not us lying in bed, swiping through strangers as if love could be sorted by checklists: hobbies, politics, job titles, zip codes, how well they photograph in good lighting. Real courtship happens face-to-face, when you can feel a person's presence in the room—their aura, their charm, the energy they carry, their social dynamics with others. Those things can't be faked. You couldn't edit them into a profile.

When you meet this way, the attraction is real. It doesn't evaporate after a handful of dates when you discover the carefully built persona online was a crafted mask. It was the value they *projected*, not the value they *truly hold*. Here, in this moment, we were alive in the banter, the teasing, the laughter—things no chat thread or emoji could ever replicate.

This is what technology has stolen from us: the spontaneity of real interactions, the thrill of playful exchanges, the unscripted spark. Online, it reduces to cheesy memes and recycled pickup lines. But here, by the pool, I looked around and saw it—this beautiful dance of courtship unfolding in real time, the kind of moments that make us feel undeniably, vibrantly alive. Everyone around us was part of it. Everyone was enjoying, swept up in the same pulse of connection.

Rhea, though, sat apart—legs crossed, her book unopened, gaze wandering elsewhere. The rest of us teased and bantered, leaning into the spectacle. But she remained unmoved—a statue in sunglasses, carrying the air of someone who had long since stopped clapping. For as beautiful as she was, she must have seen this performance a thousand times before.

And then, just as I thought nothing could crack Rhea's cool detachment, one of the men called out from the water. "You—your friend in pink—she an actress from L.A.? I swear I've seen her somewhere."

It was silly, obvious, but it worked. Rhea's lips curved, faint at first, then wider, softening into laughter. A compliment did what splashes and flexes could not.

After all, what woman on earth can resist the tug of a sweet compliment? Isn't that what women want most—to be seen for their worth, to be appreciated and cherished for who they are? And if that's what women desire above all, then what about men? What do they want most of all?

Perhaps a man's deepest desire is simply this: to impress, to prove, to win the approval of those they value most. And it is in this tension—his urge to prove, her power to decide—that the ritual of dating takes shape.

But what happens when this process is bypassed? When rewards are granted without the proving? When the courtship shrinks into the swiping? That's when everything begins to collapse. He loses his reason to strive. She loses her sense of worth. The focus shifts from the *journey* to the *reward*, from *people* to *pleasure*, and in that shift, shortcut becomes the norm—and shortcuts as we know, corrodes everything.

But here, away from the shine of pixels—past the profiles and bios—real dating reappears. Messy, spontaneous, unpredictable, and far more fun than anything an app could promise. And we watched this fun play out right before us

The compliment from one of the guys had landed squarely on Rhea. She blushed despite herself, tossing her hair, feigning annoyance but unable to hide the glow. The man edged closer in the water, his smile answering hers. A little splash, a half-joke, a glance held just long enough. The courtship dance, unfolding as it had for millennia—trial, effort, display, response.

And for a moment, watching her laughter bloom, watching the men's energy rise to meet it, I felt a strange hope. Maybe balance wasn't entirely lost—at least not in these real moments, away from technology, away from the noise of the city. The ancient rituals still surfaced when given *space*. A reminder that effort matters, and that value, when truly recognized, enables both sides to flourish: He is rewarded for impressing; she is rewarded for being worth the effort.

Chapter 55: Conquests

For three days we surrendered ourselves to leisure. Mornings drifted into afternoons over plates of feta and olives, grilled fish fresh from the sea, and wine poured with the ease of water. Afternoons melted on the sand, where the Aegean breeze tangled our hair and the sun left its amber fingerprints across our shoulders. Evenings belonged to us—our girl gang curled up in hotel lounges or perched at rooftop bars, gossiping in half-whispers that grew into laughter, the kind of laughter that left us breathless and made strangers turn their heads. Boys hovered at the edges, trying their luck with jokes or compliments, and though we toyed with their attention, it was never about them. It was about us—the delicious feeling of being young, untethered, and radiant under the Greek sky.

By the end of the third day, pleasure itself had become almost too much. Our stomachs were full, our bodies tanned and relaxed, our nights blurred into the sweetness of cocktails and secrets. And then, as indulgence always does, it left us restless. Something deeper began to stir—our minds asked for more, but something different now. Not just more entertainment or shopping stalls, but more culture, more story. We wanted to step outside the bubble of hotels and local markets and discover the Greece that lived beyond the menus and bar counters.

The Greek legends had always fascinated us—the thunderous Zeus, the fiery Ares, the empire-building Alexander The Great. We had read of them, seen their names etched into history books, but here was our chance to stand where they once stood. We wanted to walk among the ruins, to see in stone and marble what we had only imagined. So we hired a guide, a man who promised to fold time back for us, to lead us through temples and relics with stories that blurred the line between fact and fable, to weave myth and history together. And with that our days of pleasure gave way to days of wonder as we set out to explore a Greece of ruins and relics, of gods and conquerors.

Our first stop was the *Temple of Olympian Zeus.* The morning sun had just begun to burnish the white stone of Athens as we followed our guide through shaded streets into an open expanse where the ruins of another age waited. Ahead, the columns of the Olympieion rose. They reached into the sky like broken spears, the kind once thrown in Zeus's name.

The guide stopped, his hand resting lightly on the railing. "Here," he said, voice echoing against the stone, "is where Greece first built its devotion to power. Zeus—the father of gods and men. He ruled not by kindness, not by law, but by thunder. His weapon was the bolt of lightning, flung from the sky to crush anyone who dared oppose him. For the Greeks, that was divinity: raw, unanswerable force."

The columns shimmered in the heat, and I could almost hear the crack of thunder in their shadows. The guide explained how Zeus did not ask for permission. He took. He conquered women, cities and lands. His children are scattered across myth like sparks from a storm. The temples in his name were less about prayer than about awe—reminding mortals of their fragility under the sky. When you stood here in his time, you didn't feel protected. You felt vulnerable. You felt small. You felt mortal.

He led us further, until the clamor of the city dimmed, and we stood before carvings that once depicted *Ares.* Figures of warriors clashed in frozen battle—shields raised, spears lifted mid-strike, their bodies caught between motion and eternity. Horses reared, muscles etched in marble and their stone eyes wild with fury. Though chipped and weathered, the scene still pulsed with violence, the spirit of war carved into every line.

"If Zeus is the storm," the guide said, "Ares is the blood it leaves behind. The god of war."

Listening to the stories of Ares made me realize that the wars Greeks referred to wasn't about strategy, or bringing order, but it was pure rage. Ares was worshipped not because people loved him, but because they feared what happened when he was ignored. War was his feast. He walked in every battlefield, glorying in carnage, drunk on death. And the Greeks—well, they built him altars anyway. Because to live then was to know that blood and ambition would always have their price, and the Greeks paid that price in their respects to Ares.

Hours later, inside the cool hush of the museum, the world narrowed to marble and shadow as the guide led us from the gods to the mortal men—though in those days, the difference often blurred. Glass cases mirrored our faces as we drifted past fragments of helmets, tarnished coins, and weapons worn thin by centuries. Then we stopped before him—*the head of Alexander*. Chiseled in pale stone, his curls caught the light as though still damp from battle, his gaze fixed upward, imperious, unreachable.

"This is," our guide began, his voice carrying in the vaulted hall, "the head of Alexander the Great. Son of Zeus, they called him—and he believed it. He carved his legend across the earth with a sword that glittered like lightning in his hand. From Greece to Egypt, to the very edges of India, he marched—never stopping, never resting. His gift to the world?" The guide paused, letting the silence draw us in. "A vast empire that stretched as far as any man's imagination could reach."

We paused by a marble relief where Alexander's head stared forever ahead—sharp, unyielding, handsome in the way statues always are. The more I heard his stories the more I realized how he had carried Zeus's thunder and Ares's fury into the mortal realm. Where the gods demanded worship, he demanded obedience. He built cities as monuments to his dominion, and burned those that dared defy his greatness. His Macedonian sword was more than a weapon—it was his creed, his altar and his temple. Wherever it struck, cities bowed, and in its shadow empires rose.

Under the solemn canopy of the museum halls, I could almost hear the tramp of soldiers' feet on a distant victory march, their steps ringing over the marble floors, their bodies draped in bronze and iron. They seemed still alive—haunted by bloodlust, as though even centuries could not blunt their appetite for violence and chaos.

Power in Greece was always measured in conquest—who you crushed, how far your empire stretched, how many bowed before your name. Rage, ambition, destruction—these were virtues. The gods roared. The men obeyed. And the earth bled.

By the time we left the shadow of Zeus's columns and Alexander's marble gaze, my head was heavy with thunder. It was all too much. *Masculine forces* pressed against us from every angle, roaring through the ruins. Their temples stood high, their legends etched deep, but their energy was suffocating, as if we had swallowed too much storm at once.

I found myself craving something different. Not another story of swords and storms, but something gentler, steadier, more human. I longed for stories of prosperity rather than destruction—because creation must always come first, and inevitably, it rises again after the ruins.

My eyes drifted down to the folded city map in my hand, skimming past the bold print of Zeus, Olympia, Alexander. And there, almost hidden at the edge, was a smaller name: *Temple of Athena*.

The guide leaned in. "Ah," he said softly, "Athena. The goddess of wisdom, strategy, and craft. This city is named after her—Athens. She was its protector, its patron. While Zeus thundered and Alexander conquered, it was Athena who gave the people culture, harvest and nourishment, who taught them to build, to govern, to endure. That is why, when the gods competed for this land, the Athenians chose her gift. And so, her name crowns the city still."

We looked at each other, our breath caught by the sudden weight of that revelation. The goddess after whom an entire city was named. How strange that we had begun with thunderbolts and wars, yet not with her. Clearly she had left a mark deep enough to name a civilization, and yet her story lived only in the margins of our books, a whisper beneath the roar of Zeus and Alexander.

We had been raised on tales of kings and storms, history that sang praises of generals and conquests. But here, between the cracks of ruins, another story stirred—the story of a woman, a goddess, a builder. A story too easily silenced, as though the chroniclers of power had chosen to tuck her away, afraid her light might cast the men's shadows thinner.

Our minds, tired of blood and storm, longed for her.

And so we decided: tomorrow, we would seek Athena.

Chapter 56: Wisdom

The climb up to the Acropolis carried us through narrow stone paths, past olive trees with silver leaves trembling in the wind. Their roots clutched at the same earth walked by philosophers, priests, and soldiers thousands of years before. Some trunks were gnarled and massive, older than perhaps our great-grandparents' great-grandparents. A thousand years in a single tree. They had been sacred to Athena, the goddess who once offered mankind her most enduring gift.

The path bent upward, sun catching on broken marble scattered among the stones. And then, at the summit, the Parthenon revealed itself. Even in ruin, it towered—the framework of symmetry still visible against the heavens

We stopped in its shadow, carefully looking at the monument. "Here," he said, "is Athena's house. Half-broken, yes—but it is still the soul of Athens. This city bears her name. Not Zeus's. Not Poseidon's. Not Alexander's. Hers."

The guide continued, his voice softening as though revealing a truth meant only for us. "Athena," he said, "was not like the others. She was born not of a mother's body but of her father's mind—sprung fully formed, armored, from the head of Zeus himself. She carried both wisdom and war in her blood, but she did not fight for *conquest*. She fought for *protection*, for *order*, for *justice*.

He pointed upward, and for the first time we noticed details almost invisible against the glare of sun: owls carved into the stone, olive branches curling along the frieze, figures in armor whose stance was not wild rage but deliberate poise. Athena's world was written into the details.

"When the gods contested this land," the guide began, "Poseidon struck the rock with his trident. The earth split, and a spring burst forth—violent, dazzling, but salty and undrinkable. Athena, instead, planted a tree. The olive. A gift that endures beyond lifetimes. Oil to feed the hungry, to light the dark, to heal wounds. Wood for homes and ships. Branches to crown victors and to mark peace between enemies. The *Athenians saw the difference between spectacle and sustenance.* They chose her gift. They chose her."

The wind curled around us, carrying with it the faint resinous smell of the groves below. The olive trees along the slopes stood there through centuries, as if reminding us that Athena's gift was not myth alone, but a living legacy.

The guide's voice grew deeper. "Athena was unlike the other Greek Gods. The Gods lust for battle, for the chaos of blood. The Goddess enters war with strategy. She refines strength, she does not unleash it blindly. Think of Odysseus— who was intelligent, patient and disciplined. She stood at his side. But Ajax, who dragged a woman from her altar, she destroyed, for violating the sanctity of a woman. To Athena, *power without restraint is corruption.* Consent, law, and protection—these were her weapons."

A goddess that valued *consent*. We exchanged quick glances, as if to confirm we'd all heard it the same way. Us girls were impressed. In a pantheon filled with gods who took what they wanted, often by force, here was one who set limits, who drew lines, who declared that power without permission was not power at all but rot. It made her feel less like a myth and more like a vision of what women had always longed for: *a protector who understood restraint, a warrior who fought for justice rather than dominance.*

Her temple, we realized, was not a trophy to conquest; it was a container of memory. Every column is rule. Every proportion is discipline made visible. It is symmetry—it is order turned into stone. And order is what brings justice. *In Athena's world, the strong do not devour the weak, nor does the alpha prey upon the meek.* Order is kept by law and structure, and through it the city becomes a vessel—holding its people as the olive tree cradles its fruit.

To Athens she was more than a goddess. She was mother. She nourished with culture, governed with law, fed with olives, and protected with spear. That is why this city carries her name. Not from fear, not from conquest, but from *reverence*.

We stood spellbound. Her story had cast a spell; the Parthenon felt divine, its silence alive with memory.

We lingered in the hush that followed. Zeus had thundered with violence, Ares had reveled in carnage, Alexander had carried conquest across continents. Their legacies inspired awe, yes—but also unease, because their power was built on breaking. Athena was different. Her temple steadied rather than crushed. For the first time, the ground beneath us did not feel like battlefield soil, but like *foundation stone*.

Rhea's hand brushed the stone of a column, her fingers lingering as if it could answer her. For the first time since her heartbreak, her eyes did not sink downward but lifted. Not in sorrow, but in recognition. Athena was not marble alone—she was mirror. A goddess who embodied both intellect and strength, both protector and nurturer, both strategy and compassion—*all of the qualities a woman is perfectly capable of carrying all by herself.* And in doing so, she becomes a woman who was not defined by who loved her or who feared her, but by what she stood for, what she *created* and *preserved*.

We sat on the temple steps, the sun leaning westward, casting long shadows across the marble. Tourists drifted past, yet for us the ruin was no ruin—it was presence. And in that presence, I felt almost as if Athena herself bent low, whispering into the air: *You are already enough. You have always been enough.*

We stayed a long while, four women breathing under her gaze, not as travelers but as inheritors. Her strength, her steadiness, her reminder that true power is not the storm but the hand that plants a tree.

And in that moment, we believed her.

Chapter 57: Chaos

The marble steps still held the day's heat, radiating faintly beneath us. We lingered at the edge of the Parthenon, unwilling to leave just yet. Our friends had wandered off with their cameras, drawn toward the scattered ruins. Rhea and I stayed behind, sitting shoulder to shoulder in the temple's shadow.

She was staring at the horizon. Then she turned, her face sharp with sudden clarity.

"I can't believe we've been lied to this whole time."

I frowned. "What do you mean?"

Her words tumbled out fast, almost fierce. "We've always been told men are the ones who bring order, structure and reason. While women are the chaos—emotional, irrational, unpredictable. That's the story, isn't it? Men being *logical thinkers* while women being *emotional wrecks*? But look around. Look at history. Look at these legends. The truth is right here: men have created the chaos, and women have always been the ones who bring order."

Her voice struck me like the crack of a bell. It wasn't just her words—it was how much truth was packed inside them. I felt the weight of it settle into me. She was right. Over and over, women had been told they were the storm, while men were the steady hand. And yet every storm in the stories we'd heard had been carried by men.

"Think about it," she pressed on. "In every continent, the same narrative is woven into pop culture, movies, even social media. Women as messy, dramatic, hysterical. Men as calm, logical and rational. But tell me—who's wrecking economies, starting wars, crashing markets, setting entire forests on fire with one careless decision? Not women. Men."

I laughed, startled at her bluntness. She wasn't wrong.

"And we don't need to dig through history books to prove it," I added. "You don't even have to travel all the way to Greece. Just walk into a bachelor pad. There's your chaos theory right there."

Her mouth curved into the smallest smile, so I went on, warming to the humor. "I mean, compare it. A woman's wardrobe: color-coordinated rows of dresses, shoes lined like soldiers, handbags in their dust bags, jewelry arranged in velvet trays. I open my closet and it looks like a boutique. Now picture a man's closet. Shirts crumpled like hostages, socks that haven't seen their partners in years, and one suit hanging in a dry-cleaning bag—the same one worn to weddings, funerals, and job interviews. Their apartments? Piles of pizza boxes doubling as interior design. Plants dead in the corner. A fridge with one beer and mustard from 2012. But sure, we're the unpredictable chaotic ones."

Rhea laughed now, a real laugh, shaking her head.

"And it's not just closets," I continued. "Women build routines—morning skincare, workouts, hair, makeup. And then we extend it outward: the family's schedule, the kids' lunches, the bills, the birthdays, the dentist appointments. We make sure the entire household runs like a train schedule. Men?" I shrugged. "They roll into the day half-dressed, coffee spilled down their shirts, and somehow still forget their laptop chargers. And yet they're the ones preaching structure."

She leaned forward, animated now. "Exactly. Men break more traffic laws, get into more accidents, pay higher insurance. They commit the vast majority of crimes—but they call *us* irrational? They're the ones punching holes in drywall because their football team lost. But women are supposedly the emotional wrecks?"

I felt a thrill of recognition—the way her words sliced through years of conditioning. "You're right," I said. "It's almost funny. Women have more control over our emotions than men do. We name them, process them, talk about them, work through them. Men? Half the time they can't tell if they're angry, sad, guilty, or just hungry. But they're the logical ones, right?"

Rhea smirked "And don't even get me started on jealousy. They say women can't stand to see each other succeed, that we claw at one another out of envy. But honestly? That's their projection. *Hierarchy* and *competition* are what *they* thrive on. Men can't even watch their own brothers succeed without resenting it."

I clapped my hands together like a fan at a concert. "Preach, Rhea. Every single word." I could feel it in my bones— she was right "Us women? We don't thrive on competition—we thrive in *community*. Look at us. Our girl gang isn't about outshining each other, it's about pulling each other forward. We celebrate when one of us lands the job, gets the guy, buys the house. We send flowers, organize dinners, make it a party. Men fight over the throne; women build the village."

Our words lingered, pressing into the warm air between us like a weight neither of us wanted to lift yet.

I leaned back, the edge of humor slipping away as something more reflective entered my voice. "We're always told that men think with their brains and women with their hearts, but in practice it's actually the exact reverse. Men are driven by emotion, while women navigate with logic and reason." I said, shaking my head at the irony.

She smirked at that, but then her face softened after a moment. "We've been told this lie for so long we believed it. And meanwhile, we're the ones who actually live with discipline, with responsibilities. We're the ones who restrain ourselves. When have you ever seen women solve frustration with bar fights, road rage, or setting cars on fire? It's almost always men who can't stop themselves from acting on their first impulse. They are the impulsive ones, not us."

Her voice dropped, and for a moment it was less banter and more confession. "They say men build civilizations. Without them, there would be no cities, no law, no order. But look closer at history. Men burned more than they built. They left ruins, blood, chaos in their wake. And the women? We're the ones who planted, fed and nurtured. Men fight wars to win. Women fight to protect."

She turned to me then, eyes glassy. "And tell me, Sia—is every fight fought on battlefields? Don't we fight every day, in our own homes, for the people we love? For our children, our husbands, our families? We fight to keep them from losing themselves—to bad habits, to addictions, to their own self-destruction. They call it *nagging*. But it's not nagging. It's protecting. It's building order into their lives when they can't."

Her words spilled now in a rush, an outburst unspooling from somewhere deep. "But they don't listen anymore, Sia. They just don't. They scroll, they play games, they cheat, they lie, they sit idle while we do everything. They rob us of our peace of mind. Where are the good men? All I see are disappointments. We want to nourish them, protect them, help them—but how can we, if they won't let us? If they won't even hear us?"

Her breath came fast, and I placed a hand gently on her back. Sometimes it wasn't answers that mattered, but the space to let the frustration burn itself out. Like tears rinsing pain, words carried their own release—venting can release frustration, irritation, sometimes even anger.

I didn't have solutions, but I knew one thing: she was right. We had been lied to by a society that painted women as chaotic and emotional when in truth, it was women who upheld the rules, they are the rule followers— and perhaps that was why modern life felt so shaky. When rules collapsed, when relationships dissolved into "anything goes," when convenience replaced commitment, no wonder women felt anxious. We weren't built for disorder. We were built for consistency.

The thought hung between us, sinking into the marble steps as if the temple itself wanted to keep it. Our two friends joined us back lifting the heaviness of the mood.

As the sky softened into evening we rose from the steps. The Parthenon loomed above us, fractured but enduring. We walked down the stone path, the olive trees swaying in the wind. For all the ruin around us, Athena's wisdom still lingered. And perhaps it was ours to carry forward.

Chapter 58: Divinity

We said goodbye to our guide at the foot of the Acropolis, his voice still echoing with its solemn pauses and theatrical flourishes. He waved us off like disciples departing a sermon, and we clambered into our little rental—a white Fiat, one door dented, its dashboard sticky with age.

The road unspooled before us, bordered by golden fields where windmills turned like slow dancers, their blades carving the evening air with lazy precision. Windows down, hair whipped loose, voices tumbling over one another—we felt lighter than we had in weeks, as if Athens itself had pressed its blessing into our shoulders.

And then—chaos. The Fiat jolted, a violent shudder snapping us against our seats. The tire had blown, dragging us to the shoulder in a graceless collapse.

Silence held us for a beat. Rhea leaned against the wheel, laughing helplessly, though the sharp edge of her frustration was unmistakable. I craned my neck toward the fields—no cars, no voices, not even a flicker of signal. Just us, four women on a deserted road, the windmills bowing like indifferent giants in the distance.

Then, a flicker of hope. A house revealed itself beyond a narrow stream, tucked into the slope. Whitewashed walls, shutters painted the blue of the sea, a garden spreading green at its front. Chickens pecked near a wooden coop, and solar panels glimmered faintly on the roof, catching the evening light. It looked like a home carried forward from another century, yet threaded with the present—self-contained, resilient, quietly defiant.

We followed the path across a low stone bridge, our sandals tapping against the worn surface. Up close, the house was even more inviting: herbs grew in clay pots by the door, ivy climbed the walls, and the air carried the faint scent of woodsmoke and rosemary.

I knocked, half-expecting silence. But the door opened at once.

She stood there—the woman who belonged to this place. Older, yes, but in the way mountains are old: strong, luminous, alive. Her hair, silver knotted at the back, caught the light; her face carried lines, but also a glow of health that no cream could bottle. Her eyes, sharp yet welcoming, looked us over as though she had been expecting us all along.

"Come," she said, her English lilting but steady. She waved us in with a hand dusted in flour, as though four stranded girls at dusk were exactly what the evening required.

The kitchen we entered was its own world. Bread dough rested under a linen cloth, a pot of lentil stew simmered on the stove, the smell rich with garlic and herbs. She was kneading more dough on a wooden counter, her hands pressing strength into the flour. A tray of vegetables—eggplants, tomatoes, peppers—waited to be stuffed and roasted. On a side shelf sat a bottle of ouzo, already half-poured into small glasses, as if hospitality had been prepared in advance.

We slipped into chairs around her kitchen table, still shaking off the absurdity of our flat tire. The walls were hung with copper pans and bundles of dried herbs, and above the hearth was a painting that drew my eye at once: Athena, holding a pot in her hands, olive branches curling at her feet.

The old woman caught me staring and gave a knowing nod, as if to say, *Yes. She lives here too.*

Actually..." I began, twisting my fingers around the glass she had set in front of me, "our car broke down and we were just thinking—"

"Yes, yes." She smiled, wiping her hands on her apron. "I saw it." She pointed toward the window.

I turned. Through the square of glass you could see the Fiat, slumped at the edge of the road, a white toy car with one paw folded under.

"I already called a mechanic," she said, as if it were nothing.

Rhea blinked. "You called someone for us?"

"Of course," she said. "I know every car that passes this road. You were not coming here for olive oil." Her eyes twinkled. "It is easy to see."

It felt almost magical—not the storybook kind, but the kind born of awe, of wonder. It was as if she already knew why we had come, what we wanted from her. It wasn't clairvoyance, not really. What we call "premonition" is so often just heightened presence, the art of truly paying attention. The more present you are, the more the world reveals itself. Details sharpen. Threads connect. You begin to see the hidden seams of a moment, the way a sailor can read the sea in the smallest ripple, already knowing the storm to come.

What happens is you begin to see patterns. And patterns reveal design. That's why a mother can glance across a playground and, from a single reckless movement, know her child is seconds from falling. We call it intuition, but it's just the mind and the senses braided tightly enough to catch what others miss. Women are said to be more "intuitive," but perhaps we are simply more present—more willing to look, to listen, to notice. And over time, intuition seasoned with knowledge becomes something else entirely, something close to foresight: reading a person's mood in the tilt of their head, their intentions in the shuffle of their walk, the storms they're hiding in the tremor of their voice.

And yet, what does the world call such perception? Fortune-telling at best. And at its worst—Witchcraft. Words used to turn a gift into a threat. When misogyny is thick in the air, a woman's insight becomes a thing to be feared, mocked, or punished. But in rare spaces—where men aren't ruled by their insecurities, where admiration eclipses fear—the same women are seen as divine. They are called *goddesses*.

And this is how goddesses are made—not simply by beauty or charm, but by wisdom and intuition. The intuition to recognize what others long for before they can speak it, and the wisdom to lay out a path toward it. That is the divinity people glimpse—not magic, but awareness sharpened into insight.

Chapter 59: Network

"Thank you so much for calling help," Rhea said softly.

"You're a lifesaver," I added.

The old woman waved a floury hand. "Bah... It was nothing." She pushed a small bowl toward us. "Here. Munch until dinner."

We leaned forward eagerly. Inside were green olives slicked with oil, lemon, and sprigs of thyme. Hunger made them taste like a revelation.

"What are you cooking?" I asked, unable to keep my eyes from the counter.

She smiled without looking up from her dough. "Gemista," she said, rolling the word with her accent. "Tomatoes and peppers stuffed with rice, herbs, pine nuts. They bake slowly; they taste better when you wait. And bread—always bread. Bread is time made edible." She nodded toward the stew simmering on the stove. "Fakes soupa—lentils from my garden, onions from my neighbor, a little vinegar to wake it up."

I noticed how every ingredient in her dish was drawn directly from the land—vegetables from her garden, eggs from the coop, milk from her goats. She knew exactly what went into her food, and where each part of it came from. And then I thought of us: how we eat from cans and bottles, frozen packets and plastic wrappers, never asking where it came from or what it truly contains. We are so far removed from nature, from the earth that once sustained us directly.

And perhaps in that distance, we lose countless lessons. We no longer learn to sense what our bodies need or what to avoid, to recognize the subtle wisdom of life's patterns. We forget that growth is slow and requires patience. It is not as simple as walking into a store and swiping a card. To grow food is to care for it, to nurture it, to water and feed it so that it continues to give. Ignore it, and the source withers. The land teaches you that *care is not optional—it is the price of value.*

It also teaches *resilience.* You face pests and insects, sudden storms, and the need for protection. You build coops and shelters for animals, store water in tanks or reservoirs, guard what matters against harm. In all this, you learn to defend as much as you nurture. These are lessons city life hides from us, where milk and groceries appear as if conjured, divorced from the earth and paid for with nothing more than a swipe of plastic.

The old lady's gaze lingered on Rhea's hand. "Ah, that ring," she said, her voice thick with affection. "Kallíste, my child—it is beautiful."

Rhea's face fell, her eyes dropping to the ground. I hurried to intervene. "Actually... She broke off the engagement. Her fiancé cheated on her. That's why we came to Greece—to lift her spirits. She hasn't had the heart to return the ring yet, but she will once we're back."

The woman's head jerked back in disbelief. "Return the ring? Why?" Her brows knitted, her tone scandalized. We glanced at each other, equally surprised by her reaction.

"Well... the engagement is over," I said cautiously. "So the ring goes back."

She wagged her finger as though scolding a child. "Óchi, óchi—no, no, no. You keep that, korítsi mou. He wasted your time, your energy, your youth. He broke your heart. A foolish boy—What a..." she searched for a word and found one with relish, "what a malakas—to lose such a girl." She cupped Rhea's chin gently, her eyes glinting with admiration. "Pretty face, strong eyes. He will regret this until he dies."

Rhea blushed, a small smile breaking through.

"Don't you worry, paidi mou," the woman went on, her voice softening. "A hundred suitors will lay gifts at your feet. You will see."

Rhea shook her head. "I don't think that's going to happen."

The woman waved her hand dismissively. "Eh, one thing is certain—he will never marry again. Who would take him now, knowing he lies and cheats? His friends must speak of him with disgust, his family too. And his poor mother—tsóni!—she must be burning with shame, ashamed to have raised such a boy. To cheat, to lie, to betray... phéftis!"

Rhea and I exchanged a look, half-amused, as though we were sitting with someone from another world.

"I never told anyone of his cheating," Rhea said quietly. "Not his friends, not his family. I thought... it was our personal matter."

The old woman clucked her tongue, shaking her head. "Personal? Ti les, child? Lies, cheating, false promises—these are not personal matters. These are matters of honor, of character—setting expectations for acceptable behavior. He broke promises, played with a woman's integrity—it is no longer just between you two. Why protect him? You would not want the other girls to know? To be warned? This is not shame for you, but for him."

Rhea hesitated, unsettled. "Well... they'll find out on their own."

"And until then what? He continues to go around fooling women as long as he likes?" She slapped the dough once, hard enough to puff flour into the air. "See, this is the problem with you modern women. So disconnected. So private. In our village, if a man dared to be disloyal, the whole village knew by sundown. We weren't just protecting ourselves. We were protecting each other—guarding each sister, each daughter. We were a *network*, like the roots of olive trees—messages passing underground. We kept each other safe."

By now she had the whole room. *Julia* and *Marissa*, who had been buried in their phones, had set them aside and were listening intently. Something in the old woman's words landed deep, striking a chord that hummed between all of us. We wanted to believe her. A part of us even did. But the idea felt so unfamiliar, so disruptive, we didn't know how to process it. Our common sense whispered, *yes, of course—that makes sense.* But our city-bred minds recoiled: *no, that's too much...That's drama. That's slandering.*

The old woman dusted her hands together, flour softening into the air. Her voice, though calm, cut like a chisel.

"In my day," she said, "if a man broke his word, if he cheated or lied, every woman knew his name, his face, his habits. He could not hide. He would either change, or he would have to find a woman in another village which was, let's say, very difficult at the time, so guess what? Aha...*the men would change*. They would actually change their ways. I have seen it with my own eyes."

She reached for a clay bowl, dropping pinches of oregano and mint into the rice mixture. Her movements were measured, practiced—as if each herb was part of the story.

She jabbed a finger toward Rhea. "And you, with all this *technology* in your hands! With one click you could warn every woman in the city, and yet you keep it hidden. Do you not see? Silence lets him keep lying. Silence lets him go on and on, never forced to change."

Julia and Marissa exchanged uneasy glances. The old woman's words had a rawness we weren't used to. We'd been raised in a world that prized privacy, that taught us to swallow humiliation quietly, to hide our pain as though it were shameful. Her bluntness pressed against that conditioning like a hammer on glass.

She stuffed the rice into a tomato, her fingers sure, then set it upright in a pan. "When I was young, we women were a *net*. We carried *stories, warnings and wisdom*. If a man drank too much, if he hit his wife, if he gambled the money away—every woman knew. We were not cruel. We were protective. We saved each other from wasting our lives on such men. Now you live in cities, surrounded by millions, connected to everyone by technology, and yet you are more alone than we ever were. You call it privacy. I call it a lack of a support network."

Her words landed heavily. Something in us wanted to cheer, and something else wanted to protest.

Chapter 60: Information

Julia leaned forward, elbows on the table. "But it's not that simple, you know. We could be sued for defamation."

The old woman threw back her head and laughed, a full-bodied laugh that made the pans on the wall tremble. "Defamation!" she cried. "Men, I tell you. Always finding ways to escape trouble. You know what it reminds me of? When my son was a teenager, he would come home late, smelling of wine, pretending it was 'study group.' And when I caught him, do you know what he did? He dragged his older brother into the room as his lawyer!" She wagged a floury finger at us. "The big brother stood there, speaking for him, inventing stories, twisting my words. Ah! That was the first trial of our household court. And of course, I was the judge."

We burst out laughing, picturing her kitchen as a courtroom, her son squirming behind his brother's legal defense.

"You see?" she went on, chuckling. "This is why they invented lawyers. So the guilty could wriggle free, so the rich could escape, while the poor boy gets the punishment. But people have mouths—they can speak for themselves, fight their own battles. Instead, we let them tangle us up in technicalities, in details, until we forget common sense. Tell me, would a man back in the village sue every woman for *gossiping* about him?"

We all broke into laughter again, the image too ridiculous to hold back. Even Rhea, who had been quiet, let herself giggle, shaking her head.

The laughter softened into a thoughtful silence. *Gossip*—we had all done it, indulged in it, though always with *guilt*, with whispers, as if it were a sin we couldn't resist. Something tempting, irresistible, yet always mocked, ridiculed, dismissed.

The old woman's eyes gleamed. "Gossip, they call it. Men gave it a bad name. But what is it, really? It is our tool to *exchange information*. A very powerful tool." She leaned on the counter, her hands dusted with flour. "Men talk about things— cars, stocks, money, planes–of power and of greed. But women? We women, we talk about *people*. About *relationships*. About *feelings*. About how someone made us feel, how close we are, how safe or unsafe someone makes us. We talk about our husbands, our children, our families. The things that matter. And men are afraid of it. Afraid that if women share too much, their dirty secrets will be out—men will lose their power. So they called it gossip, and we believed them. We dropped our weapons. We dropped our common sense, our network. And now we wonder why we feel so helpless? That's because we have become *the victims of our own doing*."

We looked at each other in amazement. Never had anyone glorified gossip this way. It wasn't shameful chatter, but a kind of intelligence—the oldest network of information there was.

And she was right. If Rhea hadn't told me about her breakup, if she hadn't shared the details, I wouldn't have recognized my own disappointments mirrored in hers. I wouldn't have seen the pattern. It was through sharing—yes, gossip—that we realized men's betrayals weren't random but repeated. A behavior, not an accident.

Marissa leaned forward, eyes shining. "See, I always loved gossip. I just never thought why it got such a bad name. *I'd rather talk about people than money or things. People matter.*

But..." she hesitated, "what about the ethics of it? Isn't it immoral to talk badly about others?"

The old woman smiled, setting down her knife. Her tone shifted, serious now. "Morality is not so simple, *koritsia mou*. It is not only about the action, but the intention behind it. Why you do something matters more than the action itself."

Julia chimed in. "Yes, I agree. I always thought that. Like... if you lie to protect someone, it's not really wrong. But even if you say the truth, if your goal is just to hurt someone, it's still not right. Criticism should help someone grow, not cut them down."

The woman's eyes warmed. "Exactly, my child. If you speak badly of someone to destroy them, to make them small—yes, that is sin. But if you use your words to protect, to warn, to guide? That is good. That is wisdom. It is the same as any *weapon*." She picked up the knife again. "You can use it to kill someone....or you can use it to make dinner." and, with a flourish, sliced through a tomato.

We laughed, the seriousness cut by her timing, and she grinned, tapping her temple. "So it is with gossip. A lethal tool, but powerful. Use it wisely. Not alone, but together. As a tribe. As a village. As women."

Chapter 61: Femininity

Just then the doorbell chimed, a sharp little note that cut through the warmth of the kitchen. The old woman wiped her hands on her apron and went to answer. We watched her silhouette in the doorway as she greeted the mechanic with loud Greek and broad gestures, her voice carrying across the hall like a general commanding troops.

Julia was summoned, of course—the "responsible one" in our group—and she went to the door, nodding dutifully as the woman and the mechanic volleyed instructions over her head. We could only sit and watch, the rest of us, as the old lady handled everything on our behalf: explaining the problem, asking questions we wouldn't know to ask, making sure we weren't overcharged.

And as we sat there, I realized what it was: this was *goddess energy*. Not the thunder of Zeus or the rage of Ares, but the steady kind—the kind that makes everyone under one roof feel safe. You don't have to command respect when you care for people, *respect comes naturally*. We felt it in our bones. Protected, guarded, fed, even our broken car handled without us lifting a finger.

Respect flowed toward her without her demanding it. She didn't raise her voice. She didn't force us. Yet we automatically leaned into her orbit. If she asked us to grab tomatoes from her garden, we'd go without hesitation. If she needed herbs from a pot, we'd hand them over before she finished the sentence. It wasn't submission—it was the natural flow of order. Like the way gears in a watch obey the master spring. Not out of fear, but out of design.

That's what true leadership looks like: *protection first, instruction second.* And the rest falls in line.

It made me realize there are two kinds of leadership. The first is the *masculine way*—leadership through force, intimidation, raised voices, commands barked into the air. Authority built on strength, on fear, on awe. People surrender not because they want to, but because they must. It is the way *apes choose their alpha*, the way ancient Greeks chose their gods. Zeus with his thunderbolt, Ares with his rage. Even Alexander was worshipped as divine—not because he nurtured, but because he conquered. Historians crowned him *Alexander the Great,* the only man in history to bear that title, not for gentleness but for ferocity. Respect that bows instinctively to *raw supremacy.*

And then there is the second path—the *feminine way.* A leadership not demanded, but earned. Respect born of care, protection, and nourishment. This kind of leader does not drain energy from those around her; she fills them, strengthens them. She lifts spirits, offers guidance, realigns those who have strayed. Sometimes through wisdom, sometimes through strategy, sometimes even through *discipline* and *punishment*— but always in service of growth. And in return, people follow her naturally, without being told.

This is not to say that one way is better than the other— nature has given us both. But today, we only seem to recognize the masculine way. Women are taught to believe that in order to lead, they must *dominate*: they must push, compete, and command, or else risk being dismissed. And when they succeed by those rules, what do we call them? "Boss bitch." "Control Freak." "Too much." Modern lingo for women who have stepped into masculine shoes—but shoes that were never made to fit them.

And in that pursuit, we forget our own style of leadership. We forget that to lead like a goddess is *not to seize, but to create*. Is it any wonder, then, why so many women in positions of authority feel hollow, unfulfilled? It's because they are leading by borrowed rules, measuring themselves against a yardstick that was never theirs. And yet, once upon a time in Greece, it was the goddess Athena who was most revered. *Perhaps that is why the land had known prosperity, why abundance and peace had flourished for so long.*

But when we forget this kind of leadership—the feminine way, what happens? We return to conflict everywhere—pulling each other down, grasping for dominance, simmering with anger and frustration. And until we embrace the feminine way of leadership, *peace will forever remain elusive.*

Both forms of leadership have their place. But I am absolutely convinced that in today's fragile climate, what the world needs most is more of the other kind of leadership— leadership rooted in feminine energy. *Not necessarily leadership by women but by feminine forces.* Because feminine energy is not bound to gender or biology; it is defined by *style* and *essence*—the leadership of care, of protection, of wisdom, of empowerment.

Goddess leadership. The very thing the world is starving for today. And just as if to embody that truth in flesh, the old lady reappeared, her presence as grounding as it was commanding.

Chapter 62: Sustenance

The old lady returned after instructing the mechanic, Julia at her side. She clapped her hands lightly, brushing flour from her palms. "So, yes. As I was telling you, girls—do not let yourselves be taken for granted. Hold your footing. Take your stand. If someone does not meet your expectations, call them out. If they break a promise, if they betray your integrity—do not stay silent. Name them. Shame them. Make it so they cannot do it again to another."

I thought to myself—*expectations*. Such a contrast to what I had learned at the *monastery*, where the teaching was simple: if someone does not meet your expectations, *let them go*. Expect less, desire less. Do not cling to outcomes—just keep acting selflessly, without attachment.

The contrast between her words and those teachings made me restless. Because both philosophies seemed correct in their own ways. So which was it? Should we truly hold no expectations of men? Or should we demand what is rightfully ours—demand that they keep their word, honor their promises, and revolt if they fail us?

Caught in this confusion, I finally asked her, "But I was told not to keep *expectations*. Not to desire too much. *Not to focus on the outcome*. Just to give in a relationship, and not be disheartened if nothing comes back. That is what I've been practicing recently—enjoying the little moments without looking for a future promise. Are you saying what I learned at the monastery was wrong? Because what you say sounds contradictory, and yet... both feel valid. Please, enlighten us.

Should we hold expectations in love, or let them go? Should we demand more, or simply take joy in whatever little we are given?"

The old lady looked at me then, her eyes glinting with approval—perhaps pleased to see her words not taken lightly, not tossed in one ear and out the other. We girls were listening. Truly listening. Not just nodding, but leaning in like disciples at the feet of a teacher, eager to wrestle with the doubts her lessons stirred.

She gave a warm smile, her eyes gleaming. "Where is the contradiction, my child? The teachings in a monastery are for you, at a *personal level*—for your soul, for your peace. But the advice I give is for all of you, *as a group, for women together*. How can they be the same?"

"I don't understand," I admitted. "I am me, and I am a woman too. How can the advice be different?"

She smiled again, clearly delighted to explain, as if savoring the chance to pass down wisdom. "Tell me, *korítsi mou*—if your employer does not pay you for your work, perhaps because he had a bad month. Maybe he lost money, maybe he has debts. Or maybe he simply forgot. In your *personal capacity*, you may choose to let it go. *Kaneis den páthe.* It does not matter. You think, 'I can manage for a month. I will not hold grudges, I will not invite stress.' And so you carry on, you find *peace*. You still go to work, full of joy, doing your duties."

She paused, her finger raised. "But now, suppose your employer sees your silence as weakness. Suppose he decides to stop paying you altogether. Not just you—but the other workers too. Then tell me, will you still give the same advice to all your fellow employees? To just smile, keep working for free, and say it doesn't matter?"

We all shook our heads at once. Julia muttered, "No way—that's exploitation." Marissa nodded sharply. "Absolutely not."

The old lady spread her hands, triumphant. "*Na to*! You see? Even if you let something go at a personal level—because you have trained your mind to live with less, to remain happy in any circumstance—it does not mean you abandon the *fight for principles*. You may not need the money, but you still raise your voice. Not for *yourself*, but for *everyone*. Because otherwise, your kindness becomes the very tool for not only your exploitation, but for everyone else too. And that, *korítsia mou*, is when you must speak."

We nodded, every one of us, fully convinced.

She continued, her hands moving as if to weigh the air. "So you see, sometimes you do not fight only for yourself—you fight for your people, for your community, for principles that hold everything together. You may say, 'I am fine if my partner does not give back as he should. I have trained myself to be content, to enjoy the small pleasures, the casual moments. I do not need commitment, I do not need promises.' That may be enough for you, personally.

"But, *korítsi mou*, what happens when you take an exception and make it into a rule—when you start settling for less every single time, when you keep letting go again and again, and expect everyone else to do the same? What happens when you tell every wife to stop expecting from her husband? Or when you tell women, in general, to stop expecting anything from men? When you tell employers to stop expecting from their employees?"

"That's when everything begins to collapse. Marriages collapse. Relationships collapse. Companies collapse. Societies collapse."

"Why? Because *a society survives on expectations*, on structure, on predictability. The wife expects from the husband, the husband from the wife. The manager expects work from the employee, the employee expects his pay at the end of the month. This is what creates trust. This is what sustains the market. Without it—without predictability, without accountability—the economy crumbles. And the moment one group takes more than the other, imbalance sets in. And that imbalance, always, inevitably, destroys everything."

"So my dear ladies—desire not for yourself, but desire for fairness, for balance, for the sustenance of the society. That's where desire is good, that's where expectations are noble and that's the only time when putting up a fight is truly virtuous."

We sat in silence, nodding, taking in her words like a sermon.

I realized the monastery's philosophy carried its own weight. It was significant, it had merit, it mattered, but those principles were meant to guide your inner self. Its teachings focused on your own desires, your own needs, and how to cut them down. *A monastery does not instruct the whole society how to function.* Perhaps, that is why they live outside the city limits—because their work is inward, training the self to live with less.

The old lady spread her arms toward her little home. "Look at me. I have always lived with less. I have enough. I am self-sufficient. I grow my food, I gather olives, I harvest my own solar energy, the little stream nearby gives me fresh water. I do not desire much. But—" her eyes lit with mischief—"if I see a thief sneaking into my garden, stealing my figs, I will still chase him with my sandal in hand. You think I will let him get away? No, no, no! Even an old woman runs fast when her fruit is at stake." The image made us all laugh.

She leaned forward again, her tone softening into instruction. "If your child drops his ice cream, you tell him: it is fine, let it go, tomorrow we will buy another. That is the right response. But what if the same child drops it again, and again, every single day? That is no longer accident—it is a pattern. Then you teach him: hold the cone straight. Isn't it so?" We nodded.

"If someone bumps into your car, you forgive them. It is a scratch, not worth a war. But if the same man keeps crashing into every car in town, that is no longer an accident—it is a pattern. And destructive patterns need fixing. His license needs to be taken away. Or would you still let him go?

We all shook our heads, firmly no.

She raised her finger. "So listen: if someone hurts you, steals from you, even breaks your heart, you may choose to forgive them in your *personal capacity*. Forgiveness is always yours to give. But as a society—can you let him go without consequences? No, not at all. The system must ensure punishment. *Because forgiveness belongs to the self, but justice belongs to the group.* If the social order does not ensure accountability, the same man will keep creating havoc, and others will follow. Then society is no longer civil—it becomes jungle. The strong take from the weak, power rules, chaos spreads, and everything collapses."

Her voice deepened, weighty with conviction. "A society must set expectations and hold its people accountable. Because when you think of the greater good, you cannot think only of your own inner peace—you must think of everyone: of sustenance, of balance, of preserving the very order upon which civilization rests."

"And my dear girls, the sustenance of society—of its expectations and principles—is of the highest importance. On this, there can be no compromise"

She fixed her eyes on us one by one. "So yes, you should expect from men. Even if not for yourself, then for all women. Hold them accountable. Ask for what is rightfully yours. Demand that promises be kept. And punish those who play with the integrity of women—not to satisfy personal revenge, but to protect all women, collectively."

Her words hung in the air, small flames catching in each of us, still burning long after she had spoken. We exchanged glances—some solemn, some thoughtful—as if a thread had been tied between us, binding us to something larger than ourselves. For the first time, we didn't feel like we were just individuals—we belonged to a greater whole.

It struck me how often we are told to simply "move on"— don't look back, don't hold grudges, forgive, forget, keep walking forward. But here was someone offering something different, something bigger: don't just pull yourself up after a fall—remove the stones from the path so the next person doesn't stumble. Don't just heal your own wounds—leave a warning so others don't burn the same way. Don't just forgive and forget—hold people accountable, so they cannot go on unchecked.

We no longer think this way. We have stopped thinking as a tribe, as a community, as a network that protects one another. We think only of ourselves, guarding our own wounds and interests. That evening, it felt like a breath of fresh air—her words offering a perspective no self-help book, no therapy session, no classroom had ever taught us.

And then, as if sensing it was enough for now, the old lady turned her attention to the kitchen. The air shifted, and we followed her lead, moving with her, drawn by the promise of food and the ordinary work of feeding one another: knives tapping on boards, pans singing on the stove, the clink of plates. The mood shifted from argument to tending, from lesson to labor, and we followed—changed, but ready for dinner.

Chapter 63: Equality

Soon enough, the kitchen was filled with the fragrance of roasted peppers and tomatoes, bread warm from the oven, stew rich and hearty. She set everything on the table with the satisfaction of someone who has not only cooked but taught.

"And just like that," she said, brushing her hands, "dinner is ready."

We gathered eagerly, bowls and plates passed around, the first bites followed by exclamations. Julia sighed at the bread, still steaming as she tore it. Marissa closed her eyes at the sweetness of the roasted tomato. Rhea, chewing slowly, smiled for the first time that evening without shadow in her face.

I sat back, watching the old woman's hands move—pouring, serving, tending. Her words lingered even stronger than the food. Outside, the mechanic was still bent over our car, a flashlight cutting through the darkening road. The sun had already slipped below the horizon, leaving just enough glow to trace the outlines of the land. However, we were in no rush. In truth, we were savoring the company, her hospitality, and the unexpected wisdom she carried. Perhaps it was even a blessing that the car had broken down. Without it, this lesson might never have reached us. And I could tell—she had more to give, especially about the dynamics between men and women, and how their roles once worked in tandem to keep the fabric of society intact.

Wanting to dig a little deeper—and maybe spark some playful banter—I leaned in with a grin. "You must have been such a feminist back in your time."

Julia joined me in poking her further, raising her glass. "Oh, I can already see it—men scattering the moment she entered a room."

Marissa added, "Probably hiding under tables, terrified she'd catch them misbehaving." We all burst into laughter.

The old lady burst out laughing too, shaking her head. "Óchi, óchi—no, no! Not at all. Men never ran from me. They liked me. They thought I understood them best. I raised two sons, you see—I know how men think, how they are. And I also raised three daughters... and I know how very different they are. Men and women—they are not the same."

Julia sat up, almost protesting. "What do you mean? Are you saying men and women are not equal?"

Marissa joined in, half-teasing, half-serious. "That sounds so sexist! I guess people were sexist back in your day—it's not really your fault."

The old lady narrowed her eyes, clearly annoyed, and snapped with a laugh, "Do you have wax in your ears, *korítsia*? I said *not the same,* I never said *not equal.*"

The girls smiled at one another, a little mischievous, as if teasing her on purpose.

I jumped in, hesitant. "So... you believe men and women are equal, right?" My voice carried more hope than I intended—hoping that at least one thing I had always believed would remain true in her court, that not everything I'd known was about to unravel.

She looked at me calmly, still chewing her food, and said, "Equal in what way?"

I blinked, confused. "Equal... like, in every way."

She arched a brow. "In every way? That is a hard thing, my child. How can one thing be equal to another in *every* way—unless they are identical? Which men and women are not."

We exchanged uncertain looks, caught between curiosity and confusion, waiting for her to explain.

"See," she went on, "if you lined up men and women according to height, who would stand at the taller end?"

"Mostly men," one of us answered.

"And on the shorter end?"

"Mostly women."

"Yet in the middle, there are men shorter than women, and women taller than men. But clearly, men and women are not equal in height. In the same way, if you were to test patience, women might score higher overall—yet some men would still prove more patient than some women. So you see, you cannot say men and women are equal across everything—because they are not. They are different. Very different."

She rested her fork, her gaze steady. "And this, I think, is where your generation has gone wrong. To prove men and women are equal, you erase their differences and try to make them the same. But it never works—because they are not the same. Their temperaments, their strengths, their ways of thinking—all different."

Julia leaned forward, half-defiant. "So you're saying we should not ask for equality with men?"

The old lady leaned back, steady and sure. "Like I said, equality exists only within context. So yes—when speaking of *equality of opportunity*, of choices—you should indeed demand equality with men. But *equality of outcome*, my dear girls, that will never be the same. Outcomes depend on many things: your own merit, your talents, your inclinations—and those are often shaped by your nature, sometimes even by gender."

She gestured toward the yard. "For example, everyone should be free to choose any field they wish. But do not be surprised if men prefer being mechanics and women prefer walking the ramp." She pointed toward the car outside. "Now tell me—how many of you would want his job?"

We all turned to look. The mechanic was crouched low, a flashlight clenched between his teeth, both hands buried deep in the greasy heart of our Fiat. Sweat beaded his forehead, his shirt darkened with oil.

Julia burst out laughing. "Not me!"

"Not me either," another chimed in quickly.

Marissa threw up her hands dramatically. "Oh, no thank you. I'd rather not spend my life covered in grease, oil stains, and black smudges. Eww!" She wrinkled her nose, flapping her fingers like she could already feel the grime on her skin.

We all laughed, the sound filling the little room.

The old lady smiled knowingly. "So you see—men and women may choose differently even when the same choices are on the table. And that is perfectly fine. The important thing is that the choices exist."

I thought to myself—it was perhaps the most logical take on equality I had ever heard.

She wasn't finished. "Let me tell you, there are two forces in nature: *the masculine and the feminine.* They may seem like opposites, but in truth they *complement* one another. Much like yin and yang—together they bring balance. Both are needed, both are essential. But they are not the same. Men are like wild currents of energy—restless, always wanting more, always expanding, conquering, spreading. Like a beast with endless potential but little direction. Like a storm, tearing through wherever they go."

Rhea leaned forward, her eyes lit with curiosity. "And women?" she asked.

The old lady leaned forward, her eyes glinting. "And women? *Women are the harness that controls this energy and puts it to good use.* Much like taming a beast. You have seen a horse rider, no? The straps, the reins pulling just enough, the blinders fixed so the horse does not stray but stays on the path. If men are the horse, then you, girls, are the riders."

We all burst into laughter at the image.

She let us laugh, then raised her hand and pointed toward the window. Out in the distance, great *windmills* turned slowly, their blades glowing faintly against the night sky. "You see these windmills? They harness the restless energy of the wind and make it useful. They turn it into *work*—into something productive, into creation. If men are that wild energy, then women are the force that converts it into power to build, to construct, to create."

"Without the harness, the energy would scatter and be wasted. Yet, when you think about it, without the energy, the harness itself can do nothing. If no wind blows, will the mill produce light on its own? No, it will stand still, covered in darkness."

She paused, her voice soft but firm. "So you see, both forces are *equally important.*" She lingered on the word, letting it weigh in the room.

Julia sighed in relief. "Oh, so they are equal in that sense—equal in their significance to life, to society, to existence."

Marissa grinned. "Men and women equally important. I like the sound of that. I can live with it."

"*These two forces—masculine and feminine—are not only about men and women,*" the old lady said. "They are forces of nature, the currents that keep balance in the world. And *they live inside every human being.* Every one of us, whether man or woman, carries both, though in different intensities. But they are always there."

She lifted a hand, counting off with her fingers. "Some call it body and soul. Some call it mind and consciousness, some brain and heart. Some even call it ego and id. The Greeks would have said Apollo and Dionysus. The names change, but the principle is the same. *One tempts, the other restrains. One expands, the other steadies. One flares with anger, the other soothes. Without one, there is no growth. Without the other, no stability.* And so both are necessary. Run too fast and you risk falling; walk too slow and you never arrive."

Her voice softened, almost like she was sharing a secret. "I call the masculine and feminine forces of nature as *strength* and *wisdom.* And if you really ask me, I'd say, we made this big leap—the leap from being wild animals to become humans—not because of our strength alone, but because we discovered the wisdom within us. *We learned to recognize both forces inside ourselves, and to balance them.* That balance is what made us conscious beings. Without it, we would still be tearing through the wild like beasts, guided solely by our masculine forces. Lions, gorillas—far stronger, far wilder than any man. If raw power were all it took to rule, they would dominate this planet. But they don't. We do. And do you know why?"

I leaned in and answered softly, completing her thought. *"Because humans recognized the feminine within them."*

The old lady's eyes crinkled with a smile. "Exactly, *korítsi mou.*"

After a pause, the old lady continued, as if summing it all up. "So, do not hate men, girls. That is not the lesson I wanted to give you. When I say call them out—tell their friends, their family, do not hide their secrets—it is not because you hate them. *It is because you understand them.* You understand their true nature. The way you understand your children—you know exactly how they are, and how to get them to task. With children, sometimes you must be gentle, sometimes firm. Sometimes you use strategy, sometimes reward, sometimes punishment. That, *paidi mou,* is the secret to drawing out the potential from your kids. Left to themselves, they waste it. But when they grow into responsible adults, they will turn back and thank you for it."

"It is the same with men. They need to be guided, harnessed, their energy put to good use. Otherwise, they will keep getting distracted, keep chasing new and flashy things. Left unchecked, they are like a kite drifting loose in the air. But pull the string just right, and it flies higher than ever. And one day, they will look back with pride—grateful for the family, the children, the life you built together. Even the same *nagging* that once annoyed them, they will thank you for."

"So when you call them out, when you report them to other women, when you shame them—it is not to cast them out, but to remind them there are *consequences.* To show them *life will not hand out rewards for free.* They must put in the effort, clean up their act, and only then do they earn the fruits of their labor."

She paused, gave us a wicked little grin *"And girls—never give the fruit away too soon."*

She ended with a sly wink.

We all burst into laughter, clutching our stomachs, knowing exactly what she meant. Julia nearly spilling her drink. Rhea blushed furiously, shaking her head, while Marissa fanned herself with exaggerated scandal. The old lady only smirked, clearly delighted to have us squealing like teenagers around her kitchen table.

And just then—almost as if on cue—the mechanic knocked at the door, wiping his hands. "The car is fixed," he said.

The old lady threw her hands up theatrically. *"Epitelous!* Finally! I thought you'd take all night!" she exclaimed, half in Greek, half in laughter. The mechanic only shook his head, grinning as he gathered his tools.

She pressed a few folded bills into his hand before we could stop her. We rushed forward, insisting, "Please, let us pay you." But she waved us off with a firmness that brooked no argument. *"Óchi, óchi—* Children don't reach for the bill when *yiayiá* is standing. That is our way." Her voice was warm but resolute, carrying the weight of tradition. And in that moment, we melted, letting ourselves be folded into her care.

She glanced at the window where darkness had settled fully now. "Well, girls, it's late. I won't have you driving through strange roads at night." And before we could object, she had already begun pulling out extra blankets from a cedar chest, her hands moving with the certainty of someone who had done this a thousand times before.

She spread one thick quilt across the couch, tucking it at the corners as though preparing it for a daughter returning home. Julia claimed it, curling up immediately with a sigh of relief. Two more blankets she carried to the guest room, where Rhea and I stretched out side by side, Marissa pulling a pillow down between us to muffle our inevitable late-night giggles. The old lady fussed over us until we were properly nested— pillows plumped, blankets pulled, stray hair smoothed from our foreheads as if we were children.

It had been a long day, and our tired bodies sank quickly into rest. Outside, the night draped itself over us like another blanket, soft and protective. The windmills turned slowly in the distance, their arms glowing faintly against the horizon. The stream nearby kept up its gentle murmur, a lullaby in running water. And there, wrapped in warmth and the unexpected safety of her home, we finally drifted into sleep.

Chapter 64: Containment

The rooster crowed before the sun had even lifted fully over the hills. A faint, amber glow seeped into the little room where we had slept, carried on the cool breeze that rustled the shutters. Outside, the windmills were still turning steadily, their blades sweeping the sky with slow, patient grace. The stream nearby murmured on, a constant undercurrent of sound, as if it had been whispering the same story since the beginning of time.

When we stepped into the yard, our hostess was already at work. Her scarf tied snugly around her head, she moved briskly, scattering feed for the chickens, bending low to pluck a weed from the vegetable patch, then carrying a bucket of water to the goats. There was strength in her hands, an ease to her chores that made it seem less like labor and more like ritual.

We washed our faces in the cold water from the stream, shaking off sleep, and began gathering ourselves for the drive back to our hotel. The little Fiat sat in the yard, restored, waiting like a tamed mule.

Back in the kitchen, the old lady pressed a cloth sack into Julia's hands. "Here, *koritsia mou*—a little snack for the road." Inside, wrapped neatly, were wedges of cheese, a handful of olives, bread still warm, and a flask of something sweet. "And don't forget," she added, wagging her finger, "stop by *the cave of Heracles* on your way back. Every Greek child must know his story."

The girls walked ahead, laughing softly, toward the car to make sure it was running fine. I lingered behind. My eyes caught again the painting I had noticed the night before—*Athena with a pot in her hands.* The figure seemed different in the morning light, less ornament and more message.

The old lady came up beside me, almost as if she had been waiting. "You know what it means, that *pot*?"

I shook my head. "No, not really."

She smiled knowingly. "Ah, but you have seen it everywhere. In all the ancient paintings, in Egypt, in Rome, in Mesopotamia— *a woman with a pot.* Do you know why?"

I shook my head again, almost embarrassed at my ignorance.

"This," she said softly, "was *the beginning of civilization.*"

"A pot?" I asked, incredulous.

"Yes." Her smile widened. "Think back, child. In the early days, the rivers ran wild. Everyone—men, women, children—had to go to the river to drink. But riverbeds were dangerous, beasts lurking always. Only strong men could protect. So if you wanted water, you went with a man. Always dependent. Always waiting. But then—there was a woman, wise as she was beautiful. She sat by the clay of the riverbank, dipped her hands in the mud, and shaped it with patience."

Her hands mimed the motion as she spoke—cupping, pressing, smoothing the invisible vessel between her palms. "She shaped a *pot.* Simple, no? Yet everything changed. With her pot, she could store water herself. Bring it home. Give to her children, her family. She no longer needed a trip to the river for every sip, which meant, she no longer needed to depend on a man. That, my child, was the first step toward *agency.* And *it came not from strength, but from wisdom.*"

I whispered the thought as it struck me: "Because she used her wisdom to contain."

The old woman's eyes glowed. "Yes, yes. To *contain. Civilization was born the day we learned to contain the wild forces of nature.* Women have been doing this since the beginning. Ten thousand years ago, do you know who discovered *agriculture?*"

"A woman?" I guessed.

She smiled, pleased. "Yes, *paidi mou.* It was a woman who first sowed seed and grew food. That is why, throughout history, you see countless images, paintings, and myths of *women holding grain,* wheat, or harvest in their hands. Because that was the birth of *settlements.* Before agriculture, humans wandered endlessly—hunters and gatherers, moving with the seasons. But once women learned to grow crops, people could settle, build, innovate, create families, raise children, pass down skills. Villages and cities were born. *From her wisdom, men stopped wandering, and started building.*"

Something passed through me—a quiet rearranging, as if a story I'd been told my whole life had just been turned around.

"And then years later, you already know the story of Athena—how she used her wisdom to gift the *olive tree* to Greece, bringing *prosperity* and *abundance* to her people."

Her tone hardened slightly. "But then came the dark ages. When brute force ruled—ravaging villages, looting, raping women, exploiting the weak. And again, it was a woman who rose to counter it. A queen, who introduced the *concept of justice*—where men who broke the law, who violated, who disrespected a woman's consent, could finally be punished. That is when law and order entered society."

She let the words hang. "Your generation does not face famine, or thirst, or endless war. Those battles have been fought. You have abundance of resources. You also no longer live in fear of men dragging you into the streets, raping, burning, or even branding you a witch. Law and justice—those women's victories—took care of that."

Then her voice grew quiet, grave, the weight of experience pressing into each word. "No, I know the problem your generation faces. I have children, I have grandchildren. I am not out of touch. The problem you face now..." She paused, her gaze sharpening. "...is more *insidious*."

"Not famines, not plagues—your struggle is different," she said, her tone turning heavy. "You face a *flood of options, distractions, endless stimulations*. Drugs, addictions, screens in every hand. And because of this, *creation* itself has slowed, almost halted. Your generation no longer builds anything. No marriages, no families, no children, no values. Even your relationships collapse before a week has passed.

Do you know where this leads? Not to war, not to famine, not to disease—but to something far more dangerous: *the slow death of interest in men and women creating a future together*. That, *paidi mou*, is what could topple human civilization. Extinction not by fire, but by *apathy*. Not from outside, but from within.

Before long, the social fabric will fray—broken marriages, single parents, children without values, without guidance, with nothing to carry forward. They will be lost. And that loss will breed more loss, *passing trauma from one generation to the next* until society itself collapses."

The kitchen was silent. Even the wind outside seemed to hold its breath. I realized my hands were gripping the edge of the table.

She paused, her eyes steady. "I do not say this to frighten you, but to warn you. And when I say *you,* I mean women. You have always been the ones to fix it. From the beginning of time, it has been women's wisdom that steered humanity back from the edge. And now, again, it will fall to you."

"You must find the answer to this new plague—the untamed addictions that scatter your people like leaves in the wind: the glowing screens, the idle games, the poisons they call food, the powders that steal their souls, the pleasures of flesh without love, the lurking at naked images stripped of connection. All of it pulling men and women away from what matters—family, children, connection, building something that lasts. You must discover *a new vessel, a new olive tree, a new form of justice.* A pot for modern times, to hold and contain these habits before they destroy you. That, my child, will be the work of your generation."

By saying this, she reached for a small, beautifully sculpted ancient Greek pot and pressed it into my hands. "Here. Keep this with you. Let it be a reminder—*that your generation must learn to contain its desires, its pleasures, its addictions, its habits. Contain them, and then channel them into something that builds, that creates, that sustains society forward.*"

She closed my fingers gently around the pot, her palms warm and rough with years of work. Then, as if sealing the moment, she pulled me into her arms. Her embrace smelled faintly of flour and woodsmoke, the kind of embrace that carries both strength and tenderness. Rhea, Julia, Marissa had just walked in to say their goodbyes, catching some of her last words—each of us found ourselves wrapped in it before we left, her kisses brushing our cheeks, her murmured blessings in Greek trailing after us like ribbons.

We promised to return, though we knew we might never see her again. And yet it felt as though we were carrying her with us—the wisdom, the care, the fierce protection of a woman who had become, in a single evening, more than a stranger.

I stepped out carrying the pot, its weight far greater than its clay. I thought: *We can either remain a victim waiting for help to arrive or take charge and bring change by ourselves. And what should we choose? I say we choose the latter. Because we, women, have the power to invoke the goddess within—the one who makes civilizations rise from jungles, culture from wilderness, order from chaos. The one who turns recklessness into courage, brute muscle into hard work, floods into rivers that sustain.*

They say you imbibe the consciousness of what you are most connected to. Live close to nature, and you begin to carry its patience, its growth, its quiet endurance. Live long enough on a land, and its culture seeps into you—the food, the language, the habits, the ideas. And this wise old lady, who had lived her whole life rooted in Greek soil, seems like had absorbed the essence of Athena herself.

And if that was true, then it was not just an old woman who had spoken to us just now. It was almost as if a goddess Athena herself had handed us women a task: *to take the vices of the modern world and seal them in a pot, so that balance might return, and civilization could endure.*

Chapter 65: Transformation

We drove away with the little Fiat humming beneath us, the *Greek matriarch's* house shrinking in the rearview mirror, the pot resting carefully on my lap. None of us spoke for a while. It was as though we had been brushed by something divine, as if the hours inside her home belonged less to ordinary life and more to myth. We knew instinctively that this was an experience we would carry for the rest of our lives, replaying her words in moments when we most needed guidance.

But we also knew we couldn't head straight back to the hotel. Not yet. She had told us, almost insistently, to stop by the site of Heracles—Hercules, as we had learned him in childhood tales. If she had said it, it had to mean something.

It struck me then how much we can learn from the older generations, yet how rarely we bother to. We live in a world of streamlined knowledge, curated by strangers and filtered through algorithms, rarely in context to our own lives. Meanwhile, the older generation—especially those still rooted in culture and land—offer something far richer: wisdom shaped by experience, not theory.

If attraction is tied to value, then perhaps that is why our elders feel less and less "attractive" to the younger world. Everything they once offered—life skills, stories, memories, hard-earned lessons—we now believe we can pull from Google in seconds. Instead of sitting at our grandparents' feet, we scroll through Reddit threads or TikToks where stories are spun for clicks, not for us. It's tragic, really: we stop turning to our elders, and so they fade from view, made to feel irrelevant.

Yet they are the true sources of wisdom—not the rage-baiting headlines of the internet, not Twitter, not TikTok. If we cannot learn to see their value, *we are setting ourselves up for the most miserable old age.* Our generation will one day be discarded too, left to feel useless, because we ourselves failed to teach our children that old age carries treasures.

The old lady's words still lingered with us as we drove on, carrying the weight of what they had given. And yet, beneath that weight was a spark of excitement—to reach the site of Heracles. We had a feeling there would be another lesson waiting, another truth to uncover. And so we drove forward, eyes fixed on the road with anticipation.

The road wound into the countryside, olive groves thick on either side, their silvery leaves catching the sun. After some time we reached the site. It wasn't grand like the Parthenon, not polished or crowded. The site was quieter, more weathered, half-forgotten. The remains of pillars leaned into one another, inscriptions etched faintly into the stones. *A statue's torso,* muscled and broken, stared without a head.

We wandered through the ruins, our fingers brushing the cool marble, reading what little the plaques and carvings offered. *That was where we learned the story we had somehow never been told in full.*

Hercules, rage personified. A man with strength beyond comprehension, but with no compass to guide it. His fury consumed him. *And in his madness, he killed his own wife and children.*

We froze when we read it, exchanging glances. Shocked. How had no one told us this side of him before? We had always been taught Hercules the hero, Hercules the conqueror. Not Hercules the destroyer.

And then, another detail: *Hera.* It was she who had intervened, *not to erase his guilt but to transform it.* She assigned him *twelve labors*—impossible tasks, each demanding that his wild, destructive energy be directed into something purposeful. *Slay the Nemean lion. Capture the Ceryneian hind. Clean the Augean stables. Fetch the golden apples.* Twelve in total. Monsters slain, beasts tamed, feats accomplished. He was still the same man, with the same boundless strength, but no longer aimless. His force was no longer destruction. It had become creation, order, civilization.

As I stood there among the ruins, I thought: this is all of us. That same restless energy lives in every human being. It can build or it can break. It can nourish or it can burn. But too often, we forget this duality. *We label people heroes or villains, good or bad. We simplify men into red flags or green flags, ignoring the possibility of change.*

We rarely pause to consider that red flags can turn green— that villains can be reshaped into heroes when their energy is harnessed, when someone gives them a path, a labor, a reason to be more than their impulses. When someone holds them accountable, demands responsibility, and even sets the shadow of consequence before them. That is exactly what Hera did with Hercules: *she took a man who had murdered his own wife and children—a figure entirely red, hopelessly destructive—and through the discipline of twelve labors, she transformed him into the green flag every woman would later desire, a hero sung across centuries.*

Untamed, his rage destroyed everything it touched. But contained, directed, tested—it became his greatness.

I turned back to the last cracked inscription, tracing the outline of the carved letters with my hand. Hercules had begun as a danger to his own family. But in being tasked, in being harnessed, he became a legend that carried through the centuries.

And as we left the site, the lesson followed us out: *within everyone lies the same storm—destructive when unchecked, powerful when contained.*

And perhaps that was the deeper truth: *there is no such thing as good or bad in absolute terms.* There are only people with forces inside them—vices and virtues, storms and seeds—and the question is always whether anyone, or anything, can contain those forces and guide them. Show them a direction. Reward what is worthy. Punish what is not. And in doing so we gradually shape our collective identity.

Because eventually, *a society becomes what it chooses to reward.* If you reward greed, people grow greedy. If you reward violence, people grow violent. If you reward love, people learn to be loving.

And that is how you transform, not just people but entire civilizations.

****

The Auditorium

Chapter 66: The Flags

By the time we returned from Greece, I felt as though I was carrying a lantern in my chest—clarity about relationships, about men, about life itself. Julia, my friend, was part of a women's support collective in Seattle. It wasn't the kind of group that sat in circles crying over heartbreak; it was dynamic and alive. They hosted monthly events in a large community auditorium—panels, discussions, open forums—on everything that modern women must navigate: work-life balance, family expectations, equality in the workplace, dating, relationships, the messy crossroads where it all collides.

Julia had quietly submitted my name as a potential guest speaker. When the invitation reached me, I hesitated. I wasn't sure I belonged on a stage with a microphone in my hand. But then I saw the topic: "How to Avoid Red Flags in Relationships." I knew instantly that I had something to say. After all, the last two years since my breakup had been a masterclass in learning and insights. I had observed, reflected, and pieced together truths that felt too important to keep to myself.

Knowledge is a beautiful thing. It is not meant to be learned and then locked away in our minds, but to be shared— used to build connections. The more you learn about something—what it needs, what it fears, what it craves—the more deeply you begin to feel connected to it. I experienced this myself with the birds in my garden. When I knew nothing about them, they were only distant visitors, fluttering briefly through the fig tree outside my window. But once I learned about them—what they ate, what startled them, what might coax them nearer—they became more than fleeting shadows. They became part of my days.

That is what learning does: it binds us closer to what we once thought of as the "other." The more I learned about men and women—their drives, their fears, their instincts—the more compassion I felt toward both. And by sharing knowledge, you help others connect too. So when Julia told me about this opportunity to speak before such a large audience— predominantly women—it was an easy yes.

The evening arrived. The auditorium was buzzing, rows of women filling the seats—some young and restless, others older with years behind their eyes, many in between. Conversations rippled through the hall: laughter, whispered confessions, the exchange of advice that only women give one another. The air was alive with anticipation.

Backstage, I could hear the hum of voices beyond the curtain. My palms tingled, not with fear but with eagerness to share. Julia squeezed my hand, her eyes shining, as if to say this is your moment.

When they called my name, I took a deep breath and stepped onto the stage. The lights were warm against my face, the murmur of the crowd dimming into silence. Rows of expectant eyes turned toward me. For the first time in my life, I wasn't afraid of their gaze. I felt ready—ready to share, ready to connect, ready to give.

And so I began.

"Good evening, ladies.

Tonight's topic is a fascinating one—'How to Avoid Red Flags in Relationships.'

When I first received it, I sat down and started making a list. You know, the usual suspects: lying, cheating, gaslighting, manipulation, abuse... and of course, narcissism. Because let's be honest—narcissism is like the red flag to end all red flags, isn't it?

But then I thought about it a little more. I looked back at my own relationships and realized something strange: none of these red flags were visible at the beginning. Not one. In the beginning, it was all... green. A big, bright, perfectly mowed green lawn. Everything looked so healthy and fresh I could've done cartwheels on it.

And then, slowly—like weeds sneaking up through the grass—the red flags started showing. First one. Then another. And before I knew it, the whole lawn was on fire. I wasn't dating a person anymore; I was dating a walking emergency alert system.

Which made me think—maybe red flags aren't absolutes. Maybe they don't define who someone is. We like to think green flags belong to good people and red flags belong to bad ones, but it's not that simple. If it were, people wouldn't be able to switch so easily between the two—showing green flags when they want to get close to you, and red flags when they want to push you away.

Think about it. The same person who's inconsiderate and cruel in one relationship can suddenly become kind, patient, even romantic with someone else. The man who barely acknowledged you might be cooking dinner for his new partner every night. Or he's the sweetest son to his mother, the most protective brother—and yet, with you, he's distant, dismissive, or worse.

So what explains that?

It means that we all carry both—red and green flags—within us. They're part of the same fabric. And what brings one color out over the other isn't luck or astrology or 'the one'—it's the environment we create around each other.

In today's social climate, most people are walking around with their red flags waving proudly. Everywhere you look, it's a parade. Looking for green flags these days is like trying to find a blooming flower in a decaying garden—you keep searching, keep shuffling through the same withering petals, wondering where all the fresh ones went.

And even if you do manage to find one—some rare, healthy, green little sprout—the competition for it is fierce. Everyone wants that flower. You almost always lose it before it has the chance to grow.

But what if, instead of fighting over rare green flags, we started tending the garden itself? What if we, as women, decided to water it—patiently, collectively, consistently—until new green shoots began to appear? Until the air changed? Because the truth is, when one woman demands better, she lifts the standard for all of us.

That's how we truly avoid red flags—not just for ourselves, but for every woman who comes after us.

So tonight, instead of giving you a checklist of how to spot red flags, I want to talk about how to cultivate green ones. How to build connections that bring out the best in people. How to create a world where everywhere you look—there's *a million green flags.*"

The applause surprised me. Not polite clapping—real applause, the kind that rises from the gut. I waited for it to settle, steadied myself, and moved on.

Chapter 67: The Framework

"So how do we cultivate green flags? How do we build connections that last?

It starts with a choice. The choice to connect.

We take our ability to choose for granted, don't we? Yet out of all the living beings on this planet, only humans truly have it. Offer a monkey two options—a banana for itself or one for the monkey sitting next to it—and guess what? Every single time, it's going to keep the banana.

Animals act according to programming. They follow instinct, not intention. But somewhere along the line, we developed something extraordinary—wisdom. And wisdom is basically the software update that lets us override our own programming. It gives us the power to pause and say, 'Okay, I want the banana—but maybe the other person needs it more.'

We possess the power to choose not merely for our own gain, but for the benefit of others. We can choose for love, for friendship, for children, for country. We can choose to sacrifice comfort for meaning. That ability—to go against what benefits me in favor of what benefits us—that's the miracle of being human.

This is why even AI can't quite figure us out. Algorithms can predict what shoes we'll buy, what shows we'll binge, even who we'll swipe right on—but they'll never understand why, on a completely random day, we decide to adopt a stray cat, hand a rose to a stranger, offer a compliment to someone we can't stand, or text our ex 'Happy Birthday'—because honestly, what's life without a little drama?

And that's exactly the beauty of it. In those moments, when we step out of self-interest and reach toward someone else—when we choose to shift our attention from ourselves to another person—we create a connection.

Attention is the currency of connection. It's our most generous offering. When we give someone our attention, we tell them, 'You exist. You matter. I see you.' And that, right there, is the first green flag we can ever raise.

When we shift from me to you. From mine to ours.

But we seem to be losing this art—the art of connecting with others. Perhaps because no one really taught us. It has not been the focus of our generation. We are more interested in self than anything else—self-healing, self-care, self-love, self-awareness. It's always about I, me, and myself. We are so self-focused that we often forget to look at others. Should we then really be surprised if we have trouble forming relationships?

You don't find this knowledge anywhere—not in books, not in school, not even at home anymore.

So before we get into the reasons behind seeing red flags everywhere, let me give you a framework—a manual of sorts—on how a relationship actually works. Because once you understand how to build a strong, fulfilling connection with someone, you two can only wave green flags at each other. You simply stop needing red ones.

When you strip away the complexity, a relationship is just another word for a connection—one that has been established over time. And like everything that endures, it goes through stages. I think of them as three: Attraction, Reciprocation, and Co-creation.

Think of a seed. First, it's drawn toward light—that's the pull. Then it exchanges with the soil—water, nutrients, the slow give-and-take. And finally, it bears fruit—creates something beyond itself.

Or think of a fire. It begins with friction—the spark. Then it feeds—consuming and giving back heat. And if it finds new fuel, it transforms into something larger than the original flame.

Nature shows us this pattern everywhere. And relationships are no different.

Let's start with the first stage: Attraction.

When we think of attraction, we usually think only about romance. But that's not true at all. Attraction is what starts every relationship. Because attraction isn't just toward someone's physical appearance—it's toward the value they hold. We're drawn to people, places, things, ideas, even hobbies because we sense something valuable in them.

Why are you attracted to a piece of cake? Because it has calories, and calories are energy—value. The same principle applies to people. We are attracted to what we perceive as valuable: intelligence, kindness, humor, beauty, power, confidence, companionship. Every form of attraction is valid. There's no moral hierarchy between being drawn to kindness or being drawn to good shoulders—both are forms of value.

So, to have good relationships, first we need to make ourselves attractive. And how do we do that? How do we increase our value?

No, you can't do it with words or slogans. You can't stand in front of a mirror chanting affirmations, telling yourself 'I'm beautiful' twenty times a day. No amount of self-talk can build real worth—because value isn't spoken, it's earned. You build value the hard way: by cultivating grace, by refining your appearance, by staying fit, by learning skills, by shaping your character. You work on your mind, your body, your craft, your energy—you build your life.

Time and energy are the only true currencies of value. That is the law of creation: what you invest your time and energy in gains value; what you neglect loses it.

But when it comes to relationships, simply creating value isn't enough to inspire attraction—someone has to notice it too. And this is where your environment plays an important role. When you meet someone at a nightclub, you can't expect them to see beyond your physical beauty. When you meet someone through a dating app, you can't expect them to feel the warmth of your presence through a screen. People can only recognize your depth when they witness you in your natural element—in your everyday life, doing what you love, in the places where you feel most yourself.

Attraction is that intoxicating stage when dopamine runs high, when your heart races at the mere sight of someone, when every moment in their presence feels electric. It is a force strong enough to move mountains. But, like all fires, it fades if it isn't tended.

Just as a meal can't satisfy hunger by sight alone, admiration alone cannot sustain love. Because your value in a relationship isn't about what you have—it's about what you're willing to give. A high-value person isn't defined by the wealth, power, or skills they have, but by how they share and use those gifts. And that takes us to the second stage: Reciprocation."

I paused and took a sip of water. The room was still—the good kind of still, the kind that means people are following every word.

"When you recognize value in someone, you develop a drive—a hunger—to connect with it. But to desire something from others, you must also offer something in return. Nothing comes for free—not in life, not in love. That's the law of economics. And that's also the rule in relationships.

So to connect with someone of value, you have to put in the work. Except here, the effort isn't directed toward yourself but toward another person. You invest time and energy into engaging with them—offering laughter, attention, comfort, pleasure—whatever they may long for. You meet their desires and, in turn, hope they'll meet yours. This exchange—this continuous act of giving and receiving—forms the second stage: reciprocation.

And here lies the secret to mastering this stage: engagement. The more you engage with one another, the greater the opportunity for exchange. The more you engage, the better you understand them—their needs, their quirks, their desires. As your lives begin to intertwine, exchange becomes effortless. And effortless exchange is what truly defines a healthy, green flag relationship.

You may have noticed that some of your strongest bonds still come from school or childhood—because back then, we engaged every single day. Repeated exposure lets us learn one another's habits. We related to each other because we lived shared lives. And that's how the connection grew.

To build a really strong relationship with someone, you need both qualities in the same person—someone you find not only attractive but also relatable. When those two align, a bond forms that can truly thrive.

But any connection—no matter how strong—will, over time, start to feel familiar. We begin exchanging the same jokes, sharing the same stories, repeating the same patterns. And slowly, we start taking each other for granted. We build tolerance for the very things we once so strongly desired. And when that happens, we start to crave novelty—newness, excitement, growth.

There's nothing wrong with wanting growth. But here's the truth: in a healthy relationship, novelty doesn't come from replacing the person—it comes from building something new with the same person.

That's the turning point where relationships either fall apart, or they begin to deepen—evolving into the third and final stage: Co-creation.

Creation, in itself, is a beautiful process. You pour your time and energy into something and build value that's useful and attractive to the world. But when you add another person to that process, something remarkable happens. You're no longer creating alone—you're co-creating.

You build memories, rituals, traditions, families, children— not by yourself, but alongside someone else. Together, you create something that didn't exist before you met. And that act of creation—that shared building—becomes the glue that binds you.

But what happens when, instead of building together, you start replacing? When, instead of creating, you only consume? That's when the relationship falls apart—because there's nothing new left to offer each other. We drain our most precious resources—time, energy, attention—chasing replacements instead of building something lasting.

Building together requires something more than effort. It requires focus. Not the short-term kind, but long-term focus—what we call consistency.

Without consistency, nothing grows. You can pour all your effort into something—but if you keep uprooting yourself, you never grow deep roots. It's like planting seeds in a hundred different places, but never staying long enough to let a single one bloom. Or trying to build a castle in many places at once—without focus in one place, you're left with bricks scattered everywhere, but no house ever built.

Because without consistency, there's no creation. Not in nature. Not in life. Not in relationships. But with it, the relationship can continue like an upward spiral that keeps rising as long as value is being generated. Attraction intensifies. And the cycle repeats—attraction, reciprocation, co-creation—again and again, for as long as the creation doesn't stop.

Three stages. One cycle. And the relationships that last? They're the ones that never stop cycling through it."

I let the words settle. Across the auditorium, I could see women nodding slowly—some glancing at friends, others staring straight ahead with expressions I recognized. The look of something clicking into place.

"Now—if the framework is clear, the next question becomes: why isn't it working?"

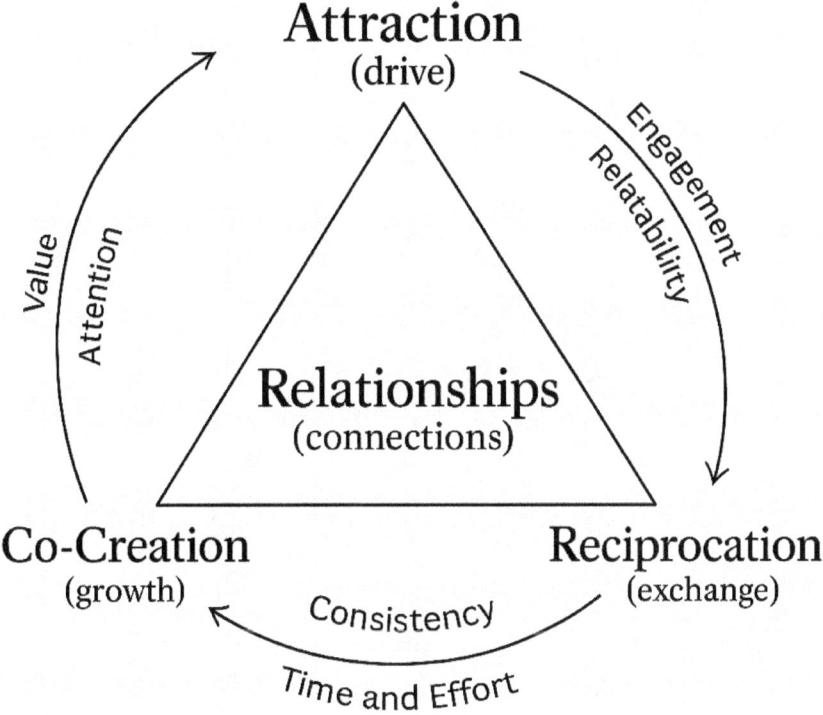

Chapter 68: The Imbalance

"Why is it that relationships are not working anymore? Why people refuse to commit or stay consistent in today's world? All we see are red flags everywhere.

We see marriages ending, families drifting apart. Many people are struggling to find a life partner or create families. Even sustaining friendships has become increasingly difficult.

So what's really going on? What is the real reason for this downfall?

"To answer that, we have to dig into something uncomfortable. Because now we're talking about the age-old dynamics between men and women—and how we function differently.

Men are typically better with short-term focus. And women? We're wired for the long game. We think of the larger picture. We are better with long-term focus.

And this difference isn't just cultural—it's evolutionary.

Nature sees men as more dispensable. They aren't born with inherent value—they have to earn it. That's why they're wired to take risks, to explore, to conquer. They're built for bursts of quick action, fast decisions, and short-term gains. Their feelings live in compartments—processing only the present moment, diving in quickly, and moving on just as fast. Perhaps that's why they're so bad at remembering things.

Women, on the other hand, are nature's more valuable assets—because we have the power to create life within ourselves. So nature made us the keepers of continuity: better at preservation, patience, nurturing, and long-term thinking. Our lives move like threads—every moment connected to the next, every feeling carried forward. That's why even an argument from weeks ago can still feel fresh in our memory.

It's important to understand this difference. Otherwise, women will keep blaming men for letting go too soon, while men will keep blaming women for holding on too long—not realizing that both operate differently. And this difference isn't a flaw. It's a design—a balance nature created between short-term and long-term perspective, each essential for survival.

Now, with this understanding, look at the modern world. It's a world largely shaped by the masculine impulse—optimized for quick wins, quick returns, quick pleasure. And in that world, the things men desire—novelty, stimulation, pleasure—are everywhere. Social media, dating apps, porn, fast food, entertainment—everything can be bought, clicked, or swiped. Desire, once earned through effort, now arrives instantly.

But the things women desire—trust, intimacy, building something together—those can't be mass-produced. They take time, presence, and consistency. You can't download them. You can't buy them. They have to be cultivated.

What men desire, and what was traditionally offered by women—attention, care, nourishment, comfort—has been devalued because it now exists in a hundred artificial forms. Who needs a home-cooked meal when pizza arrives in minutes? Who needs heartfelt conversations when endless chatrooms are a swipe away? Who needs a human touch when you can get gratification through porn?

Meanwhile, what women desire, and what was traditionally offered by men—consistency, commitment, co-creation—remains as elusive as ever. It demands cooperation. It requires men to actually show up. And that's exactly what they've stopped doing.

As a result, the balance of power has shifted. Because when what you bring is rare, your value rises. When what you offer is easily available elsewhere, your value falls.

And when value falls, something ugly happens."

I slowed down here. This was the part that mattered most.

"Think about how we treat cheap things. Think about a paper cup. You drink from it, crush it, toss it—without a second thought. You'd never do that to a ceramic mug you loved. The mug gets washed carefully, placed back on the shelf, kept for years. But the paper cup? It served its purpose. It's disposable. It doesn't even register as a loss.

Now think about how that same logic plays out between people.

When your value is high, people put effort into you. They court you. They show up. They listen when you speak. They remember what matters to you. They overlook your flaws because your worth outweighs your imperfections.

But when your value is low? Those same people stop trying. They stop noticing. They stop caring. Not because they've become cruel overnight—but because we simply do not invest in what we do not value.

And that is the first set of red flags we see today. Not cruelty. Not evil. But a quiet, steady erosion of how much women are valued in the modern world.

When a woman's value diminishes in a man's eyes, you see it in everything he does—and everything he doesn't do. The effort disappears. No more thoughtful gestures, no more planning, no more trying to impress or delight. Dates become obligations. Conversations become transactions. Her opinions are dismissed. Her feelings are treated as inconvenience. Her contributions—emotional, domestic, relational—go unacknowledged, as though they cost her nothing to give.

She is spoken to with contempt. Criticized in front of others. Her boundaries are ignored because they aren't taken seriously. Her needs are deprioritized—not because he's busy, but because they simply don't register as important. Promises are made and broken without apology, because why would you apologize to a paper cup?

She initiates. She compromises. She explains. She holds the relationship together while he contributes the bare minimum— and still believes he's doing enough. Because in his world, she is abundant. She is replaceable. She is everywhere. And you don't fight to keep what you can easily find again.

And with that loss of value comes a loss of something even more dangerous: power. Influence. Agency. The ability to shape a relationship, to set its terms, to say 'this is what I need' and have it heard. When your value is high, your voice carries weight. When it's low, you can scream and still be ignored.

The depreciating value of women is the single biggest reason we see a rise in red-flag behaviors directed toward women today. And these red flags aren't just limited to dating— they show up in workplaces, friendships, families, and in how society at large treats women.

So does that mean men are winning in this modern world?"

I shook my head slowly.

"In the short run—maybe. Men seem to benefit from the way society is built today: freedom, variety, and little accountability. But in the long run, they lose too. Everyone loses.

Picture a man in his forties. Nice apartment. Good job. Every app on his phone. He can order food, entertainment, companionship—anything he wants, delivered to his door. He has everything he ever desired. And yet he sits on his couch on a Sunday evening, scrolling through his phone, and feels nothing. No one is waiting for him. No child runs to the door when he comes home. No voice calls from the other room. He got everything the modern world promised him. And it left him hollow. He followed the script perfectly. And the script was wrong.

Because creation—real human creation—requires both the masculine and the feminine forces working together in harmony, bound by love and responsibility. It requires men and women raising children not in broken homes but in spaces built on safety, trust, and care. That is where civilization begins. Not in cities or businesses or innovations—but in the small, sacred act of two people choosing to build a life together.

And when we stop building, it doesn't just hurt women. It hurts everyone. Every part of society begins to fray. The warning signs are already here: falling marriage rates, rising divorces, an epidemic of loneliness, widespread depression, and children growing up without stable homes or examples of love.

A society that loses its capacity to build relationships becomes dysfunctional. No amount of technology can fix that. You can't automate love. You can't outsource parenting. You can't program purpose. No robot, no AI can build a family. And going to Mars won't save us if we forget how to build a home here on Earth.

And here's the part no one talks about—this breakdown doesn't just produce red flags against women. It produces a second set of red flags—shown by both men and women alike. Because when connection fails at this scale, everyone is left empty. And empty people—regardless of gender—start behaving in ways that destroy the very thing they crave."

I looked out across the room. Some women were nodding. Others weren't moving at all.

"When people are starving for connection, they don't give. They take. Think about it—when you're exhausted, depleted, running on empty, you don't have the capacity to be generous. You don't have the patience to listen. You're just trying to survive. And survival turns people selfish—not because they want to be, but because they have nothing left to offer.

You see it in the ghosting—because disappearing is easier than being honest. In the breadcrumbing—offering just enough to keep someone close, but never enough to let them in. In the emotional avoidance—the refusal to go deep, to be vulnerable, to risk being truly known.

You see it in the failure to commit—not because they don't want love, but because they've forgotten what it costs. In the manipulation—because when you can't earn affection honestly, you learn to engineer it. In the gaslighting—because when you can't face your own emptiness, you make the other person question theirs.

And then there are the ones who simply take more than they give—not out of greed, but out of depletion. They consume relationships the way they consume everything else: quickly, hungrily, and without savoring. Moving from person to person, experience to experience, hoping the next one will finally fill the void. It never does.

Because the deepest red flag of all isn't a behavior—it's an incapacity. The inability to love. Not the unwillingness—the inability. Love requires putting someone else before yourself. It requires seeing another person's needs as equal to your own. And when you are empty—when your own needs are screaming so loudly that you can't hear anyone else—you simply cannot do it. You don't have the bandwidth. Survival doesn't share."

I stopped. Let the silence hold.

"These aren't character flaws. They're symptoms of starvation. A starving person doesn't refuse to share because they're selfish—they refuse because they have nothing in their hands to give.

And this is what makes it a vicious cycle. These red flags— the ghosting, the avoidance, the inability to love—they don't just come from disconnection. They create more of it. Every time someone ghosts, a connection dies. Every time someone breadcrumbs, trust erodes. Every time someone takes without giving, the other person learns to guard themselves a little more. And so the distance between people grows wider—not because anyone chose it, but because emptiness breeds emptiness. Disconnection breeds disconnection.

And the worst part? The markets have learned to profit from this starvation. If a product truly lasted, you'd stop buying it. If an app truly gave you love, you'd stop scrolling. If social media truly made you feel connected, you wouldn't need to check it twenty times a day. So instead, they give you just enough—a drip of dopamine, a flicker of validation, a crumb of joy to keep you hooked. That's not connection. That's distraction.

Think of the last time you felt truly lonely and reached for your phone instead of a person. That's the trade the market wants you to make—every single time.

And so our attention—the very currency of connection—keeps draining into things that offer quick pleasure, leaving us too exhausted to invest in what actually matters: real people, real relationships, real growth. We are surrounded by more ways to communicate than ever before, and yet we have never been lonelier. We chase and chase—scrolling, swiping, consuming—and the chasing itself becomes the trap. Not a path toward fulfillment, but a treadmill that keeps us running in place, too busy to notice that no one is running beside us.

That is the ultimate red flag of our times. Not the liars. Not the cheaters. Not even the narcissists. But a world that has forgotten how to connect—where women are devalued, where everyone is hollowed out, and where red flags have quietly replaced the relationships we were born to build.

So the question becomes: how do we fix it?"

No one reached for their phone. No one whispered to the person beside them. They just sat there.

Chapter 69: The Solution

"I believe the answer lies with us—women.

Because let's be honest, men have already done what they do best: they've built systems that fulfill their desires. Every latest technology, every new platform, every new algorithm has been carefully crafted to multiply their access, expand their reach, and satisfy their impulses.

Look at social media—Facebook, Instagram, Snapchat. Look at dating apps—Tinder, Bumble, OnlyFans. Pick up any new-age invention and you'll see how they're all tools for people to simply do more: meet more, reach more, experience more, see more, f*ck more.

And what have we, as women, created in return? Have we built anything that truly speaks to our primal needs—the need for deep connections, lasting relationships, communities, co-creation? To bring wisdom, balance, and sustainability into the world?

For too long, our innovations have been confined to the realm of fashion, cosmetics, and beauty—to what pleases, what appeals, what attracts. But this is not working anymore. Now, we need something else—something more powerful."

I reached beneath the podium and lifted the pot—the clay pot handed to me by the Greek matriarch, weathered and ancient, its surface rough beneath my fingers. I held it up so the light caught its edges.

"We need something like this pot—the oldest invention of women—to hold the chaos. Because every civilization is sustained by a vessel: something that contains, that preserves. Without it, everything spills.

We need a modern vessel for a modern age—a pot not of clay, but of boundaries—to hold the chaos of our times before it consumes us.

We, as women, must set standards for what kind of behavior we wish to see, and use this vessel to guide people there—by rewarding what is collectively desired, and discouraging what isn't. Because when one woman raises her standards, she does it for all of us.

This is how order is restored. This is how structure returns. And we—the women—have always been the ones to do it.

We do this through our greatest gift—our ability to connect. In a healthy relationship, both men and women reciprocate; they reward each other. And by rewarding the right actions, we spark small changes—changes that, over time, bring about transformation.

Throughout history, women have shaped the world by choosing what men are rewarded for. When women rewarded resourcefulness, men became hunter-gatherers. When we rewarded innovation, men became inventors. When queens rewarded exploration, men discovered new lands. When damsels celebrated courage, men became knights. When maidens valued art, men became poets. When we admired wealth and status, men became ambitious and driven. When we rewarded effort and integrity, men built stable homes and societies.

But today? Today, we reward swipes, emojis, and empty compliments—and men have simply adapted. They've become cheap because our rewards have become cheap.

This isn't entirely our doing. The flow of rewards no longer comes from women alone—it comes from screens, from products, from services. Somewhere along the way, we lost our agency.

Yet despite all of it, men still crave something only a woman can give: real softness, real touch, real love. And that's where our power still lies. If we can redirect those rewards—not toward low effort or instant gratification, but toward hard work and consistency—we can restore balance.

It's time for women to step up and remember our power— to once again become the force that brings meaning to the madness. Because when we rise, civilization rises with us.

So let's build something together.

A collective well of knowledge. Of information. Of experience. Of trust.

Because to truly reward someone for their behavior, we need information about them—their history, their actions, their patterns. What we need is a safe space where women can share their truths: who made them feel loved, safe, and seen—and who made them feel small, dismissed, or hurt.

We need a platform where women can bring their personal stories and insights from their past experiences with men. Because when women share their stories, we teach one another to choose more wisely—with clarity rather than confusion. We begin to reward people not through curated profiles and polished images, but through their lived truth.

We've done this before with money. When people defaulted on loans, we created credit scores—to hold them accountable, to prevent them from deceiving others again and again. Now it's time for something far more vital: an integrity score. A way to recognize those who have proven themselves trustworthy, kind, and consistent over years—the ones who keep their promises not only in moments of convenience, but over time, when it truly counts."

I set the pot down gently on the podium, but kept my hand on it.

"I know this idea is uncomfortable but this is not anything new. Once upon a time, this kind of information was communal. In villages where everyone knew everyone, a person's character couldn't hide behind charm or performance. Women would call such men out, hold them accountable, and ensure consequences followed. But in today's fragmented world—where cities are vast and lives unfold on the internet—we've lost access to real information about people. We know their selfies, not their souls. We know their bios, not their truths. And without truth, accountability disappears, consequences fade, and betrayal continues.

If we manage to build this database—where we can track integrity and behavior—we can finally begin to choose wisely: who to trust, who to love, who to build with. And with the right choices we can surely bring a transformation in men.

Whether we believe it or not, transformation is possible. History has witnessed it time and again—when movements reshaped societies, toppled empires, and sparked revolutions. When people align around a common cause, our collective consciousness awakens—powerful enough to alter the course of civilization itself.

So let's come together. Let's build this collective pot of wisdom—this shared well of knowledge, this living database of truth—that can serve as the moral compass of our time. A quiet oracle guiding us toward better choices, healthier relationships, and a world worth passing on to our daughters."

I lifted the pot one final time, holding it above my head so the whole room could see it—this small, ancient, imperfect thing that had traveled from a Greek village to a stage in Seattle. For a moment, I felt every woman who had ever held it before me.

"Toward a world no longer defined by red flags—but illuminated by a million green flags."

Chapter 70: Reflections

And with that my speech was over. Longer than I expected, but filled with words that needed to be said. The applause came like a wave—rising, swelling, breaking over me in thunderous warmth. I stood beneath the lights, the clay pot raised high above my head, the symbol of everything I had lived, learned, and finally found the words to share. The stage shimmered—a blur of faces, hands clapping, voices merging into a hum that filled the room like music.

When I stepped down, people gathered around me—women first, their eyes bright, their smiles full of something deeper than politeness. Gratitude, maybe. Recognition. One by one, they came—hands on my shoulder, brief hugs, quiet thank-yous. Then more women, each carrying their own stories, their own emotions, pouring them into my hands like offerings.

I felt a joy unlike any I had known before—the pure joy of expression. The kind that rises from somewhere deep within you, demanding release. When you have an idea, a truth, a vision—it's restless within you until it's shared, much like the breath you can't hold after the inhale.

Perhaps that's nature's design—to learn, and then to teach. To absorb, and then to give. Knowledge isn't meant to be kept; it's meant to flow, passed from one to another like flame, lighting the way forward.

The Sanskrit mantra I learned at the monastery captures this sentiment beautifully: "*Asato Ma Satgamaya, Tamaso Ma Jyotirgamaya, Mrityor Ma Amritamgamaya.*"

"*May we find the courage to express freely, bringing out the thoughts from our mind & imagination into the realm of reality. May we find the motivation to learn everyday, leading ourselves from the darkness of ignorance to the light of knowledge. May we find the inspiration to create something that lasts, transforming our fleeting life into an immortal legacy that we can leave behind.*"

I didn't go home after the event. I couldn't. The day was too radiant to end indoors, too full of something new and unnameable. So I drove—two hours south of Seattle—to the cliffs along the Pacific coast.

The sun poured gold across the water, the horizon shimmering where the sea met the sky. Below, waves clashed against the dark rocks with a rhythm that seemed eternal, like the heartbeat of the earth itself. I stood there at the cliff, eyes tracing the line where blue met blue. The air smelled of salt and pine, clean and infinite.

In that vastness, I felt small but complete—not diminished, but expanded, as though I finally belonged to everything I once thought was beyond me.

Happiness, I realized, is never just one thing. It is a delicate blend of *joy* and *pleasure*—two halves of the same whole.

Joy rises quietly from within; it's the calm that fills you when your inner world is aligned. Pleasure, meanwhile, comes from the world outside—from feeding your senses, from engagement with others, from indulgence with the world. And when the two meet—when what is within you finds harmony with what is around you—that is when happiness takes form.

Today, I felt both. *The joy of creation* and *the pleasure of connection*. A perfect balance, brief but complete.

Sharing my story, my thoughts, my learnings with the women around me had given me an overwhelming sense of connection to womankind itself. For a few moments on that stage, I felt my life stretch wide—larger than my body, larger than my story. I felt revived, as if the essence of womanhood had passed through me and settled in my bones.

And by connecting deeper with my own femininity, I felt something else awaken—a yearning for its counterpart. For the masculine force that complements, challenges, and completes.

I love being a woman. I love my softness, my intuition, my quiet strength. But I also love men—with all their wild, uncontainable masculinity, as ancient and untamed as the ocean itself, thrilling and unpredictable, never fully within reach.

And by men, I don't mean the modern-day *manoids* you see around these days—scrolling their lives away, picking up fights on twitter, arguing on podcasts, ranting on Reddit, lurking over naked images, snickering at women's expense, or wasting hours in video games from their mother's basements. Not the ones simply drifting through life too dazed on substances to know what's really happening around them. No. Not them.

By men, I mean real men—the kind who can bear the weight of others on their shoulders. The ones whose charm and wit can lift spirits when all else falters. Men with the courage to take responsibility, not only for themselves but for their entire tribe. Those with the skill to lead their people and the strength to face their enemies—not in pursuit of dominance, but in defense of what they hold dear.

Looking out at the Pacific, it was impossible not to think of men like that—men who, like the sea, could draw you in with their beauty and vastness, only to toss you helpless when they turned. Men born of thunder and salt, carved by the storms. Those that moved with the tide and struck like lightning, carrying the heart of Poseidon—vast, restless and untamed. Their power was undeniable, but so was the danger. To love such a man was to risk drowning, and yet history was filled with those who willingly stepped into the tide, awed by their force.

Such men are rare now, almost mythic. But when you meet one, you know. The air changes. The noise quiets. The world suddenly feels smaller, and safer, all at once.

To engage with such men is to risk the tide. To love them is to test your balance against the waves. But when you manage to learn their currents—when you learn not to fight their force but to move with them—and when you finally learn how to ride the waves, with both courage and surrender, the pleasure you experience is unlike anything else you can experience on this earth.

Because nothing delights the feminine spirit more than turning chaos into calm, roughness into rhythm—making what is crooked, straight. Nothing stirs the feminine spirit more than the art of taming the beast—not by diminishing its strength, but by dancing with it, in all its vigor and vitality.

The ocean below me roared louder, the sunlight spilling diamonds across the Pacific. I stood there smiling, wind in my hair, salt on my lips, holding a business card between my fingers, handed to me by a charismatic man at the event—a tiny symbol of possibility fluttering in my palm. Somewhere beyond that horizon lay the next chapter of my life, uncertain but full of promise. As I looked at the card reading his name, I whispered to myself, almost laughing, *"Let's see where this wave takes me."*

****

www.ingramcontent.com/pod-product-compliance
Lightning Source LLC
Chambersburg PA
CBHW060405130626
46555CB00005B/1994